Academic Literacy
in the Social Sciences

Academic Literacy
in the Social Sciences

Judy Eaton and David N. Morris

CANADIAN
SCHOLARS

Toronto | Vancouver

Academic Literacy in the Social Sciences
Judy Eaton and David N. Morris

First published in 2019 by
Canadian Scholars, an imprint of CSP Books Inc.
425 Adelaide Street West, Suite 200
Toronto, Ontario
M5V 3C1

www.canadianscholars.ca

Library and Archives Canada Cataloguing in Publication

Eaton, Judy, 1966-, author
        Academic literacy in the social sciences / Judy Eaton
and David Morris.

Includes bibliographical references and index.
Issued in print and electronic formats.
ISBN 978-1-77338-091-9 (softcover).--ISBN 978-1-77338-092-6
(PDF).--ISBN 978-1-77338-093-3 (EPUB)

        1. Social sciences--Research--Textbooks. 2. Social
sciences--Research--Methodology--Textbooks. 3. Academic
writing--Textbooks. 4. Critical thinking--Textbooks.
5. English language--Rhetoric--Textbooks. 6. Textbooks.
I. Morris, David, 1961-, author II. Title.

H62.E27 2019   300.72   C2018-906444-7
                                              C2018-906445-5

Cover and type design by Elisabeth Springate

Printed and bound in Ontario, Canada

Canadä

TABLE OF CONTENTS

ACKNOWLEDGEMENTS

Although our names may appear on the cover, we share credit for this book with many colleagues: 469 of them to be exact. That's the number of students enrolled in our BF290 course at the Brantford campus of Wilfrid Laurier University in Fall 2017. That term, we asked our students for feedback on a draft of this textbook. We were overwhelmed by the insightful and intelligent (and sometimes saucy) suggestions they made. This version of the textbook is infinitely better because of their feedback, and we are tremendously grateful to them. Incidentally, readers should be grateful to them too, as this text is also quite a bit shorter, in response to their requests that we be more concise.

We are also incredibly fortunate to work with an amazing group of instructors who have contributed to the contents of this book in various ways. We thank Karin Archer, Rebecca Beausaert, Annette Chretien, Bryce Gunson, Jennifer Long, Michael MacLean, and Zipparah Stephenson for caring about social science as much as we do, and for inspiring our students to as well. We also thank John Corr, Karley Doucette, Pauline Dewan, and Michelle Goodridge, who not only help our students get excited about searching for literature and writing about it but also gave us excellent feedback on the related chapters in the text. They, along with Jenna Olender and Irene Tencinger, have been instrumental in shaping how we approach research and writing in the social sciences both in our courses and in this textbook.

We are also grateful to Scott Annandale, who not only touched up our author photos and magically made us look younger, but he also did the graphic design of the initial draft chapters that we asked our students to comment on. He converted our double-spaced, plain-looking draft chapters into nicely designed documents students might actually want to read.

We are grateful to Canadian Scholars for their support of this project. Many thanks, in particular, to Lily Bergh, Karri Yano, Nick Hilton, and Ashley Rayner.

Judy Eaton would like to thank Scott and Lauren for their love, support, and silly jokes, and for being the two most awesome people in her world.

David Morris would like to thank Monica Kaminski for her unceasing support and thoughtful comments. With her help, all tasks seem much lighter.

INTRODUCTION

Why Am I Reading This Book?

You may be asking yourself how it's come to pass that you are reading a book on academic literacy in the social sciences. You may even be asking what academic literacy in the social sciences actually is. Although it's possible you just happened to see this book in your local bookstore and picked it up because you thought it looked fun, we suspect a more likely answer to the first question is you have been asked to read this book as a requirement for a course you are taking. So, now that we have established why we're all here, let's address your second question: What is academic literacy in the social sciences?

SOCIAL SCIENCE

First we should clarify what we mean by the term **social science**. Social science is "the scientific study of social, cultural, psychological, economic, and political forces that guide individuals in their actions" (Hunt & Colander, 2011, p. 1). Although this definition mentions specific areas of social science like sociology, psychology, economics, and political science, the social sciences are very broad and can also include the fields of anthropology, criminology, and education, and some aspects of history, geography, and health studies, to name a few. Note also the use of the term *scientific* in the definition. Social science often follows many of the same methods as natural sciences like physics and chemistry. Although humans are less predictable than, say, gravity, you may be surprised to learn they can be studied in a scientific way. The benefit of using scientific methods to study why individuals do the things they do is that we can be more confident that the conclusions we make are based on solid, reproducible evidence, rather than less reliable methods like hearsay and urban myths. It is important to note, however, that not all social science researchers embrace all aspects of the scientific method. As we will discuss later, some social scientists embrace paradigms that see human experiences as too unique to be adequately or properly investigated by the scientific method.

Fields within the Social Sciences

Sociology	Criminology
Psychology	Education
Economics	Health studies
Political science	Geography
Anthropology	History

ACADEMIC LITERACY, AND WHY IT'S A GOOD THING

Academic literacy is the ability to find, understand, and communicate information. As such, this book has a very practical purpose: to help you develop the skills you need to understand and critically evaluate research in the social sciences. These skills involve developing a topic for a research paper, conducting a thorough literature search, critically evaluating the research you find, and effectively summarizing and sharing the information you have found.

This is important for three reasons.

1. Academic literacy → better grades
    In your university or college career, you will probably be asked to write an essay, research paper, or critical analysis, or even to conduct original research, on a topic related to the social sciences. Even if you are not majoring in one of the traditional social sciences, it is likely you will take at least one course that uses social science to help understand how and why humans do the things they do. Thus, this book is designed to help you succeed in meeting the requirements of the different courses you will take. Many of the skills you will develop, such as finding information, evaluating it, and presenting it both in writing and verbally, are easily transferrable to any course you might take, whether it involves social science or not.

2. Academic literacy → better life choices
    You may not realize it, but in your daily life you encounter many different forms of social science research. For instance, news reports are full of claims about social issues like new medical breakthroughs, which cities are the safest in which to live, which political party has the most public support, and how we, as individuals, can be happier. Sometimes these news reports are conflicting: Some say crime is decreasing while others say it is increasing; some say chocolate is good for you, but others say we should avoid sugar completely; some say babies should be fed "on demand" while others stress babies should be put on an established feeding schedule. This book will help you wade through and critically evaluate the information you read, helping you to make informed decisions about the issues that affect you.

3. Academic literacy → better job
    If the first two reasons haven't convinced you, perhaps this third one will. Being able to do the things this book will teach you to do will help you find a job. This book covers a lot of practical skills, including oral and written communication skills, project management, and critical thinking. Do those terms sound familiar? They will if you have ever looked through job ads. These are the kinds of skills employers are looking for. Graduation may seem a long way off, but if you can start developing these highly valued "transferrable skills" now, you will be much more competitive on the job market.

Transferrable (i.e., Marketable) Skills

Critical thinking	Analytical skills
Problem solving	Interpersonal skills
Decision making	Presentation skills
Creativity	Time management
Verbal communication	Research skills
Written communication	Project management skills
Digital/technological fluency	Numeracy/computation
Collaboration	

PRACTICE MAKES PERFECT

This book is meant to provide you with the basic skills of academic literacy in the social sciences. Like any newly acquired skill, it will take practice for you to become an expert. If you are reading this book as part of your course requirement, as with any course, you will get out of that course what you put into it. If you attend class, do all the assigned readings, and work hard on the assignments, you will learn more and better develop your skills. Hopefully the benefits of doing so will be apparent long after the course is over, not only in your ability to meet the requirements of your other courses but also in your life after university. As you navigate the social world of family, work, community, and politics, being a critical consumer of social research will help you make the best decisions for yourself and those you care about.

1

The Social Science of Learning: How to Social Science Your Way to Success

You're smart. You made it this far in school, and we're going to assume that if you're reading this book, you are working toward getting even more education. Well done! You have much to be proud of. But even though you may be a smarty pants, brains alone won't ensure that you succeed in your courses. Success is not based solely on intelligence; it also requires effort. As Thomas Edison apparently said, "Genius is 1% inspiration and 99% perspiration" (Rosanoff, 1932, p. 406). If that sounds terrifying, it doesn't have to. Social science can save you.

Does your study strategy involve reading a chapter over and over until you feel you know it? Have you gone through more than one highlighter on a single textbook? You may be surprised to learn that those are not necessarily the most effective study habits. Social scientists have spent a lot of time learning about how we learn. Cognitive psychologists, for example, study how the brain works—how we take in information, how it's stored in our brain, and how we recall it. Educational researchers, including psychologists, educational specialists, and sociologists, take what we know about what happens in the brain when we learn and develop strategies for the most effective ways to teach, study, and learn. This chapter summarizes that research and presents some very simple, evidence-based strategies for you to use not only in this course but also in all your other courses. In other words, from this chapter you will learn how to use social science to learn about social science!

LEARNING OBJECTIVES

1. Learn how social scientists study the learning process
2. Understand some misconceptions about how to study
3. Develop practical academic strategies for succeeding in school
4. Learn about how wellness is related to learning
5. Develop practical, non-academic strategies for improving your well-being

A NOTE ON EVIDENCE

Throughout this book you will hear a lot about evidence. Hopefully, by the end of the book, you will become the kind of person (if you aren't already) who says, "Show me the evidence" when you read or hear about some outrageous claim. What's so great about evidence? What if someone told you that in five years, aliens from a distant planet will invade our planet—would you believe them? This would probably depend on many factors: who this person is, what authority or expertise they have to be making such a claim, and, perhaps, how much you've had to drink. But the first thing you would probably want to know is what evidence there is for such a claim. How do they know aliens are coming? If the person can't provide evidence, you likely won't believe them.

It's easy to dismiss claims when they are ridiculous; most people would not be convinced that we are in danger of an extraterrestrial invasion. But not all claims are so hard to believe. What if we told you that simply *thinking* about exercising is as effective as actually doing some form of physical activity? Would you be at least a little bit tempted to believe it? We would, and we know it's not true (because we just made it up). Why might some people be fooled by this? First, because it kind of sounds plausible, and second, because it would be awesome if it was true. We are more likely to be convinced by claims if we are motivated to believe them (Bastardi, Uhlmann, & Ross, 2011).

We'll talk more about how to evaluate outrageous claims made about social science later. You'll be an expert at saying, "Show me the evidence" by the time you finish this book. For now, even if you haven't become used to asking for evidence, we're going to show it to you anyway.

There are plenty of myths about learning. You may even believe some of them. For example, many people study by reading information over and over, believing that repeated exposure is enough to help them learn. In fact, several different researchers have found that this is one of the most popular study techniques (Dunlosky, Rawson, Marsh, Nathan, & Willingham, 2013). However, researchers have tested this method of studying in actual experiments, and the results of these experiments suggest that this is not the most effective way to study. In fact, through conducting experiments in which they compare the methods of studying and the amount of time spent doing it, researchers have found that you can actually spend less time studying if you do it more effectively. Evidence is important!

This chapter provides many suggestions and techniques for improving your studying and learning, all supported by evidence. Without the evidence, this chapter would be much shorter, but it would also be less useful. By demonstrating for you where these techniques come from and why they are effective, we hope to convince you to adopt them for yourself to make your studying more effective.

A BRIEF INTRODUCTION TO YOUR BRAIN

Can you remember what kind of birthday cake you had when you turned five? Do you remember how to calculate the circumference of a circle? Do you remember what you had for lunch yesterday? Some of these questions may be harder for you than others, but chances are this information isn't on the top of your mind. Your brain is not a machine that stores everything you put into it, retrieving it for you effortlessly whenever you need it. Our brains are amazing and complex, but they are also limited in how much they can do.

What follows is a very brief introduction to how memory typically works. If you are interested in this topic, there are entire courses devoted to how we encode, store, and retrieve information. For now, we hope to give you enough of an understanding of how your brain works so that you will understand how to study better.

Memory is a three-part process. First, the information needs to get into your brain (encoding), then it needs to be catalogued properly (storage), and finally, it needs to be available when you need it (retrieval).

Figure 1.1: The Memory Process

Encoding

Encoding refers to getting the information into your brain; it's kind of like inputting data into a computer. Encoding is important, because, like the computer, improperly entered data can cause problems later on. Have you ever read a paragraph in your textbook, and then realized you have no idea what you just read? The information did not make it into your brain; it was not encoded. Have you seen the famous gorilla basketball video? If you haven't seen it, check it out before reading any further. You can find it at http://www.theinvisiblegorilla.com/gorilla_experiment.html.

In the video, as you are counting the number of passes one team makes to the other, an interesting visitor walks through the game, but 50 percent of people who watch the video do not notice the visitor. If you don't notice the guest, your brain will not record this information. There is a good reason why eyewitness testimony is controversial in the criminal justice system: Sometimes we do not notice things, or we think we see things that did not actually happen. These are problems with encoding. Encoding is an important part of the memory process, because if the input is flawed, the memory will also be flawed.

Storage

Storage refers to how your brain holds onto the encoded information. Even if you manage to encode information properly, it needs to be managed in such a way that you can get at it later. Take a look at the following number:

8360374691

Read each digit aloud once and then cover the number up with your finger. Now look around the room where you are reading and think about what you are going to do tomorrow. Now, try to remember the number without looking at it. How'd you do?

If you are like most people, you probably didn't remember the entire number accurately. Why not? Chances are you encoded the number correctly.

If you read the digits aloud, your data input was probably flawless. If you couldn't remember the number, it was probably due to a storage problem. Your memory does not store all the information you input into it. If it did, you'd be a walking encyclopedia.

Although there are different theories about how memories are stored, one of the most influential and enduring explanations is from Atkinson and Shiffrin (1971), who proposed that there are different levels of memory storage. According to their model, the first type of storage our memory performs is called sensory memory. Sensory memory is fleeting, lasting for less than a second. It allows us to determine whether to attempt to retain the information for any longer or to discard it. If the information is retained, it moves to short-term memory. Our short-term memory is also limited; unless the information is rehearsed, it only lasts for about 20 seconds. Think about the last time you had to remember a postal code or phone number. Unless you keep repeating it to yourself, it will quickly leave your memory, causing you to have to look it up or ask for it again. Information that is not lost in short-term memory moves to our long-term memory, which is not limited; it can store information indefinitely.

Retrieval

Effective storage of information is meaningless without a **retrieval** process; you need to be able to retrieve it when you need it. Think of a non-waterproof phone that has been dropped in water: It still has all your contacts on it, but you can't access them. Storage is not the problem, but getting stuff out of storage is. Even when access shouldn't be a problem, some memories are easier to retrieve than others. Many things can affect the ease with which information is recalled: the order in which it went in and the order in which it is retrieved, other information it is stored with (called retrieval cues), and even emotions you associate with that particular memory. In other words, the way you store information can help with retrieval.

As you can imagine, this all has implications for studying. If you aren't doing as well as you would like on your tests, it is not because you aren't smart (because we have already determined that you *are* smart). It may be because you are either not encoding the information properly, or it is not making it to your long-term memory, or you are not retrieving it efficiently. This is great news for you, because you can do something about it. What follows are a number of suggestions and practical tips for using what we know about memory to help you learn more effectively. Thanks, social science!

HOW TO LEARN AND STUDY MORE EFFECTIVELY

Practice Testing

If you are reading this, chances are you've got a test or two (or more) in your future. Tests are an inevitable part of education, and although they can come in many forms, one thing they all have in common is that they cause stress for many students. Few students like taking tests, and instructors tend not to like marking them either. So why not just do away with tests?

As it happens, one of the most well-supported findings in the literature on learning is that **practice tests** are important for learning and remembering material. In their book *Make It Stick: The Science of Successful Learning* (2014), Peter Brown and his colleagues use an analogy of stringing beads to make a necklace. If you don't tie a knot at the end of the string, the beads will fall off, and your necklace will just look like a sad piece of string. In the same way, if you don't practise retrieving information from memory, eventually that information will fade from your memory. Testing is like tying a knot at the end of the string. By practising retrieval of the information from your brain, you are firming up the beads so your necklace is there when you need it, with all the beads in place.

Where's the Evidence?

Remember when we talked about the importance of evidence? Well, there is a lot of evidence to suggest that testing is one of the most effective ways to learn. In one of the earliest studies that demonstrated the benefits of testing, Spitzer (1939) had sixth-graders read a passage of text, then tested them on their recall at various times over the following two months. He found that the longer he waited to test them, the more they had forgotten, which is not too surprising. The more interesting finding was that once students had been tested, their subsequent test scores stayed about the same. In other words, testing them on the material seemed to have cemented that knowledge in their brains, stopping them from forgetting it.

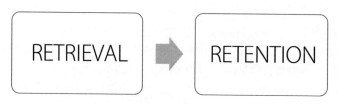

Figure 1.2: Why Practice Makes Perfect

Many studies have replicated this finding. In 2006, Roediger and Karpicke sought to determine whether testing was better than simply giving students another chance to study the material. They gave students a short passage of text to read, then randomly assigned them to either have a chance to study the passage again or do a free-recall test on the content of the passage (without having the opportunity to re-study it). One week later, all the students were tested on their ability to recall details about the passage. The students who had done the test rather than re-studying did significantly better on the test, which indicates that testing was more effective in helping students learn and remember the material than re-studying. Many other studies have demonstrated that testing is a much better study strategy than re-studying, with the best outcomes coming from repeated practice tests (Rawson & Dunlosky, 2011; Roediger, Putnam, & Smith, 2011).

Why Does It Work?

Social science does not only seek to learn "what," it also seeks to learn "why." The evidence is pretty clear that testing does improve learning and memory, but why does it work so well? What is actually happening in your brain when you retrieve information, and what implication does this have for your long-term memory and recall?

One theory as to why practice testing works is that it enhances your ability to retrieve information later (Carpenter, 2009). Each time you recall a piece of information, it activates related information in your memory. That related information then becomes encoded with the original piece of information, giving you more ways to access the information. In effect, searching for a memory creates a bigger web of connected memories, and those connected memories can also serve as cues to make it easier to retrieve the information you are looking for.

Putting It into Practice

You may think testing is up to your instructors, so there's nothing you can do about whether you are tested on the material or not. This is not true at all. It isn't about how your instructors should test you; it's about testing yourself while you are studying. It doesn't have to be complicated, but it should be effortful. Here are some practical tips for testing yourself:

Continued

- Use flashcards.
- Do the practice quizzes provided by the textbook publisher. You can often find them at the end of the chapter, or possibly even online.
- Make up your own practice questions. This is also a good test of how well you understand the material.

Doing practice tests requires more effort than simply rereading a chapter, but this effort is worth it. You'll remember the material much better, which will pay off when it comes time for those dreaded tests.

Spaced Practice

It's the end of term, and you've got four exams in the next week. Do you:

a) study for each exam the night before; or
b) invent a time machine so you can go back and start studying earlier in the term?

You probably haven't been able to invent a time machine or else you would have set time forward so you would have already written your exams. And you probably already know that (a) is not the best option. Since you are reading this chapter at the beginning of the term, you're in luck. You don't have to pick (a) or (b). You can instead choose to do spaced practice. **Spaced practice** simply means spreading your studying out instead of doing it all at once. In other words: not cramming. By starting earlier in the term and spreading your studying out over time, you can reduce your stress level and get better grades!

Where's the Evidence?

In 1998, psychologist Frank Dempster claimed that the spacing effect was "one of the most remarkable phenomena to emerge from laboratory research on learning," but its lack of actual use made it a "case study in the failure to apply the results of psychological research" (p. 627). This may sound a bit dramatic, but the point Dempster was making is an important one. Researchers have been studying the effects of spaced practice since 1885 (yes, 1885!). Hermann Ebbinghaus, who was the first to study the notion of the learning curve, was a pioneer in using experimentation to study memory. In his research, he discovered that we forget much of what we learn rather rapidly (the forgetting curve), but all it takes is some spaced repetition to help us retain that information. Ebbinghaus (1885/1913) recommended that "with any considerable number of repetitions a suitable distribution of them over a space of time is decidedly more advantageous than the massing of them at a single time" (p. 89). Considering Ebbinghaus published this work in 1885, students have been soundly ignoring this advice for well over 100 years.

Since then, countless studies have replicated his findings and made similar recommendations. In a meta-analysis that compared the results of 271 different studies of cramming (or "massed practice") versus spaced practice, Cepeda, Pashler, Vul, Wixted, and Rohrer (2006) found that, overall, spaced practice resulted in grades that were nine percent higher than massed practice. You may think nine percent is pretty small, but consider this. Improving your grade by nine percent could take you to a pass from a fail, or to an A from a B. And it's important to keep in mind this nine percent improvement does not require working nine percent harder—just nine percent smarter.

Why Does It Work?

There are a few theories as to why massed practice is less effective for long-term learning than spaced practice. One theory is that when you review something immediately after learning it, you are less likely to process it in as much detail because your review of it will not require much effort (Bahrick & Hall, 2005). If you read this chapter once, then reread it immediately after, it will still be fresh in your mind, so you will probably skim over some of the content. However, if you waited a week or even one day to reread it, you would have forgotten more of what you read, and you would probably read it more thoroughly the second time. We often mistake the ease with which we read something for an indication of how well we know it, so if you find your immediate review easy, you'll think you know all the material. This is why cramming makes us think we know more than we do.

Another theory as to why distributed practice works is that when there is a time lag between when we first study something and when we return to study it, our second study session serves as a type of practice test—it causes us to retrieve the information from our first study session from our memory (Dunlosky et al., 2013). This tends not to happen when we don't space out our study sessions, because the information hasn't found its way into our long-term memory yet. We know from our discussion on the benefits of practice testing that retrieval aids in retention. Therefore, having the material not *too* fresh in your mind is a good thing.

Putting It into Practice

Admittedly, a number of courses are not set up to encourage distributed practice. Given our understanding of human nature, it's easier to put off studying and hope for the best (or a time machine) than to plan ahead and start studying for an exam that's a month away. Although you may like the idea of a course with only one or two midterms and a final exam, having weekly tests would actually encourage more distributed practice, because it would force you to study every week. Then you wouldn't have to cram for the final exam, because you would have been practising all along.

You can't control how your courses are set up, but you can control how you approach your studying. Here's how to plan ahead for distributed practice.

- At the beginning of the term, put all of your deadlines for each course on a calendar. It's helpful to be able to see an overview of what your entire term will look like.
- Notice how you probably have fewer tests and assignments at the beginning of the term? Start studying then! We promise it won't be wasted effort.
- Make a plan to study a bit each day (or week, depending on how much time you have before your exams).
- If you drop the ball during the term (and that's likely to happen at least once), keep enough of an eye ahead to give yourself at least a week to study. Spacing out your studying over a week is going to get you a better grade than cramming the night before.

Interleaved Practice—Mixing It Up

Have you ever become really involved in learning something new, like a video game or a musical instrument or even some type of sport? Maybe you were so immersed in it you didn't do anything else. You probably did it as a baby, when you were knocking off developmental milestones such as learning to walk and eat solid food. But let's face it, it's not like babies have much else to do, so they have time to focus on one particular skill. However, if you are a full-time student, or even if you are taking a few courses on a part-time basis, you don't have the luxury of focusing on learning just one thing at a time. Even within one course there is a diversity of material to learn, and when you multiply that by all the other courses you are taking, it equates to a lot of studying all at once.

Fortunately, research has shown it's actually good to shake up your studying a bit and do **interleaved practice**; in other words, mix up the way you practise learning related content. Say, for example, you are studying for a test on 20th-century British literature, in which you will be asked to write about a number of novels from this time period. You might be tempted to study each novel separately, until you know each one really well. That's called blocking—practising one thing at a time until you perfect it. If you interleave your studying instead, by studying a bit of each novel at a time, or maybe focus on common themes or stylistic elements in the novels, you will actually increase your recall of those novels on the test. You could do it with a statistics course too: Rather than just studying one type of statistical test before moving on to the next one, try studying, for example, the assumptions of all the statistical tests, then the formulas, and then the interpretations.

Where's the Evidence?

The idea of interleaved practice has been popular in sports and other areas involving the learning of physical skills, and the evidence in favour of it for this purpose is pretty convincing. For example, researchers were able to significantly improve the batting ability of baseball players by having them do interleaved practice, in which they practised hitting various types of pitches (e.g., curveball, fastball) in one session, compared to when they did blocked practice focusing on only one type of pitch (e.g., curveball) at a time (Hall, Domingues, & Cavazos, 1994).

Since you likely aren't being tested on your ability to hit a curveball, you'll probably be more convinced by research in the field of education. Taylor and Rohrer (2010) were able to *double* the test scores of their students (77% vs. 38%) by having them do interleaved practice rather than blocked practice on a math test. And students who were being tested on their ability to correctly match painters with their paintings performed significantly better when they learned about all the artists and their works at once (i.e., interleaved practice), rather than studying one artist at a time (i.e., blocking; Kang & Pashler, 2012).

Why Does It Work?

There are a couple of theories as to why interleaved practice works. One theory is that the learning that takes place during blocked practice involves less processing because you are learning the same type of thing all at once. Similar to what happens when you do massed practice, you may spend less time processing this material because you think you already know it, and thus you don't learn it as well. With interleaved practice, it's likely that more advanced processing takes place as you are learning (Dunlosky et al., 2013). Another theory as to why interleaved practice is better than blocked practice is that when you only study one thing at a time (i.e., you use blocked practice), you aren't practising discriminating between concepts (Dunlosky, et al., 2013). For example, if you practise just one type of pitch at a time, that blocked practice won't help you figure out what type of pitch you are about to get when you're playing an actual game of baseball. If you had used interleaved practice, you would have not only practised hitting various types of pitches, but you would have also practised how to anticipate what kind of pitch you were going to get. With blocked practice, when you're only learning one type of pitch at a time, you don't have to discriminate between types of pitches, which is a skill you need in an actual game.

The same reasoning works for academic studying. If you only study one type of statistical test at a time, it won't help you as much when you are asked what type of statistical test to use in a given situation, because you won't have practised interleaving the various types of statistical tests. Interleaving helps you integrate the material better, which is often what you are asked to do on a test.

Putting It into Practice

How to use interleaved practice may vary depending on what you are studying for. The key thing to remember is to mix it up a bit—don't try to memorize one thing and then move on to another thing. This doesn't only apply for individual courses, either. If you can, try to interleave your studying for your courses too. This is especially relevant if you are taking a number of courses in the same discipline or area. That may not happen in your first year of study, but as you get further along in your studies and your courses become more specialized to your program, try interleaving your studying for your courses. It's likely that they have interrelated content. For example, if you are studying criminology, some of the theories of crime would be relevant in many of your courses. Rather than just memorizing these theories separately, organize and study them by their features instead. Then, when you are asked to choose a theory to apply to a particular criminological issue, it will be easier to discriminate between theories.

Elaborative Interrogation and Self-Explanation— It's Okay to Talk to Yourself

These are fancy names for two very simple strategies. Before reading further, ask yourself what you think they mean, and either talk out loud or think explicitly about the reason behind your answer. Do you see what we did there? We just got you to engage in elaborative interrogation and self-explanation! **Elaborative interrogation** simply means attempting to figure out the reasoning behind some stated fact, or asking "why?" So, for example, if you are studying for a test in developmental psychology and you come across a section on risk taking in adolescence, before reading further, think about why adolescents might be more likely than adults to engage in risky behaviours. Generate your own reasons first, based on your prior learning and your own experiences. **Self-explanation** is similar to elaborative interrogation, but it focuses more on explaining the concept to yourself to ensure that you fully understand it. For example, if you are studying how various drugs affect the brain, explain the process to yourself, stopping to clarify if you come across anything that doesn't make sense to you.

Elaborative interrogation and self-explanation are similar strategies, in that they both involve active processing of the material. By stopping and asking yourself questions or verbalizing your thought processes, you are working with the information at a much deeper level than if you simply read the material. This is a very active technique, and it actually encourages you to talk to yourself! Just be sure to do it quietly if you are in the library or study hall.

Where's the Evidence?

The benefits of elaborative interrogation and self-explanation are pretty well established. In a simple but elegant study, Pressley, McDaniel, Turnure, Wood, and Ahmad (1987) gave students a list of sentences, such as "the hungry man got into the car," to study. Some of the students were asked to explain why they thought the man got into the car, some were told why he got into the car (because he was going to a restaurant), and some were not given anything other than the original sentence. When they were tested later on their recall of the content of the sentences (for example, "Who got into the car?"), guess who did better? Why? (See? We're doing it again—getting you to use elaborative interrogation!) You probably guessed the group who was asked to generate explanations performed better, and you're right. Not only did they do better, but their accuracy was approximately 72 percent, compared to 37 percent for the other two groups.

This study technique works well in groups too. Woloshyn and Stockley (1995) had students work either alone or in pairs, using elaborative interrogation or not, and found that regardless of whether they were working alone or with a partner, those who used elaborative interrogation performed better.

Why Does It Work?

When you are forced to generate your own reasons for things or when you have to articulate your understanding of a concept, you are not just relying on retrieving information from your working memory. Instead, you are organizing and integrating that knowledge with existing information in your memory. In other words, you are expanding your current knowledge, rather than just adding another separate box of facts to your memory. Elaborative interrogation and self-explanation also help with discriminating between concepts, because they often involve thinking about the similarities and differences, or comparing or contrasting them (Dunlosky et al., 2013). This makes it easier when, on a test, you are asked to explain the differences between concepts or to choose the most appropriate one in a given situation.

Putting It into Practice

To make full use of this technique, try channelling your inner toddler, and ask "why?" after everything you read. Resist the temptation to look for answers before generating your own. And then explain everything—to yourself, your study partner, even your dog. This will also give you a good idea of how well you understand the material.

Less Effective Study Strategies

There are some popular study strategies you may have been using that are not as effective as you might think.

Highlighting

Many students use highlighting to flag important information in the textbook, and there's nothing wrong with doing so. We tend to remember things that stand out, so if there is one yellow term highlighted on a page, you will probably remember it better. The problem is when you highlight too much, in which case all you are demonstrating is your artistic ability in turning a white page yellow. It may make it look pretty, but it's not very useful. When the page is all yellow, nothing stands out. The other reason why minimal highlighting is better is that by highlighting only a small amount of material, you probably have to put some mental effort into deciding what is important. This extra processing will help you remember it. However, if you're going to put the effort into figuring out the most important material in order to highlight properly, you may as well put that effort into a more effective learning technique. So, don't let yourself be fooled into thinking that just because you have covered your chapter with yellow highlighting, you have studied effectively.

Rereading

The more times you read something, the better you'll know it, right? Wrong! We bet you could move your eyes through this entire paragraph while thinking about something else, and you wouldn't remember anything you read. The problem with simply reading the material over and over again is that it is passive. If you aren't processing the material in some way as you read it, it won't stick. Reading something multiple times will not get the material into your long-term memory. Remember, effective encoding and storage are essential for retrieval, and if you haven't encoded and stored the material you just read, you won't be able to retrieve it. The other problem with simply rereading a chapter is that after you read it the first time, you may think you know it. When you read it a second time, you read it less carefully, and even less carefully the third and fourth times you read it. Because you read less carefully, you probably also read faster, which may make you (mistakenly) think that you know it better. You would be better off spending the time reading once with one of the more active strategies we discussed previously.

Summarization

You might be surprised to know that summarizing the material you need to learn is not always the best strategy. Although being able to pull important points out of a longer piece of work is a very good skill, it doesn't always work. Think about this chapter that you're reading now. How confident are you that you could summarize the entire chapter in a few short points? Could you do well on a single essay question about what the chapter was about? Could you do well on a short-answer test, where you were asked to summarize the various learning strategies? Could you do well on a detailed, multiple-choice test? Summarizing tends to not be effective when you have a lot of material to learn.

It might be a good choice if you have a short quiz on a few main points, but it won't help you ace that exam covering the first six chapters of your Introduction to Sociology text.

TAKING CHARGE OF YOUR LEARNING

How to Get the Most Out of Your Classes

Throughout your time in school you will take many courses. Some of them you will love and will look forward to attending class, even if it's at 8:30 in the morning. Others you may not look forward to so much, either because they are too challenging or too easy, or they're not directly related to your chosen program of study. Some of them will be optional, and others will be mandatory. Regardless of your reasons for taking a course, you probably still want to do well in it, right? What would be the point of taking a class and failing it? That's not a good use of your time or your money.

Below are three ways to get the most out of your classes. They're simple, but you'd be surprised at how many students don't do all three.

1. Attend every lecture
    If you were to ask instructors to list the most aggravating questions they get from students, the most common—and for some, the only—one would be "I missed class last week. Did I miss anything important?" In fact, this question has even inspired a poem by Canadian poet Tom Wayman (1993), entitled, "Did I Miss Anything?" Here's the first stanza:

    Did I Miss Anything?

    Nothing. When we realized you weren't here
    we sat with our hands folded on our desks
    in silence, for the full two hours.

    We recommend reading the entire poem (you can find it online)—it's pretty funny.
        You get the picture. While not every lecture will be packed full of information that you find fascinating, every one is important. Your instructor has a limited amount of time to cover an entire course worth of material, and they would not waste an entire week on something that

wasn't worthwhile. "But my instructor just follows what's in the textbook," you might say. If that's the case, then attending lectures will save you time when you are studying. Even if it's the same material as in your text, hearing it rather than reading it will encode it differently in your memory, helping you retrieve it later (Michael, Keller, Carpenter, & Just, 2001). If nothing else, you might miss important information about an upcoming assignment or test.

There is always *something* you can get from every single lecture. For those courses where finding the motivation to go to class is a bit harder, try making a game of it. Instead of going in with the assumption you won't learn anything, try to actively look for the purpose of the lecture.

Maybe breaking it down into dollars will convince you. According to Statistics Canada, the average yearly tuition for regular degree programs at Canadian universities in the 2016/17 academic year was $6,373. Although the value of a course isn't only based on what you get out of lectures, if a typical student takes 10 courses per year, with each course being three hours per week and lasting for 13 weeks, that works out to a cost of $16.34 per hour. If your class meets once a week for three hours, that works out to just under $50. If your class meets twice a week for 1.5 hours, that's about $25.

You may be thinking about all the things you could do with that $25 or $50: Go out for a nice meal. Take a friend to a movie. Make a donation to charity. But here's the thing. You've already decided your education is worth investing in. The fact that you made the decision to apply to college or university, accept their offer of admission, and pay your tuition indicates you realize the value of an education. You believe, at some level, that this is an investment in your future, so why waste it?

Finally, think about school as practice for life. Treat your education as your job—a job you don't want to get fired from. Could you get away with not going to work? Not for long. Could you get away with not getting your work done on time? Again, probably not. Think about your courses as an opportunity to develop the habits that will help you succeed in your life. Habits are important—when you do something often enough, it becomes automatic and eventually will become a habit. When actions become automatic, you don't have to think about them anymore; you just do them. That saves you mental energy, because your brain doesn't have to think about what to do. If you develop good habits in school, like going to class regularly and on time and getting your work done, it will become a habit that will serve you well in your life after school.

2. Take notes (but not with a computer)

Computers are amazing, right? You probably rely on yours for lots of things and would feel a bit lost without it. You may even see it as an essential tool for your education, and you're probably right. It would be hard to make it through school without one. You may be surprised to learn, however, that your trusty laptop could be doing you more harm than good in the classroom.

Recent research suggests that taking notes by hand during class is more effective than taking notes by computer. In a series of experiments, Mueller and Oppenheimer (2014) randomly assigned students to take notes either by hand or on a computer, and then tested them on their memory and understanding of the lecture content. They found that even though students took more notes when they typed their notes on a computer compared to when they wrote them by hand, those in the handwriting condition did better on tests.

One reason for this might be that the notes you type are more likely to be verbatim—word-for-word what the instructor says. As long as you can type pretty fast, this might seem like a good way to get the most out of the class. However, this eliminates the need for you to process the material before you make your notes. Think about it this way: When you are handwriting your notes, you need to be selective because it's unlikely that you can write down everything the instructor says. The mere act of deciding what is important and what isn't, and trying to paraphrase it in order to write it efficiently, is a form of encoding. When you are typing word-for-word, encoding does not happen because you are not as likely to be actively processing the information. Mueller and Oppenheimer (2014) tested whether giving the computer note-takers a chance to catch up with the handwriting note-takers by allowing them time to study before the test would help, but it didn't—they still didn't do as well on the test as the handwriting note-takers. So taking notes by hand actually gives you a step up on studying! Although it might seem like more effort at the time, it actually saves you time when you are studying.

Taking notes by hand doesn't work for everyone, and it may not be possible for you to leave your computer at home. If that's the case, you can still take advantage of the benefits of early encoding. Try not to write down everything the instructor says during class. Make your note-taking more effortful by thinking about what's most important and writing it in your own words. Talk to your instructor or teaching assistant for advice on how you might approach this in their course. Your school may even offer workshops on how to tailor your note-taking strategies to your unique strengths and abilities.

3. Pay attention

   Here's another good reason to take notes by hand if you can: Your computer is a distraction. Every time you turn your attention to your computer, you are turning your attention away from what's happening in class.

   Our brains are limited in how much information they can process, and while we may think we are good at multitasking, research suggests we're actually pretty bad at it (Ellis, Daniels, & Jauregui, 2010). You can't write a funny comment on your friend's Facebook status while paying full attention to what your instructor is saying. No one can. Short-term memory is limited in capacity, and it takes effort to move information into our long-term memory, so unless you pay attention to the information coming in, it won't stick. Remember the pathway to enduring memory: encoding, storage, and retrieval. You may successfully encode it (in other words, you will hear it and think you understand it), but it won't be stored in your memory properly and you won't be able to retrieve it.

   If you do use your computer in class for taking notes, close all the other programs. Maybe even turn off your WiFi. Reduce the temptation to just quickly check social media or watch YouTube by not even having them open.

Managing Your Time

You will probably receive lots of advice about how to manage your time in school. Buy a planner or use an app to get organized. Make lists. Create a schedule; be sure to include some down time. At the beginning of the term you will probably be very motivated to stay on top of things, and you'll likely be pretty good at it at first. Unfortunately, the beginning of the term is not when you most need to be an organization wizard—it's the middle and the end of the term when you have three midterms to study for and two papers to write, or five final exams in three days.

If you use the learning and studying strategies in this chapter, you'll probably save yourself some time because you'll be studying more effectively. We don't have the space in this book to cover all the great time-management strategies out there, but here are two evidence-based strategies for planning your study time, and for dealing with the inevitable lapses in your planning.

Don't Be a Hero—Take a Break

You may think the longer you study, the more successful you will be at learning. Actually, the opposite is true. Research shows that we can sustain our attention on focused work for about 1.5 hours; after that, our attention drops off sharply. In the interest of maximizing the return on your study investment, you should take breaks rather than trying to study continuously in one marathon session. One way to build breaks into your study time is through the Pomodoro method. It's a simple process, developed by Francesco Cirillo, whereby you set a timer for 25 minutes, and commit to focused work/studying during that period. When your timer goes off, you get a short (five-minute) break. Then set the timer for another 25 minutes and do the same. Once you've had four 25-minute sessions, you get to take a longer break (30 minutes). You can do a Web search for "Pomodoro" to find out more about it, and there are free apps you can download to help time your study sessions.

Eat Your Frogs for Breakfast

Not real frogs—they're too cute to eat. There's a famous quote, sometimes attributed to Mark Twain, that says, "Eat a live frog first thing in the morning and nothing worse will happen to you the rest of the day." In other words, get those tough/boring/anxiety-provoking tasks out of the way in the morning so you aren't worried about them the rest of the day. The problem is we tend to put off things that scare us or make us anxious. So, there's the initial anxiety a difficult task creates in us. But then, because we put off the task, we become more anxious because, at some point, we'll have to do it. Procrastination is funny that way: In the short term, it may feel good because we are putting off something we don't want to do, but in the long term, it causes us a lot of grief. Therefore, procrastination is painful! But here's the thing—when you actually complete the task you don't want to do, the pain goes away. If you eat those frogs in the morning, not only will it feel good to get them out of the way, but also they won't be hopping around in your brain for the rest of the day.

What to Do When Things Don't Go as Planned

The Value of Failure

Even if you take every piece of advice in this chapter to heart, studying effectively, making the most of your classes, and generally being a hard-working, dedicated student, chances are your academic pursuits won't always go the way you want them to. Maybe you didn't do as well on a test as you would have liked or you handed in a paper you didn't have time to polish or you got nervous before a presentation and didn't handle questions well. To our knowledge, social scientists have not yet estimated the exactly probability of this happening, but we're going to suggest that it's pretty high. You aren't perfect, and neither is anyone else. So, failure happens, and at some point we all have to deal with it.

As this section heading suggests, instead of beating yourself up over a setback, it might help you more to see it as an opportunity. Research has shown that failure is actually essential to success, because without failure we don't learn, adapt, and develop resilience (Sitkin, 1992). Imagine a world where no one ever made a mistake: We would not have penicillin, the Dyson vacuum cleaner, or even the colour mauve (Dyson, 2003; Garfield, 2000; Lax, 2004)! If you always succeed, what motivation do you have to try new things or do things differently? Sitkin (1992) suggests that continual success is actually detrimental because it can lead to a number of negative outcomes: failing to look for alternative (and perhaps more effective) ways to do things, a reduction in the amount of attention we pay to things, complacency and inertia, risk aversion, and homogeneity (in other words, being boring).

The good thing about small failures, Sitkin (1992) argues, is that they push us out of complacency. When things don't go as planned, it forces us to think more about them. Remember from our discussion of how the brain works that when we engage in deeper processing, we tend to learn and remember more. When you are forced to rethink a problem, such as why you failed a test, it actually helps you process the material, making you more likely to remember it in the future. That's why practice testing helps: When you practise and get something wrong, it results in more complex thinking, which results in better and more enduring learning.

So the next time things don't go the way you planned, be grateful. Think of it as an opportunity to grow, learn, and become stronger. Don't let failure overcome you; instead, use it as a stepping stone to success, and "fail forward" (Maxwell, 2007).

It's All in Your (Growth) Mindset

Do you believe your intelligence is unchangeable, or do you believe you can increase your intelligence? Your answer to this question can affect how you approach difficult tasks. According to **mindset theory** (Dweck, 2006; Dweck, Chui, & Hong, 1995), people tend to make one of two assumptions about the malleability of various personal attributes or characteristics. Those with an entity theory perspective (also referred to as a "fixed mindset") believe personal attributes are fixed and unchangeable, while those with an incremental theory perspective (also referred to as a "growth mindset") believe personal attributes are malleable. Your mindset is part of your worldview, and thus it can affect your attitudes and behaviours (Dweck et al., 1995).

How? Let's say you don't do as well on a test as you would like. If you believe your intelligence is fixed and unchangeable (in other words, you have a fixed mindset), your response to not doing well on the test may be to think you are not intelligent. Since you believe you can't change your intelligence, you might not be motivated to seek help or try harder on the next test. Conversely, if you believe your intelligence is malleable, failure on a test may motivate you to try harder because you believe you can become more intelligent through increased effort.

When it comes to picking yourself up after a disappointing test performance, having a growth mindset is useful because if you believe you can do better, then you will try again. You'll seek extra help, study more, and work harder. If you don't think you can do better, then you'll be more likely to give up.

The good news is that if you do tend to have a fixed mindset about some things, you can change—even mindset is malleable!

Carol Dweck, the researcher who originally developed the theory of mindset, has a really helpful website on which you can take a quiz to find out whether you tend to have a growth or fixed mindset. You can find it at mindsetonline.com. It also provides a four-step plan to help you strengthen your growth mindset.

Four Steps for a Growth Mindset

1. Learn to hear your fixed mindset "voice"
Pay attention to how you approach challenges. Do you tend to take a defeatist attitude ("I can't do it; I'm not good enough")?
2. Recognize that you have a choice
You can't control most of the challenges you are faced with, but you can control how you respond to them.
3. Talk back to it with a growth mindset
If your fixed mindset says, "I can't do it," consciously and deliberately respond to it with a growth mindset response, such as "I won't know unless I try. If I can't do it this time, I'll get it next time."

4. Take the growth mindset action

You may always have that fixed-mindset voice in your head saying you can't do it, but with practice, you will also have the growth-mindset voice that says you can. Choose to listen to the growth mindset action. Take on challenges with a positive attitude and learn from your setbacks.

Adapted from: https://mindsetonline.com/changeyourmindset/firststeps/index.html

Seeking Help

It may seem like the easiest thing in the world to do, but many people find it difficult to ask for help. This is especially true for some students. You may get to a point in your studies where you don't understand the course material and can't figure it out on your own or you have something going on in your life that makes it impossible for you to hand an assignment in on time or you are struggling with your mental health and need someone to talk to. Universities and colleges are set up to provide exactly this kind of support to you. Your instructors are there to help you with the course material and to discuss concerns about due dates, and the campus wellness centre has trained counsellors on staff to make sure you get the help you need.

There is a connection between academic performance and help seeking: Those who ask for help tend to get higher grades (Alexitch, 2002). This is a correlation, so we don't know whether seeking help results in higher grades, or whether those who perform better academically are simply more likely to ask for help. What we do know for sure is that if you need help and don't ask for it, you won't get what you need.

Although you will be surrounded by helpful, friendly people, they won't necessarily know you need help unless you tell them. A big challenge for many students when they first arrive at university or college is learning how to advocate for themselves. Some schools are larger than others, but even at a smaller campus, your instructors won't necessarily know if you are struggling. You need to take that first step.

Where to Find Help on Campus

- Your friends: They may not be able to help you write that essay, but they will give you social support and make you laugh, and that's often all you need to get through the challenging times.

Continued

- Academic advisors: Try to visit them every year to make sure you're on track to graduate on time. They can also refer you to other sources of help if you need it.
- Study groups: Some courses may have formal study groups, but you can always start your own.
- Professor/course instructor: We have spent many lonely hours in our offices waiting for students to come for help during our office hours. Please come to see us—we don't bite!
- Teaching/lab assistant: These are the trained professionals who often end up marking your essays and exams. You should make sure they know who you are, and ask them lots of questions.
- Writing centre: Free writing consultation and help with assignments and essays—why wouldn't you use them?
- Librarian: Did you know that librarians are experts at finding sources? And that part of their job is to help you become an expert too?
- Counselling or wellness centre: Your school understands that wellness and academic success go hand-in-hand. They can help you with the physical or emotional challenges that can make learning harder.
- Accessible learning: If you have a disability, they can help make sure you have supports and accommodations in place so you can do your best.

IT'S NOT ALL ABOUT STUDYING: THE SOCIAL SCIENCE OF WELLNESS

Sleep

How much sleep did you get last night? And how do you feel today? The connection between sleep and mental functioning is well established: the more tired you are, the less well your mind works. There's a reason why sleep deprivation has been used as a form of torture. Going without sleep for too long has pretty serious consequences, ranging from confusion and irritability to disorientation and even death. Don't worry—pulling an all-nighter before a test is not going to have any serious, long-term effects on your health, but it can have a negative effect on your grades.

When we sleep, we are actually consolidating information in our memory. Our brain takes advantage of the "downtime" while we are sleeping to code the new information it acquired during the day and integrate it with our existing long-term memories, making it easier for us to retrieve this new information later (Diekelmann & Born, 2010). That sounds like it would be pretty helpful when you are studying, doesn't it? Not getting enough sleep before a test means your brain doesn't have the opportunity to consolidate the new information, making it harder to remember. Research has shown that when students sacrifice sleep for studying, it negatively affects their academic performance. Sleepy students report having trouble concentrating and processing new material, doing poorly on tests, and not getting their assignments done (Gillen-O'Neel, Huynh, & Fuligni, 2013). Researchers have found an overall positive correlation between hours of sleep and academic performance, with more sleep being associated with better grades (Curcio, Ferrara, & De Gennaro, 2006). If not getting enough sleep has been shown to negatively affect memory, then consistently not getting enough sleep could result in lower grades.

Life gets busy, especially at the end of term when you have lots of assignments due and final exams coming up. You might be tempted to sacrifice a bit of sleep to make more time for studying. According to the research mentioned above, sleep should be the last thing you sacrifice. If you can, try other options first, like taking one less shift at work or postponing that Netflix marathon. Your memory, and hopefully your grades, will thank you!

Exercise

Regular exercise is another healthy activity that often falls by the wayside when we get busy. You don't have to be an elite athlete to appreciate the benefits of exercise; anything that involves moving, such as going for a walk, shooting baskets, doing yoga, or even dancing, counts. As a student, exercise is especially important, because it can positively affect your academic performance. In other words, a healthy body = a healthy mind. It's simple, so why don't we do it more?

When you are studying or writing a paper, it's easy to tell yourself you don't have time to exercise. You may find yourself sitting at your desk for hours on end, focusing on your upcoming test or essay. You may have even spent an entire day working, only getting up to get food and use the bathroom. You don't need a textbook to tell you this isn't good for you—your body will let you know that. The good news is that researchers have discovered you don't necessarily have to run a marathon to reap the benefits of exercise.

Fenesi, Lucibello, Kim, and Heisz (2016) found that taking a short exercise break can help you learn better. They were interested in whether short bursts of exercise during a lecture would help students pay attention and focus more. There were three conditions in this study: no break, exercise break (where students did short bursts of jumping jacks), and non-exercise break (where students played computer games). The researchers included a non-exercise break because they wanted to know whether just taking a break would be helpful, or whether it had to be an active break. They tested students on the content of the lecture 48 hours later, and compared their grades. Those in the exercise break group reported they felt they had concentrated better on the lecture, and their tests scores were higher than the other two groups. Those in the computer break group performed no better on the test than those who got no break. In other words, taking a break was only beneficial to both concentration and retention if it involved exercise. So, the next time you are studying and want to take a break, try doing a few jumping jacks or push-ups instead of playing the latest addictive game on your phone.

The research described above recommends incorporating exercise into your studying, but it's not just your grades that can benefit. The physical benefits are clear, the most important being that exercise can help you live longer (Paffenbarger & Hyde, 1988). However, being active has also been found to have psychological benefits. Research has shown that people report more positive moods after they exercise, especially if they were in a bad mood before exercising (Gauvin, Rejeski, & Norris, 1996). University students who exercise regularly report lower rates of depression than those who do not exercise (Steptoe et al., 1997). There is much promising research on the use of exercise to treat stress, depression, and anxiety (Salmon, 2001). As a student, you will likely experience times when you feel stressed, anxious, or even just a bit grumpy. If you're overwhelmed by these feelings, you should seek help from your doctor or the school wellness centre, but a quick fix for mild symptoms might be to try to get more exercise.

Remember your mind and your body are not separate. When you take care of your body by eating well, exercising, and getting enough sleep, you are also taking care of your brain.

Go Outside

Did your parents ever tell you to go outside and play if they felt you were lazing around the house too much? They (and you) may not have realized it, but they were giving you sound advice on how to be happier. Interesting research on the science of happiness has shown that being in nature can increase our happiness. It stems from what is referred to as the **"biophilia hypothesis"** (Wilson, 1984), which suggests that humans have an inborn need to connect with nature and other living things. According to this theory, connecting with the natural world has a positive effect on us because it fulfills this innate need. That's one reason why cities have parks and green spaces, offices have plants, and Canadians will endure mosquitoes and black flies in the spring just to get into the great outdoors.

It's an interesting theory, but what does the evidence say? Researchers have approached this question in various ways, but the overwhelming conclusion is that nature is good for our well-being; people are happier when they are in nature. In an effort to better understand this relationship, and to rule out the possibility that happier people just tend to go outside more, MacKerron and Mourato (2013) designed an innovative study in which they created a smart-phone app that prompted participants to self-rate their well-being at various times in the day. Using GPS data, the researchers connected the participants' well-being with their location (whether they were in a natural or urban environment). From this, they were able to test the connection between well-being and natural environments, while controlling for things like weather, time of day, who the person was with, what they were doing, and what day it was. The results were clear: Participants were significantly happier when they were in green or natural environments compared to when they were indoors or in areas where there was no green space.

In addition to self-report measures of well-being (which are, after all, subjective), researchers have also examined the physiological effects of spending time in nature. Bratman, Hamilton, Hahn, Daily, and Gross (2015) studied the brains of people who had walked outside in a natural setting for 90 minutes, and compared them to people who had walked in urban settings for the same amount of time. They found significantly less activity in the subgenual prefrontal cortex (sgPFC) for those who walked in nature. The sgPFC is the part of the brain associated with the kinds of self-focused, obsessive thoughts that occur when we ruminate. Rumination happens when we focus our attention on the causes and consequences of the negative emotions associated with our emotional distress rather than on possible solutions. So, for example, if you don't do well on test, you might replay over and over in your mind how you felt when you got your mark back, blaming yourself for not studying enough. It's okay to feel sad or disappointed and to try to understand why we feel the way we feel, but it becomes maladaptive when we only focus on what happened and why rather than on what can be done about it. Chronic rumination has been linked with depression, anxiety, impaired problem-solving ability, and reduced social support (Nolen-Hoeksema, Wisco, & Lyubomirsky, 2008). So these results suggest going for a walk in nature can protect us against the obsessive thoughts that can lead to the kinds of things that can reduce our well-being.

How can this help you as a student? If you can, take your breaks outside. Hug a tree. Plant some flowers. Buy a plant for your room. Walk in the woods. Go play outside. Maximize the benefits of nature by exercising outside. Research shows that if you do it with a friend, the benefits are even greater (Plante, Gustafson, Brecht, Imberi, & Sanchez, 2011).

Calm Your Mind

If you get enough sleep, exercise regularly, and get fresh air, you'll have gone a long way toward keeping your body working properly (we haven't talked about healthy eating, but we're assuming you already know you can't live on beer and Doritos). And while it's true that if your body is healthy, your mind will function better, there are additional things you can do to keep your mind and mood well-tuned.

If you've ever felt that your mind is racing and you can't concentrate on anything because you have too many thoughts rushing around in your head, don't worry—you're not alone! There's even a name for it; Buddha called it "monkey mind," maybe because it can feel like there's a bunch of wild and/or drunk monkeys in your brain, all battling for your attention. Monkey mind can be especially distracting when you are trying to study. The monkey that represents all the other essays you have due might be wrestling with the monkey that is stressed about the test tomorrow, and the monkey that represents the very strict budget you are on might be chasing the monkey that wants to go shopping or out to a show. Then the Doritos monkey steps in and undoes all your healthy eating efforts for the week.

Buddha had a solution to monkey mind: meditation. You don't have to be a Buddhist monk or own the latest yoga gear to meditate. And there are so many different ways to do it that you can easily fit it into your day. You don't have to sit in an uncomfortable position and chant for an hour. There are lots of resources, including guided meditation videos and quick breathing practices you can do wherever you happen to be.

A review of all the literature on the benefits of meditation for physical issues would take up an entire textbook, but suffice it to say it has been used with much promise not only in the treatment of chronic pain (Hilton et al., 2017) but also for insomnia, hypertension (high blood pressure), dealing with cancer treatments, and even to reverse the effects of aging. No one is claiming meditation is a cure for illness, but it can help individuals deal with various medical issues and perhaps make them more manageable. Psychologists have also found benefits of meditation for various psychological and emotional issues. In a review of 57 studies of mindfulness meditation in college students, Bamber and Schneider (2016) found pretty clear evidence that meditation results in a decrease in stress and anxiety.

Teachers have been embracing meditation as a way to help their students focus. Meditation programs have been used to help students lower their anxiety before exams, self-regulate their behaviour, and even improve their memory. It's important to note this research is still in its infancy. While it seems to work and researchers are beginning to study it, the evidence is still a bit sketchy (Gould, Dariotis, Greenberg, & Mendelson, 2016). We're not claiming it will make you a Zen master, but it might help give you the focus you are looking for before a long study session.

Online Meditation and Mindfulness Resources

This is not an exhaustive list—there are lots of videos and articles out there. These are just a few to get you started.

http://mindfulnessforstudents.co.uk/students/
https://www.ted.com/talks/andy_puddicombe_all_it_takes_is_10_
     mindful_minutes
https://www.mindful.org/meditation/mindfulness-getting-started/
http://headspace.com

If meditation isn't your thing, there are other ways to tame those crazy monkeys. Yoga is a great way to combine both exercise and meditation/mindfulness. Or try immersing yourself in music or art, volunteering your time, or even prayer. The key thing is to find what works best for you.

Be Grateful

Your parents probably taught you how to say "please" and "thank you," and you're probably pretty good at using them by now. Saying "please" is a very good strategy for getting what you want, so you probably don't need to be convinced that it's a good idea to continue doing this in university. But what purpose does saying "thank you" serve? It's polite, and politeness is part of what makes society civilized. But in addition to making other people feel good, being grateful can actually be good for you and your mental health.

In a typical day, lots of good and not-so-good things happen. You may sleep through your alarm, but then a friend brings you a coffee in your early class. You may have had trouble accessing the Internet in your residence, but then you bond over your lack of connectivity with a nice neighbour. For many of us, our default is to focus on the negative things that happen, and with good reason. When negative things happen, we are motivated to figure out why they happened so we can avoid similar things in the future. So, we spend a fair amount of cognitive energy trying to figure them out. Conversely, when good things happen, we usually don't need an explanation for them, so we don't spend as much cognitive energy on them. We tend to focus more on negative events. But think about it: Which makes you feel happier—thinking about good things or thinking about bad things?

Research has shown that simply thinking back over your day each evening and writing about the things you were grateful for can significantly improve your mood (Emmons & McCullough, 2003). As crappy as your day might have been, you can always find something good that happened, which you can be grateful for: a nice sunset, a tasty lunch, or a smile from a stranger. By doing this regularly, you can retrain your brain to focus more on the positive things that happen to you during the day and less on the negative things. In time, you will actually begin to look for things you are grateful for, and while you are paying all that attention to these positive things, you spend much less time focusing on the negative. This isn't to say you should ignore stuff you need to deal with (being grateful will not make your statistics exam go away, no matter how hard you try), but it will help you focus less on things you have no control over.

Here's a very simple exercise to help you develop your gratitude muscles. Every evening, write down three things you are grateful for. They don't have to be big things, and try to avoid general things like "my family." Try to think of specific things that happened during the day, so choose something like "my sister texted me right when I needed a break" rather than "my sister is awesome."

A FINAL WORD ON THE SOCIAL SCIENCE OF LEARNING

Hey, you're still here! Thanks for sticking with us until the end. We've covered a lot in this chapter, and we discussed plenty of strategies that might help you make it through your courses a little more painlessly. All of our advice is evidence-based, which means there is social science research that backs up our claims. Don't discount the evidence just because a particular strategy doesn't work for you or because you don't agree with the advice. Also keep in mind this research is based on the "typical" student with a "typical" life situation and "typical" abilities. We understand that you may not fit into the mould of a "typical" student, and not all of these strategies will work for you. We also know there probably aren't enough hours in the day to do all the things we suggest, despite the fact that some of our strategies can actually save you time. All we ask is that you try some of them out, and hopefully you'll find something to make your studying more efficient and effective and your journey through school a little easier.

A Checklist for Success

STUDYING

Practice testing—Test yourself as you study. This actually helps you remember the material better at test time.

Spaced practice—Spread your studying out over the term instead of one long study session the night before the exam. This can actually save you time: More frequent, shorter study sessions are more efficient than one long session.

Interleaved practice—By switching things up and not just studying one concept after another, you'll remember connections between concepts rather than just the concepts themselves.

Elaborative interrogation and self-explanation—Practise explaining the material to yourself, your roommates, your friends, and even your pet. If you can explain it to them, you'll be able to explain it better on a test.

WELLNESS

Sleep—Not only does getting a good night's sleep before a test help you feel more alert and focused during the test, sleep helps consolidate information in your memory, so you'll remember what you studied better if you don't pull an all-nighter.

Exercise—Your brain is part of your body. Having a healthy body will help you have a healthy mind.

Go outside—Nature is good for you. Getting outside can help clear your mind, and make you less stressed.

Calm your mind—Meditation and/or mindfulness training can help you manage stress and anxiety, and learn to focus better.

Continued

Be grateful—Appreciating the good things that happen to you will help you focus more on the positive and less on the negative.

OTHER STUFF

Go to class and pay attention—You can miss a lot by not going to class, and attending class usually means better grades.

Think about your note-taking strategy—Consider leaving your laptop at home and taking your notes by hand if possible.

Failing can be good for you—Use small failures as opportunities to learn and grow.

See yourself as a work in progress—Take on challenges with a growth mindset; know that, with effort, you can always do better.

Get help when you need it—Successful students have one thing in common: They ask for help when they need it.

Be organized—Be sure to schedule time for work and play.

REVIEW IT

1. Memory is a three-part process. Describe each of the three parts. Now try describing the memory process without comparing it to a computer or using computer terminology.
2. Why will practice tests help you to learn and remember course material?
3. How do spaced practices help you to learn and remember course material? Why is "cramming" for a test less efficient than spaced practice?
4. Highlighting text in your readings can sometimes be a counterproductive study strategy. Why?
5. Which is more conducive to learning course material: taking notes on a computer or taking notes with a pen and paper? Why?
6. Why can small failures be helpful?

APPLY IT

How do your study habits compare to those outlined in this chapter? What good habits did you already have? What habits did you learn about that you could try?

2 Doing Social Science: Theory and Research in the Social Sciences

Notice the use of the word *science* in the term *social science*. And remember way, way back in Chapter 1 when we talked about evidence? Well, this chapter is about how social science combines those two concepts. For many people, the term *scientific evidence* brings to mind images of people in lab coats with test tubes, particle accelerators, or electron microscopes. In this chapter, we're going to talk about how social scientists find scientific evidence, albeit with equipment that's not quite as cool.

Why do we care about how social scientists construct theories and carry out their research? If we understand how to do research properly, then we can separate bad research from good research. You shouldn't believe everything you read, nor should you doubt everything you read. The only way to know if research findings are sound is to understand how the research was conducted.

LEARNING OBJECTIVES

1. Understand the use of theory in the social sciences
2. Learn the different approaches to social science
3. Learn the steps in the research process
4. Understand the different uses for social science research
5. Understand the different types of qualitative and quantitative research
6. Understand how theory and research work together in the social sciences

HOW WE UNDERSTAND THE WORLD

You know a lot of stuff. Take a minute to think about how you have accumulated all this knowledge. Were you born with it? Nope—babies, cute as they are, are kind of basic. Did you make it up? Hopefully not. You probably learned it from various places, like school, your parents, your friends, the Internet, books, and television. Those can be very good sources of information, but they can also be flawed. Let's take a look at a few of these ways of understanding.

Non-scientific Ways of Knowing

Authority

One way we come to learn things about the world is through someone telling us, also known as authority. This is a very useful and time-saving way to learn things. If Stephen Hawking, who was a brilliant theoretical physicist, writes, "a black hole can be supertranslated by throwing in an asymmetric shock wave" (he really did say that: Hawking, Perry, & Strominger, 2016, p. 1), we're probably going to believe him. Why? Because we know him as an expert on this type of stuff. He is considered to be a trusted authority on theoretical physics, he did a lot more thinking about black holes than we have, and he guest-starred in both *The Big Bang Theory* and *The Simpsons* television shows (then again, so has Charlie Sheen, so perhaps you should ignore this last point). Anyway, let's agree we have it on good authority that you can supertranslate a black hole by throwing in an asymmetric shock wave.

But what if we told you that it's possible to train a dolphin to walk and chew gum at the same time? Would knowing that the people who just tried to get you to believe this (i.e., us, the textbook authors) have PhDs help convince you? Hopefully not. Information received from an authority is not always accurate. We readily admit we are not dolphin experts, so you should not believe anything we tell you about dolphins. We are, however, experts on social science, so you can trust the information you read in this textbook.

It may be tempting to believe what you hear from an authority because it saves you from having to figure it out yourself, but the challenge comes in determining whether the authority can be trusted. Authorities can be incorrect, biased, prejudiced, imprecise, or have hidden agendas. This doesn't mean you should never believe anything you hear from someone who appears to be an authority, but you also shouldn't assume everything they say is true.

Tradition

We know some things simply because we seem to have always known them, or they are "facts" that have been passed down from generation to generation. This use of tradition as fact can be problematic for two reasons. First, tradition can be incorrect. For example, before the year 1915, women in Canada were not allowed to vote because it was largely believed they were better off staying at home making babies than doing complicated things like reasoning, critical thinking, and understanding politics. Today, most people (including social scientists) see this as a ridiculous notion, but with children being taught this distinction between the sexes from a very young age, it was so ingrained that it was held to be true by many people. The second problem with relying on tradition is things can change or our understanding can become more sophisticated. For example, builders used to install lead pipes and asbestos in homes because they were considered to be the best choice. Now that we have a better understanding of the harmful effects of these materials on human health, they don't use them anymore. We're not suggesting tradition is bad—imagine a world without weddings, high holidays, Sunday dinners, hockey playoff beards, and the Tooth Fairy—but it's important to think about why you know the things you do.

Common Sense

Some things just make sense, don't they? Like the fact that you tend to miss your loved ones when you are separated from them. As they say, "absence makes the heart grow fonder." But wait, don't they also say "out of sight, out of mind"? You've probably agreed with both of these statements at some point or another, simply because they made sense at the time. Just because something makes sense to you at the time does not mean it is true. Many compulsive gamblers think they are more likely to win because they've had a long string of losses (not true). Some people think it is less safe to fly after they read a news report of a plane crash (not true). Many things that make sense are actually true—for example, if you are nice to people, they're more likely to be nice to you (you really can catch more flies with honey)—but don't assume everything that makes sense to you is actually true.

The Internet and Other Media

For better or for worse, much of our information comes from the Internet. While it is an unprecedented luxury to have all this information (not to mention all those cat videos) available to us at any time of day or night, we would

venture that the Internet is probably one of the leading causes of misinformation in our modern world. And given that many of us use the Internet for
research, this can be problematic. How do you know what is correct and what
isn't? In addition to the Internet and its abundance of sketchy facts and advice,
other types of media can also be a source of misinformation. For example, if
you got your information about what professors and other academics are really
like from the television show *The Big Bang Theory*, your impression of professors would be pretty far removed from what actual professors are like (well,
most of us, anyway). Depending on which news channel you watch, you may
think climate change is either a real threat to our survival or a complete hoax.
Television shows are meant to entertain and they take liberties with reality,
and news shows are meant to attract viewers and perhaps further the agenda
of their producers, so they also may take liberties with actual facts.

Facts and "Alternative Facts"

It's difficult to know what to believe sometimes. In a world where we have
access to so much information, it's almost more of a challenge to know the
truth because so much of that information isn't accurate. To add to the challenge of figuring out what's true and what isn't, there is a recent trend to
discount information one does not agree with as "fake news," and to reframe
incorrect information as "alternative facts." These are tools designed to
deliberately convey false information. The key is to be critical and, as we've
said before, ask for evidence. And this doesn't just apply to information you
receive from others; you also need to question your own beliefs and opinions.
We are all biased—we have our own preferences, ideas, and overall worldviews that may make us more open to believing certain things. The key is to
recognize our biases.

Scientific Ways of Knowing

Although the ways of knowing outlined above can save you time, they are
sometimes flawed. The benefit of using social science to understand the
world is that it gives us more confidence in the knowledge we have. As we
mentioned above, social science is a science, and many social scientists have
adopted the methods of science as a way to better understand the world.
The scientific method isn't perfect and not all social scientists follow it, but
it does have advantages over our more loosey-goosey ways of understanding
the world. One reason why this is true is because social science research tends
to follow the four canons of science. A **canon** is a fundamental principle or

rule. The **canons of science** are four principles or rules that scientists hold to be true: determinism, empiricism, parsimony, and testability. These canons give researchers a starting point for their inquiry.

Determinism

Determinism is the assumption that all events or phenomena have causes; things happen for a reason. This may not seem all that interesting at first glance, but think about how you view the world. For instance, do you say "please" and "thank you"? We're going to assume you said "yes" to this question. Why do we act politely to others? Because it's the right thing to do, but also because we follow a basic assumption that if you are nice to others, they will be nice to you. "Could you please get me a glass of water?" will be much more likely to get you a glass of water (especially one without spit in it) than saying, "Get me a glass of water, NOW!" But what if being polite made no difference at all, and you couldn't predict whether you'd get a glass of water or a punch in the face, regardless of how polite you were? What if we had no way to predict how people would respond in any given situation, and all our behaviour was completely random? Life would be very complicated, and it would be advisable to get your own glass of water, that's for sure!

A belief in determinism, then, can give us a lot of comfort. If we know the cause of something, we can predict it, and being able to predict what will happen makes us feel in control. In addition to helping us feel in control, if we believe things have causes (i.e., they are not random), then we can study them. In other words, if we have a theory, we can test it.

For example, at our university, students wear lots of university-branded clothing (like sweaters). We have observed this over and over in the many years we have taught here. Because we are social scientists who understand the canon of determinism, we have developed a theory to explain this observation. Our theory is that students at our university wear branded clothing because they have lots of school spirit—they are proud of their school and want to share their affiliation with it. Now, we may not be accurate in our explanation of this behaviour. Students may wear university-branded sweaters because the residence rooms are so cold or because they are less expensive than other clothes or for a host of other reasons, but the point is because we now have a theory, or competing theories, we can test it.

Determinism is important in science because if we didn't believe that events were determined—in other words, if we believed that things had no underlying causes—then we couldn't study them or predict them. It may not matter, in the overall scheme of things, whether students in our classes wear logo sweaters or not, but for many issues in the social sciences, prediction matters a fair bit. Imagine a criminologist trying to discover the best way to prevent crime or rehabilitate offenders if crime was not caused by something. Imagine trying to resolve social issues like poverty and homelessness if we believed that they were completely random and could happen to anyone at any time.

Empiricism

Empiricism is the idea of learning about things by observing them. The important thing to note here is that these observations must be systematic—they need to have some method behind them to try to control for bias and error. You've probably heard the story of the blind men and the elephant. There are various versions of this Indian fable, but the one contained in a poem by John Godfrey Saxe (2017) tells the story of six blind men who approached an elephant and felt the elephant to determine what it looked like. The first man felt the elephant's side and concluded elephants look like walls. The second man felt its tusk and concluded elephants are like spears. The third man felt its trunk and concluded elephants look like snakes. The fourth felt its knee and decided elephants look like trees. The fifth man touched the elephant's ear and concluded elephants must look like fans, while the sixth man touched the elephant's tail and concluded elephants look like ropes. Obviously none of these observations accurately describes what an entire elephant looks like, even though individually they are correct. Empiricism comes from using more than one observation to draw conclusions about the world.

Just like these blind men, we all make observations that are technically correct but do not tell us the entire truth. For example, are you, or is anyone you know, afraid of flying? Fear of flying tends to become especially salient after a plane crash is reported in the news. Don't get us wrong: Plane crashes are terrifying, and often have very tragic consequences. However, those who are afraid of flying are only using one or a few observations to come to the conclusion that flying is dangerous. If you look at the statistics of how often planes crash compared to how often they land perfectly with nothing out of the ordinary happening, you'll see that the chance of any type of tragedy occurring when you are flying is extremely low. Do you know what's more likely to kill you than a plane crash? Being stung by a bee. Driving to the airport. Food poisoning. Lightning. So should you worry that the airplane you are about to board will crash? We can't tell you what to worry about, but we would suggest there are more pressing things to spend your mental energy on when you travel by airplane, like whether you'll have a toddler kicking your seat the entire flight or whether you'll be able to find your luggage when you get to your destination.

Recall our observation that students at our university seem to wear a lot of clothing branded with the university logo. You may have concluded (rightfully) that our observations are not exactly systematic. A true empiricist would actually count the number of students wearing university gear, and then also the number of students who don't wear branded gear. They could then calculate the percentage of our students who wear school logos. If they wanted to know if the percentage is higher at our school than at others, they could do the same elsewhere, and then compare. By collecting data on all students, or at least a representative sample of them, we could learn about this particular student behaviour. Empirical research doesn't have to involve numbers. If you wanted to study school spirit, rather than counting university logos on shirts, you could visit universities and talk to the students to see how they feel, or even just observe them to see how they interact with other students and how they behave at events. A researcher who goes into the field to watch how people function in certain environments would also be considered to be doing empirical research—there are many different ways to make observations.

Parsimony

The law of **parsimony** is that the best explanation is the simplest one. This applies to whether you are developing a theory or trying to determine the best-fitting theory. When you are attempting to develop a theory that will explain some aspect of human nature, you should begin with as simple and straightforward an explanation as possible. Sometimes these explanations don't work, but you should always start out with a simple one, in part because they are easier to test. Sometimes we are not developing our own theories but trying to determine the best theory when faced with competing explanations for a particular phenomenon. In that case, the canon of parsimony would be to go with the simplest one that explains the phenomenon. You may have heard of this referred to as "Occam's Razor."

Let's go back to our university logo gear example. One theory as to why students wear so much branded gear is that they love their school and want to let others know it. It's a pretty straightforward theory. However, another theory might be that students wear branded gear because humans have a deep-rooted desire to be noticed, and one way to be noticed is to spend a lot of money on a university degree. However, people don't know you spent a lot of money on your university degree unless you tell them. Wearing a branded sweater is one way to advertise this fact and, hence, be noticed. Given that both of these theories could explain the clothing decisions of the students, you should start with the less complicated of the two. You can still test these theories to see which actually explains the phenomenon, but start with the simpler one.

Testability

In order to conduct a scientific analysis of any theory, it has to be testable. **Testability** refers to the ability to determine whether the theory actually explains the phenomenon. For example, we could make the claim that goldfish are very good at reading and that they have a preference for mystery novels, but it would be very hard to prove or disprove this. If you have taken any courses on children's development, you may be familiar with Sigmund Freud's theory of psychosexual development. According to Freud, young girls, as part of their normal psychosexual development, experience "penis envy" upon realizing they don't have a penis. Apparently this leads them to resent their mother and fight with her for their father's affections. Oh, and by the way, this all happens out of these young girls' conscious awareness, so you can't ask them if it's true. It's okay to roll your eyes at this—lots of respected scholars have. But it's not okay to dismiss it just because you think it's silly. It may seem to be a ridiculous theory, but the best reason to dismiss it is because it cannot be empirically tested, and not because you don't agree with it.

Theories are often not testable because they involve concepts that are not clearly defined in a way that makes them measurable. Think about a concept such as height. We know the height of a person is the distance between their head and their feet, and we have an accurate way to measure it. We refer to this as **operationalization**: the process of specifying how a variable is measured. You can operationalize height further by stating that it is the number of centimetres between an individual's head and their feet when they are standing up. Even a socially constructed concept like "crime" can be operationalized, using the criminal code as a catalogue of illegal activities. The operational definition of crime, then, might be that it is an activity that contravenes the rules set out in the Canadian *Criminal Code*.

But let's go back to Freud's theories. He certainly defined all of his constructs—you can look up definitions of psychosexual development and penis envy—so the problem is not one of lack of definitions. The problem is that his constructs cannot be *operationally* defined. How would you measure unconscious processes, especially when Freud claimed they are happening in infants and young children? Not only are they too young to tell you, but even if they could tell you, it all happens in their unconscious, so they won't know. Convenient, isn't it?

THE ROLE OF THEORY IN SOCIAL SCIENCE

Think about the last time you noticed something interesting or different happening in the world around you. Maybe you saw someone stop to help a young woman pick up some papers she had dropped. Your interpretation of this event is shaped by how you see the world: your assumptions about human nature, your specific theories about why people help each other (or don't), similar and different observations you have made in the past, and maybe even what kind of mood you are in at the moment. In the same way, social science is informed by paradigms, theory, observations, and bias.

Paradigms
Paradigms are ways of looking at the world. Think of them as a frame of reference, or a worldview, without which you would not be able to organize and make sense of the things you see around you. Thomas Kuhn, a philosopher of science, defined paradigms as "universally recognized scientific achievements that, for a time, provide model problems and solutions for a community of practitioners" (Kuhn, 1996, p. 10). For social scientists, paradigms provide a standard set of assumptions, rules, and methods for conducting research.

It's important to note, though, that different social scientists may work under different paradigms, which tells you one important thing: These are not universal truths. For example, there are many ways to view mental illness. Some social scientists see mental illness as some type of deficiency within an individual that can be treated with either drugs or therapy or a combination of both. However, other social scientists may not view mental illness as a deficiency needing to be treated at all. Instead they may see it as a construction of society, and believe mental illness has been stigmatized as an illness because society is not comfortable with those who act in odd or unexpected ways. Another social scientist may see mental illness as a gendered issue, because there are particular types of mental illness that tend to show up more in women than in men (and vice versa), without any biological reasons for these gender differences. Obviously, these vastly different assumptions about mental illness are associated with vastly different methods of studying it. Thus, the paradigm that individual social scientists work under plays a role in how they conduct their research. Also, the notion of paradigms may suggest to you that social scientists tend to pick one and stick to it, but that's not necessarily the case: Social scientists may work under multiple paradigms.

There are many different paradigms used in the social sciences. We can't cover them all, but here are some very broad examples. Keep in mind these paradigms are not "truths." They are ways of looking at the world, and as you are reading about them, you may find you don't agree with the outlook they present. You may also find that one paradigm fits well with a certain issue, while another paradigm fits better with another issue. The diversity within the social sciences means there will be diversity in the ways in which social scientists view the world, and we believe that's a good thing.

Positivist Paradigm

Those who subscribe to a positivist paradigm believe that social science, being a science, should follow the same principles as the natural sciences. In other words, they believe social behaviour can be measured and interpreted using the same techniques used to measure and interpret the natural world. Positivists work on the assumption that social reality consists of objective facts that can be measured.

Interpretive Paradigm

The interpretive paradigm builds upon the philosophical foundations of post-structuralism and postmodernism. Rather than seeing the world as being composed of objective facts, researchers who subscribe to the interpretive paradigm concentrate on the study of meanings created by groups and individuals. These meanings are the result of lived experiences within both broad and specific historical and cultural contexts. Within this paradigm, it is believed that human behaviours and social structures can be best understood from the analysis or interpretation of these meanings. Since reality is viewed as subjective and socially constructed, truly objective data is difficult to obtain and measure; thus, positivist approaches of study do not fit. Instead, interpretivists concentrate on the study of cultural "texts," objects or behaviours that can reveal meaning.

Critical Paradigms

Like the interpretive paradigm, the critical paradigm suggests that research is not value free: Scientific facts can only be understood within their social and historical context. As Max Horkheimer (1972) noted, "The facts of science and

science itself are but segments of the life process itself, and in order to understand the significance of facts or of science, generally one must possess the key
to the historical situation, to the right social theory" (p. 159). Thus, adherents
to this paradigm hold the view that if there is an objective reality, one must first
deal with the biases, distortions, and prejudices that mask this reality.

The critical paradigm does not merely seek to develop theories to explain
social realities. It is also a goal-oriented paradigm that seeks "human emanci-
pation from slavery ... to create a world which satisfies the needs and powers"
of people (Horkheimer, 1972, p. 246). Since the slavery targeted by critical
theorists includes all forms of human domination and oppression, it is a paradigm that has been subdivided into distinct critical paradigms with similar
aims but different foci. For example, critical race theory holds that racism is
the value that has masked and distorted objective reality, and feminist theory
holds that sexism is the value that distorts objective reality. These paradigms
are much more nuanced than this, but what they have in common is a desire
to strip away traditional biased notions of reality to get to the "truth," as well
as a desire for social transformation.

Theories

While paradigms represent an overarching view of how a particular social
scientist might view social phenomena, theories involve more specific ideas
about individual phenomena. In its simplest form, a **theory** is "a statement of
the suspected relationship between and among variables" (Gelso, 2006, p. 2).
Theories help us make sense of the world around us; they aim to explain why
things happen. You probably have a number of theories about how the world
works. Any time you see something happening that doesn't appear to have a
clear causal explanation, you probably develop a theory about why it happened.
If a driver cuts you off, you may explain their behaviour with a theory you have
developed about the relationship between the kinds of cars people drive and
how they drive. If you are visiting another country and notice different behaviours in the people who live there compared to where you are from, you may
develop theories about cultural differences. You may even have theories about
how men and women are different from each other.

Theories in Social Science

The thing to remember about theories is that they are just theories; they are
not statements of fact. That's the role of science: to test/develop theories and
provide evidence that either supports or refutes them. You might have a theory

about driving behaviour and car models. This is your statement about how cars and driving are related. Your theory may be based on observations, but they are probably not systematic observations. They are not systematic because your sample is probably pretty limited, and you have not controlled for bias. Don't worry; it's not just you. The things we notice about the world are inherently biased: We often see what we want to see and ignore the things we don't want to see. And those things we want to see tend to be the things that "fit" with our theory, and the things we don't want to see tend to be those that don't fit with our theory. See how that works?

Psychologists call this phenomenon **confirmation bias**, and it shows that evidence matters! It helps explain how two individuals can hold very different beliefs about the same thing. For example, it explains why some people are afraid of flying when the evidence shows flying is actually safer than a lot of more mundane activities: Those who are afraid of flying have not systematically reviewed the data on incidence rates of plane crashes but instead have only focused on what they expect to see (i.e., high-profile but rare plane crashes). It also explains why people hold stereotypes of others who are different from them. Let's say you are visiting Canada, and you hold a stereotype about Canadians being very polite. In your travels within the country, you will encounter a wide variety of Canadians, some polite and others not so polite. Because you already hold this belief that Canadians are polite, you'll tend to ignore the ones you meet who are not polite and only focus on the polite ones. This selective attention on polite Canadians will reinforce your stereotype that Canadians are polite. Now, Canadians probably don't mind that people think they're polite (with our sincere apologies to those who do), but you can see how a lack of systematic observation can fuel much more damaging stereotypes, leading to racism and prejudice.

Building Theories: Induction versus Deduction

Let's say you have a theory about studying. You believe the more you study, the better you will do on your exams. There are two ways you could have arrived at this theory. You could have read Chapter 1 on how to learn more effectively, paying attention to the content on memory and how information gets from our short-term to our long-term memory and is then retrieved when we need it. From this information, you developed a theory that studying should improve your exam performance. If your theory comes from abstract reasoning, using existing general principles about learning but not from any direct observation of your own learning, then you have used a **deductive approach** to theory building. This is a top-down method of developing a theory, where you theorize first, then look for evidence to support your theory. The second way you might have developed this theory is to look at your prior history of studying and exam performance. You may have noticed that when you have studied for exams, you tended to do better on them, and when you didn't study as much, your performance was not as good. Therefore, you reason, studying must lead to higher grades. When you first make observations about some phenomenon and then develop a theory based on those observations, you are using an **inductive approach** to theory building. This is a bottom-up method of theory development, where you start with specific observations, then develop a more generalized theory that explains those observations.

Sometimes researchers use both deductive and inductive approaches to a research question. Let's say you were interested in the reasons why people attend folk music festivals. You may have some vague idea about some of the reasons: People like music, they like being outside, they like the sense of community, and so on. Since you don't really know the reasons, and there may be others you haven't thought of, you might start with an inductive approach. You might go to a few folk music festivals, observe what people do, and interview them to find out their motivations for attending. From the data you collect through your observations and interviews, you may then develop a theory of why people attend these music festivals. This would be a bottom-up, inductive approach, where you start with the data and generate a theory from that data.

After developing a theory of why people attend folk music festivals, you may then take a deductive approach, where you test your theory to see if it holds true for other types of music festivals, like bluegrass festivals, EDM festivals, or even Highland Games. For this research, you might interview people, using a fixed set of questions or a questionnaire specifically designed

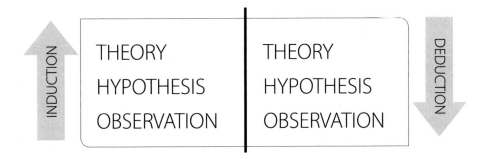

Figure 2.1: Induction vs. Deduction

to test your theory. This would be a top-down, deductive approach, in which you have a theory and then collect data in order to test this theory. Using both of these methods, you would be able to develop a solid research program on this particular social phenomenon (and you'd get to hear some pretty great music too).

RESEARCH AND THE SCIENTIFIC METHOD

Research. It is a term whose meaning seems self-evident even though it is frequently used to describe a wide variety of personal, academic, and professional activities. For example, if you are interested making a major purchase, you may spend considerable time doing online searches to find reviews about your intended purchase. If you have an assignment, you will likely invest a good deal of effort looking for relevant sources at the library or online. While these types of searches involve little more than browsing or "surfing," if you do this browsing/surfing in a focused and methodical way, it would be considered to be a type of research.

However, can we describe these activities as "scientific research"? To answer this question, it is useful to explore the nature of scientific research a little further. Fundamental to the understanding of scientific research is an understanding of science. When many of us think of science, we often think of the disciplines of the **natural sciences**, such as biology, chemistry, and physics. These are disciplines that study phenomena and processes in nature. Sometimes they are referred to as the "hard" sciences, but we're not going to call them that because (a) they are not "hard," at least not harder than the social sciences, and (b) the term implies that social sciences are "soft" sciences.

While it is common to define science in terms of the natural sciences, the existence of social sciences suggests that such definitions of science are inadequate. The nature of science must be something common to both the natural and social sciences; it must be more about the way of studying a problem than about the subjects of study. Indeed, most of the sciences—at least those that embrace the positivist paradigm—rely on a systemic and organized approach for investigation: the scientific method. Because the scientific method is about testing hypotheses and not about proving anything, science must also be considered to be a humble way of thinking about the subjects being studied. New ways of understanding the natural and social world will inevitably replace older ones. Even the findings of the greatest scientists of one generation may be supplanted by insights of the next. Finally, science can be thought of as the body of the knowledge produced by practitioners using the scientific method. Thus, science can be defined as a way of thinking about the world, a systemic way of studying it and the body of knowledge it creates.

Steps in the Research Process

When you boil it down, the research process is really just the asking and answering of a research question. Social scientists don't know everything, so they develop questions, and then conduct research that provides answers to those questions. Think about your own informal research. Let's say your phone died and you need to get a new one. Your question might be "What kind of phone should I buy?", and you would set out to answer this question. You might start with a quick look at one of the major phone providers in your area or perhaps you'd search for sales on phones or maybe you'd just ask your friends what they have. It's important to note, however, that not all questions that are asked and answered would be considered scientific research. Chances are your search for a new phone would not start out being very systematic or methodical. For that reason, it would not be considered to be scientific. When scientists conduct research, whether it's in physics or biology or sociology or criminology, they follow a set series of steps.

1. Select a topic

   Scientists first need something to study. Topics tend to be broad and very general. In social science, examples of topics would be homelessness, stress, voting behaviour, cyberbullying, or altruism. There is a saying among social scientists that "research is me-search." All researchers, if given the choice, study topics that are meaningful to them, but we've found that social scientists in particular tend to study topics that resonate with them on a personal level. When you are taking courses in which you get to choose your own topic, we recommend that you pick something that is meaningful to you. It will be much more interesting to learn about, you'll feel more motivated to work on it, and—who knows?—you might actually learn something about yourself!

2. Develop a research question

   Topics are too broad to do much with, so the next step in the research process is to narrow down the topic and turn it into a question. For example, within the topic of homelessness, one could study the causes of homelessness, societal responses to the homeless, possible solutions to homelessness, and so on. A focused question might be "To what extent does increasing shelter beds keep people from sleeping on the street?" or "What factors contribute to youth homelessness?" Researchers draw from prior research in order to develop their questions. Before setting out to do any research, they normally conduct a search for and review of existing research (referred to as a literature review) to find out what has already been done on their topic, or to help them refine their question.

3. Design the study

    Once a researcher has a question in mind, they need to figure out how to answer that question. This is where good research design comes in. There are many ways to conduct research and many different ways to design a scientific study. We can't cover them all here, but if you're interested in learning more about them, we encourage you to take a research methods course. One of the most important things to consider when choosing, or evaluating, a research study is whether the study design is appropriate for the question being asked. You don't need to be an expert researcher to evaluate whether the design fits the question. Think about, for instance, a study on youth homelessness. Would it make sense to design a study in which you only interview the parents? No, because they may have no idea why their children left home. Maybe it is worthwhile talking to the parents, but you'll probably learn more about why the children left home by talking to the children themselves.

4. Collect the data

    When it comes to social science research, "data" could be many different things. Data might be numbers, such as the average age of homeless youth or the amount of money they make panhandling in a day, or data could be the words of the youth themselves, explaining how they feel about being on the street. Data could even be a combination of numbers and words, with a count of how many times the media use certain words to describe homeless youth, and whether they use the same types of words when describing homeless adults. Data could consist of the photos of homeless youth published by the media, or the tone of voice passers-by use when declining to give them money. Generally, data can be divided into two main types: **qualitative data**, which is expressed as words, images, sounds, or objects, and **quantitative data**, which is expressed

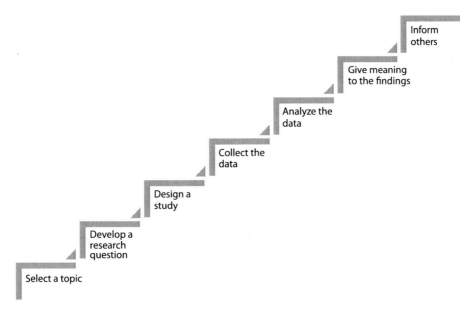

Figure 2.2: Steps in the Research Process

as numbers. We'll talk more about types of qualitative and quantitative research in a minute.

5. Analyze the data

Analyzing data involves looking for patterns or meanings in the data. With qualitative data, this is done by looking for themes in the data. For example, the researcher, upon reading all of the transcripts of interviews with the homeless youth, may find that two points came up frequently in their interviews: Respondents often mentioned fighting with their parents when they were younger, and many of them felt that they could not live up to their parents' expectations. These would be considered themes in a qualitative analysis. With quantitative data, the analysis is done with statistics. Researchers might ask the youth how much they make panhandling in a day and see how this relates, statistically, with their self-reported well-being, and whether there are differences depending on their age, gender, or race. As with the collection of data, analyzing the data must be done systematically and carefully. For example, if a researcher interviews five young homeless people, all of their voices should be given equal weight in the analysis/coding of the data. The researcher must not put more focus on the response of one or two participants just because their responses fit best with the study's hypotheses. Similarly, quantitative data must be managed carefully, making sure the proper statistical tests are done, and extreme scores that may skew the results are handled properly.

6. Give meaning to the findings
    Data analysis results in either a group of themes, in the case of qualitative data, or a number and significance level, in the case of quantitative data, but they don't tell the entire story. Giving meaning to the findings involves linking them back to the research question (i.e., answering the original questions that were asked in Step 2) and also putting them into a broader context. For example, if the results of the study identified high expectations from parents as a factor that affects youth homelessness but more so for males than for females, the researcher should interpret what this might mean and what can be done to support young males and their parents. If a quantitative analysis showed a significant difference between youth from larger urban centres (e.g., Toronto) and those from smaller cities (e.g., Brantford), the researcher should explain what this means, and what implications it has for the allocation of resources to these cities.

7. Inform others
    It is important to conduct high-quality, meaningful research, but that effort is wasted if the results are not shared with others. Our understanding of humans, culture, and society is composed of many small facts. Each research study contributes a small part to this understanding, but in order to make this contribution, it must be shared with the scientific community. This is usually done through journal articles, conference presentations, and books. Before being shared in the scientific community, research must undergo a **peer-review** process, which means that it has been read by colleagues in the field to ensure that it is not biased, poorly conducted, or otherwise unsuitable. The work of social scientists can also be valuable to policy makers and the general public, and thus it is also often shared through technical reports, books, and the popular media.

Types of Study Design

Qualitative Research Methods
Qualitative research aims for an in-depth understanding of various aspects of the human condition, focusing on the words people say, the gestures they

make, or the photos they take, among other things. There are many diverse methods researchers can use that would be considered qualitative. Below we outline the most common.

INTERVIEWS

One of the most common qualitative methods is the **interview**. In its simplest form, the interview involves a researcher asking a respondent questions and then documenting the answers (either by recording it or taking notes). It may seem like a pretty simple technique—you're just asking people questions, right?—but it actually takes skill and practice to do it properly. How you frame a question can significantly affect the answer, so researchers need to think carefully about the questions they ask. For example, "I'm getting a coffee. Can I bring you one too?" would probably get you a different answer than "I'm getting a coffee. You don't want one, do you?" Think about how people might respond differently to "Do you agree that police use too much force?" compared to "What are your feelings about the amount of force used by police?" In addition to making sure your questions aren't reflecting your own bias, it also can take skill to ask them in such a way that your respondents feel comfortable giving you full answers. Questions with simple "yes" or "no" answers don't tell you much; interviewers need to be skilled at probing for more detailed answers while still being respectful of the respondent.

Interviews can be highly structured or not. In its most structured form, all the questions are predetermined beforehand, and the interviewer sticks to this script. This type of **structured interview** can be useful if you are interviewing many people and want to be able to compare their answers to specific questions. The downside is that one person might say something really intriguing about an issue you hadn't thought of, but if you only have pre-set questions you can't explore it more fully. In this case, a **semi-structured interview** might be best, whereby you do have predetermined questions, but you also have the flexibility to ask new questions. The loosest form of an interview is the **open-ended interview**, where you may start with a set question (e.g., "Tell me about what it was like moving to Canada from Syria"), but then you let the interview follow its own path, asking questions directly related to what the respondent has said.

FOCUS GROUPS

A **focus group** is a group interview. Like interviews, focus groups can be structured or not, and the responses by participants are recorded in some way, to be analyzed later. Focus groups usually have some form of moderator (often the researcher) who runs the group. This role is important, as this person must not only ask the questions but they also need to ensure that everyone has a chance to speak, that the group doesn't stray too far off topic, and that everyone is respectful. The advantage of asking questions in a group setting is that participants can feed off each other—one person's answer might prompt another person to reflect on a similar experience they might not have thought of otherwise. Interesting data can arise from group discussions. However, for sensitive topics, people might not feel comfortable speaking in a group, so researchers should take this into account when deciding whether to do individual or group interviews.

FIELD RESEARCH/ETHNOGRAPHY

In order to gain a better understanding of a culture or group, social science researchers often conduct **field research**, where they collect their data in a natural setting. For example, in order to learn about how senior citizens enjoy living in retirement homes, a researcher might spend time in the retirement home, not only interviewing the residents but also simply hanging out with them, playing games and eating dinner, all the while observing and making notes on how they interact with each other and with the staff. To learn about bullying at school, a researcher might observe children in their schoolyard, at recess and after school, to see first-hand what happens before, during, and after a bullying incident (of course, they would first obtain ethical approval to do this, which we'll learn about in Chapter 6). Ethnographic researchers take this one step further and actually try to immerse themselves in the culture they are studying. There are limits to this; a person with no musical talent could not immerse themselves seamlessly into an orchestra, and it might be unwise to try to fit in with a group involved in illegal activities. Ethnographic researchers also need to be culturally sensitive and must respect the communities they are studying. The Canadian legislative body that governs the ethical treatment of research participants (you'll learn more about them in Chapter 6) recently added special regulations for conducting research in Indigenous communities, to address the fact that, historically, research in these communities has been conducted by non-Indigenous researchers, and it has not necessarily adequately represented or benefited the Indigenous peoples or their communities. These guidelines are intended to ensure that the best interests of First Nations, Inuit, and Métis communities are represented in research and that their cultural practices are respected.

Quantitative Research Methods

Quantitative research aims to learn more about phenomena by measuring them with as much accuracy as possible using numbers.

EXPERIMENTS

An **experiment** in social science research follows the same structure as an experiment in other sciences. It involves manipulating a variable under carefully controlled conditions and observing whether any changes occur in a second variable as a result. Using experiments, for example, researchers could determine whether being frustrated causes people to be more aggressive (i.e., the frustration-aggression hypothesis), whether monitoring the number of steps you take in a day makes you more likely to engage in additional healthy behaviours, or whether rehabilitation programs are effective at lowering recidivism rates in young offenders. In fact, experiments are the best way to determine whether one variable causes another.

In an experiment, a researcher manipulates a variable to see what effect it has. The variable that the researcher manipulates is called the **independent variable**. The variable that is measured (to see if it changed) is called the **dependent variable**. To keep these two types of variable straight, think about the dependent variable as the variable that changes because it is *dependent* on what is done with the other variable. Often (but not always), experiments are set up so the independent variable has two or more conditions: at least one that serves as the **experimental condition**, and one that serves as a **control condition**. The experimental condition is where the researcher expects the action to happen. The control condition serves as a comparison group, so the researcher can determine if doing something (i.e., the experimental condition) has more of an effect than doing nothing (i.e., the control condition). For example, let's say a researcher is interested in whether meditation has a positive effect on well-being, so she conducts an experiment where she has one group of people meditate and another group of people not meditate, and at the end of a week she measures their well-being. What is the independent variable? (Hint: It's the variable being manipulated). What is the dependent variable? (Hint: It's the thing being measured or assessed.) In this experiment, the independent variable would be meditation, because the researcher is manipulating whether people meditate or not, and the dependent variable is well-being, because she is assessing whether well-being is dependent on, or affected by, meditating. The experimental group is the one that meditates, and the control group is the one that doesn't. The researcher's expectation, or hypothesis, is that those who meditate should have higher well-being than those who do not meditate.

There are a few important rules about experiments. First of all, in a true experiment, the groups you are comparing must be equivalent to start with. If you have an experimental condition and a control condition, they must not be different before you actually start your experiment; if they are, you won't know whether any difference you find between them at the end of the experiment is due to the effects of the independent variable or because they were different at the outset. One way researchers ensure that their two groups are equivalent is to randomly assign people to groups. With **random assignment**, everyone has an equal chance of being in either group. For instance, if you happen to have some people who are more introspective or open to meditation, random assignment ensures that they don't deliberately pick the experimental group (i.e., the one that gets to meditate)—the group they end up in is completely due to chance.

The next step in an experiment is to introduce the independent variable (i.e., conduct the experiment). Another important rule of experiments is that when you have an experimental group and a control group, the only thing these two groups should differ on is the independent variable. For example, in the meditation study, the only difference between the meditation group and the non-meditation group should be whether they meditate or not. You can't ask the meditators to get up early to meditate, while letting the control group

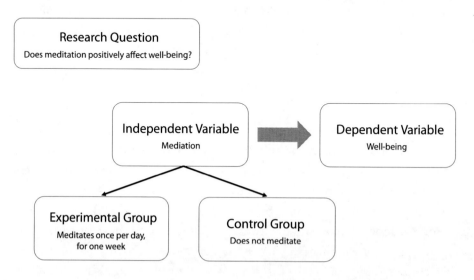

Figure 2.3: An Experiment on the Effectiveness of Meditation

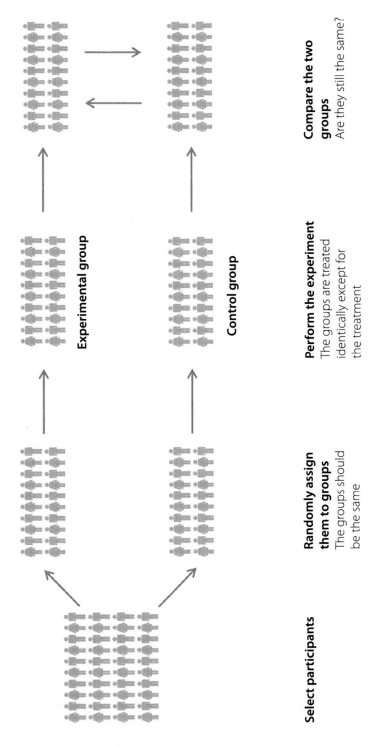

Figure 2.4: The Experiment

sleep in. If you do this, you've introduced a **confound**—an additional variable that could affect the dependent variable. If, at the end of the study, your meditation group seems to have lower well-being than your non-meditation group, it might be because they are sleep deprived and not because meditation is detrimental to well-being. Since both meditation and wake-up time varied in your experiment, you won't know which one actually had the effect on your dependent variable. If all else is equal between the two groups and the only thing that is different is the independent variable, then if the two groups differ in their well-being at the end of the study, it must be due to the meditation because everything else was the same.

If you carefully plan an experiment, and you find a statistically significant difference between your two groups, you can be confident that it was because your independent variable caused it to happen. This high level of control over the variables is why experiments are the best way to assess whether one thing causes another.

CORRELATIONAL STUDIES

Sometimes, rather than testing whether one thing causes another, a researcher might want to know if two things are related. A quantitative (i.e., numerical) assessment of whether two things are related is referred to as **correlation**. A study that assesses the degree to which two variables are related to each other is called a correlational study. Let's say you were interested in whether people who had a lot of Facebook friends actually were more socially active. In other words, is Facebook popularity related to, or *correlated with*, real-life popularity? You could easily quantify the number of Facebook friends a person has; it's listed on their Facebook page. You could also ask them to tell you how often they go out with friends in a month; that number would be a quantification of their real-life popularity (of course, it's self-reported, and it's possible that people might not be completely accurate). You could then conduct a statistical analysis that mathematically assesses whether there is a significant correlation between these two measures. Is it true that the higher a person's number of Facebook friends, the more often they go out with friends? And is the reverse also true: The fewer Facebook friends a person has the less often they go out with friends?

Correlation, Causation, and Nick Cage

Now might be a good time to make a very important point about the design and interpretation of research studies. Consider the following:

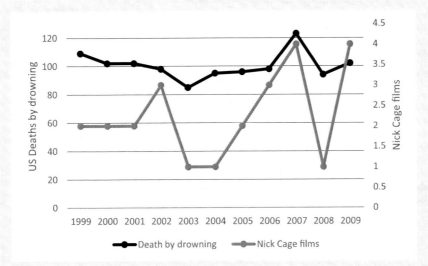

Figure 2.5: Drowning and Nick Cage Films

www.tylervigen.com/view_correlation?id=359

There is a significant positive relationship between the number of people who have drowned by falling into a swimming pool and the number of movies Nick Cage has appeared in. If you don't believe us, take a look at the graph below:

Looks pretty convincing, right? The actual correlation is $r = 0.66$, and since r ranges from 0 to 1.0 (and can be positive or negative), this is a pretty impressive correlation. It's also a significant correlation, which means there's less than a 5 percent chance the correlation occurred randomly. And, with a further statistical calculation (squaring r), we can determine that $r^2 = .44$, which means that 44 percent of the variability in pool deaths is attributed to the number of films Nick Cage has appeared in. In other words, if you think about all of the reasons why people drown by falling into swimming pools (e.g., being pushed, drinking too much, not knowing how to swim), those reasons all added together would equal 100 percent. According to this correlation, 44 percent of accidental pool deaths can be attributed to Nick Cage movies.

We'd all be better off if Mr. Cage retired from the film industry, right? Wrong. And here's why: Correlation does not equal causation!

Going back to our Facebook popularity example, a correlation between number of Facebook friends and real-life popularity does not mean that Facebook makes you popular, or that real-life popularity makes you

Continued

a Facebook superstar. All it tells us is that these two things are related to each other. Many of you probably learned this in high school, and you're sick of hearing it. However, mistaking correlational evidence for causal evidence is probably one of the most common mistakes made by people reporting on social science research. Why? Humans prefer certainty over uncertainty, so maybe it's because claiming that X causes Y is more definite than saying X is related to Y in some way. Causal claims are also probably more likely to capture our attention. Which story would you be most likely to click on: "Nick Cage responsible for 44 percent of drowning deaths" or "Completely random correlation between Nick Cage movies and drowning deaths"?

CONTENT ANALYSIS

Content analysis combines elements of both quantitative and qualitative methods. It involves quantifying traditionally qualitative things, like words or images, in an attempt to identify common themes. This helps researchers compare themes over time. For example, social scientists conducted a content analysis of themes used in car advertisements from 1983 to 1998. They examined all of the ads, and coded them for the kinds of things they mentioned about cars. They found that the most common theme over time was an emphasis on performance. Incidentally, they also noted that safety was only a predominant theme in one year—1993—which also happened to be the year airbags became mandatory in new cars (Ferguson, Hardy, & Williams, 2003).

Content analyses can also be used to challenge our perceptions. There have been a number of content analyses conducted on themes in Disney films. You may think these films are simply harmless entertainment for children, but this research suggests that they are much more than that. Many themes have been identified, such as depictions of gender roles (Hoerrner, 1996), prosocial behaviour (Padilla-Walker, Coyne, Fraser, & Stockdale, 2013), death (Cox, Garrett, & Graham, 2005), and even mental illness (Lawson & Fouts, 2004). These social scientists take a closer look at common themes in these films that may influence children in unintended ways.

A thorough content analysis involves deciding what the sample will be (i.e., all Disney films or just the ones with princesses; all car ads from 1983 to 1998), reviewing all of the content carefully and coding for the themes under study, and then using some type of statistical analysis to determine what the most prevalent themes are.

Existing Statistics/Secondary Analysis

Some researchers conduct quantitative research by collecting their own data, either in experiments or in correlational studies, using direct measurements (e.g., reaction time, number of times the person goes out with friends) or surveys or questionnaires. Sometimes data already exists that can help answer a research question. Criminologists, for example, often rely on crime reports and statistics to help test their theories of crime. Economists might want to know the average income in various parts of the country. Health researchers might want incidence rates of certain diseases. Statistics Canada collects this type of data and makes it available to researchers; in fact, their mandate is to "produce statistics that help Canadians better understand their country—its population, resources, economy, society and culture" (Statistics Canada, 2018a).

This type of research does not involve collecting data so it is often referred to as **secondary analysis**. The advantage of using data that has already been collected is that a researcher has access to a much larger pool of participants than if they did the study on their own. Most individual researchers could not collect the type of data organizations like Statistics Canada can, because it is costly and time consuming, and also because people may be more likely to fill out a Statistics Canada survey than a survey by a researcher they have never heard of. For crime statistics, local police stations must report their data to Statistics Canada, so researchers can get a fairly complete (although not perfect) picture of reported crime throughout Canada by using these existing statistics. The disadvantage of using existing statistics is that researchers cannot ask their own questions; they are limited to the questions that have already been asked. A criminologist, for example, might want to know whether female victims are more likely to confide in male or female officers about their experience, but if the survey conducted by Statistics Canada did not ask this question, the researcher will be unable to study it.

Qualitative or Quantitative: Which Should You Use?

Often you'll find that researchers identify themselves as either a qualitative researcher or a quantitative researcher. It takes a long time to become an expert in either, so it makes sense that researchers tend to use one method over another because it's what they are best at. As a consumer of social science research, it's important to be able to think critically about whether the best method was used. Would it make sense to only use data from police reports to assess how safe people feel in their neighbourhood? Given that not all crimes are reported to the police, and given that there are many factors that can contribute to an individual feeling safe or not, a qualitative approach might be a better way to assess this. Interviews may reveal issues the researcher had not thought about. However, if you were interested in how often people access the healthcare system and how this relates to their income, a qualitative approach might not be the most appropriate. For one thing, our memories are notoriously inaccurate, so asking someone how many times they visited the doctor in the past year may or may not accurately reflect the number of actual visits they made. In addition, some people may not feel comfortable sharing this information in an interview—they may feel that both their medical visits and their income are too private to reveal to an interviewer. In this case, you'd be more likely to get accurate data by directly accessing their health records.

Sometimes the most convincing research studies are those that use both qualitative and quantitative methods. If you ask a question in two different ways and get the same answer, you can be more confident in the accuracy of the answer. In the same way, researchers who find they get similar results when they conduct interviews and use surveys can be more confident that their research findings accurately represent reality.

What's the Point of Research?

By now it's probably pretty clear that we do research in order to gather evidence so we can be more confident in the accuracy of what we know (or what we think we know). That's a general, one-size-fits-all explanation for what the point is of research. However, there are more nuanced reasons for why research is conducted. And being able to identify the point of a research study can help you determine whether it reached its goal.

Exploration

Some research is conducted in order to learn about a new topic that has not been studied before. **Exploratory research** is the starting point for when we don't know enough about a topic to even know what specific questions to ask. One purpose of an exploratory study might be to figure out what the key variables are so we can plan a study that either measures or manipulates those variables. For example, in the long history of social science's attempts to understand humans and their behaviours, social media is a very new thing. When tools like Facebook and Twitter first appeared on the scene, social scientists were fascinated, as they represented a very different method of engaging in social interactions than people were used to. At the same time, they raised lots of questions about existing social science phenomena, such as how people interact with each other, what implications social media had for face-to-face interactions, how conflict is handled, and so on. Although we already knew a lot about human interactions and conflict, social scientists had no idea how they would play out online. So the first studies about social media were very exploratory—they tended to involve observing how people used the various tools. Another use of exploratory research is to develop methods for measuring and assessing variables. Social media has presented challenges with regards to how to deal with the huge amounts of data generated. A single Twitter post can generate thousands of responses. Social scientists get excited about lots of data, but that much data can be terrifying. How do you save, catalogue, and code it all? Exploratory studies have investigated ways to do this and have led to the development of software to make this task easier.

Description

Some social phenomena are not new, but researchers simply want to know more about them. **Descriptive research** is a way to empirically ask questions regarding how often a phenomenon happens, who is involved, under what conditions it occurs, and so on. For example, once researchers had a better understanding of what Facebook and Twitter were and how to manage the massive amounts of data these tools generated, they were able to ask more specific questions that would enable us to better understand who uses them and how they use them. For example, given that Facebook is a place where people can share diverse kinds of information, researchers are interested in who posts what. Descriptive research might ask the following kinds of questions: Which personality types are more likely to post pictures of themselves? Who is more likely to share news stories and try to educate others with their posts? How cute does a cat video have to be before people will share it? There is a lot of diversity in how people use Facebook, and having a better understanding of this can give us a better understanding of human nature.

Explanation

While descriptive research is about questions regarding the "who," "what," "where," and "how often" of social phenomena, **explanatory research** is about asking "why." To have a full understanding of human nature, it's not enough to ask *what* people do; we also need to know *why*. Think about your own reasons for using social media. It's probably fairly easy for you to identify and quantify your behaviour (Do you use it? How many times a day do you check it? How often do you post?). But now think about why you use (or don't use) social media. What do you get out of it? Researchers are interested in why people use Facebook, for example, because it can help them advise people on the best way to use it. This isn't so they can control people's behaviour or anything sinister like that, but they have found that checking social media doesn't always have positive effects. What if a person who is feeling lonely checks social media to feel connected, but all the pictures and posts of their friends looking happy and doing fun things make them feel even lonelier? This actually happens (Burke, Marlow, & Lento, 2010), and one reason why is because of our basic human tendency to compare ourselves to others, referred to as social comparison theory. If you are feeling good about yourself, you can handle seeing others having fun and looking awesome. However, when you are feeling down and in need of some positive feedback, the last thing you should do is check social media, because seeing other people having fun and looking awesome will just cause you to compare yourself negatively to them, and you'll possibly feel even worse about yourself. Social comparison theory helps explain one of the "whys" of social media use, and in this case, knowing "why" helps us advise people on how to use social media in a positive way.

Programmatic Research
Sometimes a research study will focus solely on exploration or description or explanation, but sometimes researchers will tackle two or more of these purposes in a single study or a series of studies. You may run across scholarly articles that contain two or more research studies. Often this is so the researcher can both explore and describe, or describe and explain, the phenomenon under study. The first study might identify the phenomenon and present some new information that helps to describe it, and the second study might test whether a given theory can explain why the phenomenon happens. Good social science research tends to be **programmatic** in this way: It aims to first explore the phenomenon, then describe it, and then provide an explanation as to why it happens.

Basic and Applied Research
In addition to a desire to explore, describe, or explain some social phenomenon, social science researchers may have different reasons for conducting research. Some research is intended solely to help us better understand human nature on a more abstract level, while other research is intended to be put into practice, to directly address some particular problem. The former is called **basic research**, and it is conducted for the purpose of understanding. Basic research

may develop or test a theory of human social behaviour or try to discover why a particular social phenomenon happens. Although the practical applications of this research might not seem evident, it serves as a building block for the development of practical applications. Without basic research on human memory, Chapter 1 of this textbook would not exist. All of those very practical suggestions for how to learn and study more effectively are based on basic research. **Applied research** is designed with a purpose, to address some specific problem or issue. Social scientists who conduct applied research are less interested in theory building or testing and more interested in making an immediate difference. Examples of applied research might be a study of the effectiveness of a particular social program (known as evaluation research), a study assessing various ways to make people pay more attention when they are driving, or a study of racial differences in arrests.

Although it isn't always the case, basic research tends to be more explanatory, while applied research tends to be more exploratory or descriptive. This doesn't mean that one type of research is any "better" than another. All research serves a purpose, whether it is for understanding or for making change, or both.

THEORY AND RESEARCH: PARTNERS IN CRIME

Good social science research includes both theory and research. A theory without evidence is just a theory, and evidence without a theory is just data. By linking theory and research, social scientists are able to better understand the world. And if they understand the world better, they can make better-informed predictions. Imagine how difficult it would be to convince people to change their behaviour if you just had a theory with no evidence. Or evidence with no theory. It's hard enough to change people's behaviour even with a solid theory supported by lots of evidence (just ask a climate change scientist)!

Another important purpose of linking theory and research is to be able to make sound, evidence-based decisions about how to make a positive change. Imagine you are working with people who have been recently released from prison, and your goal is support them so they do not reoffend. If you had no theoretical understanding of why people commit crimes, it would be difficult for you to know how to support them. For example, one prominent theory of crime is called strain theory (Agnew, 1992), and it suggests that people commit crimes when they do not have the resources or abilities to achieve "success" in society through regularly accepted means. There are many different theories of why people commit crimes, and it's unlikely that one of them can explain all crime, but let's say this is the theory you are using. If you know this, then your first priority might be to find this person a job or get them job training so they can obtain the basic resources they need to feel successful. If you had no idea why people commit crimes, not only would you not know how to support them, but you might inadvertently do something that would make them more likely to reoffend.

ONE MORE THING ...

This might be a good time for us to make a confession: We found the topic of research methods a bit boring when we first encountered it as undergraduate students. Reading about research is one thing, but actually being involved in it is an entirely different (and way more exciting) thing. The thrill of coming up with a research question and then answering it with real evidence can't be adequately conveyed in a chapter in a textbook on academic literacy in the social sciences. You need to experience it to really understand our unabashed (and admittedly geeky) love of research. There may be ways for you to get involved in the research being conducted on your campus (as a volunteer or a research assistant), or even to conduct your own research. Some research methods courses even include an assignment in which you design and conduct your own research. If you're still not convinced, think about the skills required to do research (critical thinking, data analysis, communication skills, project management, etc.)—who wouldn't want these abilities?

REVIEW IT

1. What is a potential problem with common sense as a way of knowing?
2. Distinguish between a theory and a paradigm.
3. Distinguish between inductive and deductive approaches to theory building.
4. Describe the seven steps in the research process.

5. Compare the different types of qualitative and quantitative research. How are they different? How are they similar?
6. What is the difference between basic and applied research?

APPLY IT

If you were going to conduct research in the social sciences, which paradigm would you choose to work under? Why? Would it be just one of those described in the chapter, a combination of two or more of them, or something different?

3 The Literature Search: Finding Social Science Research

You probably do some kind of research almost on a daily basis. When you check the weather, look to find out what movies are playing, or search for the best guacamole recipe, you are seeking answers to questions. This is considered research. And, thanks to the Internet, we can find the answer to pretty much any question we could think of online. In fact, we do so much online research that doing research is often simply described as "Googling it." However, as we learned in Chapter 2, scholarly research is qualitatively different from the casual research we do on a day-to-day basis. The questions you are researching are likely to be different. The sources you use will undoubtedly be quite different. The audience for the final products of your research is also likely to be quite different. Because of the important ways in which scholarly research is different from casual research, you won't be surprised to learn that "Googling" to find an answer is likely to be an insufficient approach to research in the social sciences. In this chapter, we'll describe some better ways to make sure you find the best social science research.

LEARNING OBJECTIVES

1. Learn how to find a good research topic
2. Learn to differentiate between scholarly and non-scholarly work
3. Learn how to find information in library databases

THE RESEARCH QUESTION

Finding a Topic

In our experience, one of the most challenging things for students when writing papers and assignments is picking a topic. We can certainly understand this. You may be just learning about the area and don't really know what a good topic might be. Conversely, you may already be familiar with the area and can think of many potentially good topics, but can't decide which one to write about. Or you may not be that motivated to write a paper at all.

Your assignment might involve writing about a particular topic (for example, "victims of crime"), which gives you a good place to start, but you'll still have to narrow it down. Sometimes you will have less direction about a topic. Your instructor might just ask you to write about a topic related to the course. You may think this a great thing, as it opens up a world of potential research topics. Or you may find this vast amount of choice to be paralyzing. Regardless of which camp you are in, you're going to need to come up with a topic.

There is no magical solution to finding a research topic, but here are a few suggestions:

1. What interests you?
    It may seem obvious, but if you are going to put all that work into writing a paper, it should be about something that interests you, that you'd like to learn more about. There must be at least one thing you've learned about in the course that interested you, right?

2. Do some reading
    You might get some ideas from your course textbook or readings. If you run across something you found interesting, but it doesn't work well as an assignment topic, dig a little deeper, either by reading further or searching online. You may find something related to it (or even something completely unrelated to it) that would make a good topic.

3. Pick something doable
    You might be tempted to choose something complicated or difficult in the hopes of getting a better mark on it. Sometimes this works, but it's a risk, because if you don't do it well, your instructor may not be willing to give

out marks for bravery. It's okay to want to do something a bit different, but don't bite off more than you can chew.

Turning Your Topic into a Research Question

Once you've found a topic that interests you, you're going to need to narrow it down into a manageable research question. "Victims of crime" may be an interesting topic that you are excited to write about, but it is much too broad: People have written entire books about victims of crime, so it's going to be difficult for you to do the subject justice in a ten-page paper. It's much better to pick a very narrow, specific topic that you can cover well rather than a vague, general topic. Not only is it difficult to write a comprehensive paper on such a large, broad topic, but researching something so vague is also challenging. If you were to do a search for articles on victims of crime, you would find a lot of them. And we mean a lot. Google, which includes non-scholarly references, gives you over 16 million results. Google Scholar, which tends to give more scholarly references, gives you over 94,000 results. Even the Criminal Justice Abstracts, a database specific to criminology that only searches for scholarly references (more on this later), gives you over 2,000 peer-reviewed references. Regardless of what kind of paper you are writing, that's too many references to wade through.

Idea Mapping

When working on your research question, "victims of crime" is a good place to start if it is a subject that interests you, but you'll need to do a bit more work to turn it into a research question. One way to narrow down your topic is to create an **idea map**. Write your large topic in a circle in the centre of the page, and then write other questions or ideas related to your topic. Then write questions or ideas related to those topics. As you move out from your original topic, your ideas should get more specific. You can start with some online research to get some ideas. For example, if you search for "victims of crime" with Google, one of the first sites that will come up (at the time of writing this book) is the Ontario government site for victims of crime (http:// www.ovc.gov.on.ca). It's not scholarly, but it does cover many issues related to your topic. For example, the purpose of the site is to provide information to victims, because a common concern of victims is where to turn for help. This would be a good thing to include in your idea map. Other ideas that come up from looking through this website might be financial costs for victims, legal rights of victims, and victim impact statements. Keep searching until you start seeing the same issues come up.

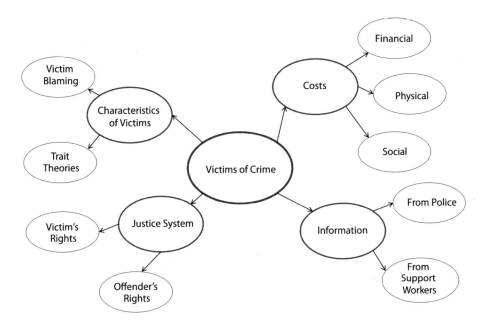

Figure 3.1: Sample Idea Map for Victims of Crime

The Research Question

Once you are familiar with some of the issues and sub-issues of the topic, you can turn it into a question. That question is what you will attempt to answer in your paper. There are two things to keep in mind when developing your research question. First, it should be debatable, meaning that the answer to the question is not so obvious that everyone knows it. For example, "Does crime hurt victims?" would not be a debatable question—there is no doubt crime hurts victims, so this question would not yield an interesting paper in which you can show off your research and reasoning skills. Second, you should choose a question you don't know the answer to. In reality, not many questions in the field of social science have definitive answers; what we mean is that you should not be so sure of the answer to your question that you are not open to learning about other perspectives on it. For example, the question of whether victims should have a say in the sentencing of offenders is debatable, but if you feel so strongly about it that you firmly believe one way or the other, you may not be able to present a balanced argument about it. Not only will a biased, one-sided paper not get you a good grade, but it also won't give you the opportunity to learn something new.

When developing your research question, keep in mind that it should fit with the length of your paper. If you've been asked to write a ten-page paper, you will need a fairly specific question, whereas if you have 20 pages you can be a bit more broad in your question. In our experience, you will most often have to narrow down your question rather than make it more broad. How can you tell if your research question is too narrow or too broad? One way is to seek expert advice; your instructor, writing support centre, or librarian might be able to help you. Another way is to try to search for articles on your topic (see below). If your search turns up 16 million results, your topic may be too broad. However, if you find only five results, your topic may be too narrow.

ACADEMIC SOURCES

You'll find social science research in many different places—books, articles, the Internet, newspapers, television. Not all of these sources are considered "scholarly" however, which means that, while they may be interesting, they will not be appropriate for an academic paper. When you are seeking out sources for an assignment or paper (such as a literature review), it can be a challenge to figure out what's scholarly and what isn't.

Scholarly vs Non-scholarly Sources

Most likely you've been asked to use scholarly sources in your writing assignments. A literature review would contain mostly, if not entirely, scholarly sources. A **scholarly source** within the social sciences is an article or book written by an expert in the field, often describing original scientific research.

Table 3.1: A Comparison of Scholarly and Non-scholarly Sources

Scholarly Source	Non-scholarly Source
Written by an expert in the field of social science	Written by a non-scientist, such as a journalist, a blogger, or a member of the general public
Often reports on the findings of an original research study conducted by the author	May report on the findings of a research study conducted by someone else
Includes citations and references	May not include citations and references
Is peer-reviewed, meaning it has been reviewed by other experts in the field	Is not peer-reviewed
Often written in a formal, academic way	May use casual, informal language

You can tell the difference between a scholarly source and a non-scholarly source in a number of ways. If you are in doubt about whether a source is scholarly or not, ask a librarian.

The other distinction between types of sources is whether they are primary or secondary. A **primary source** is a description of original research, conducted by the author. This might include articles about the author's study based on experiments, surveys, interviews, content analyses, or any other type of study that social science researchers use to answer a specific question. In the social sciences, primary sources are usually journal articles, but sometimes they can be books, if the book describes a particularly large or complicated research study. Primary sources are scholarly sources. A **secondary source** can also be a scholarly source, but it isn't always. Secondary sources are a step removed from primary sources, in that they tend to summarize, describe, analyze, or contextualize primary sources. Secondary research articles may include, but are not limited to, literature reviews and academic opinion articles. A textbook would be considered a secondary source, because it describes the research of others in order to provide information and perspective on a larger field of study. Other books can also be secondary sources. For example, a book about victims of crime that pulls together all the research on victims conducted by various social scientists would be a secondary source.

Appropriate Sources of Social Science Research

You'll come across many different types of sources in your research travels. A quick Internet search will give you books, journal articles, newspaper articles, websites, blogs, photos, videos, and more. Many of these will be interesting, but not all of them will be appropriate for an academic paper. The two best sources for social science research are academic journal articles and scholarly books.

Academic Journal Articles

Most original scientific research is first published in academic journals. Academic journals are collections of research articles put together by publishers representing the scientific community. Although there are some interdisciplinary academic journals, most tend to be focused on one discipline, or even a specific topic within a discipline. For example, within the field of sociology, there are journals on the general field of sociology, such as *Canadian Sociological Review*, *Journal of Sociology*, and *Current Sociology*, but there are also journals that focus on specific issues within sociology, such as *Teaching Sociology* and *International Journal of Sociology of the Family*. Most academic journals have a peer-review process, whereby all articles they publish are first reviewed by other experts in the field to ensure that the research study is well designed, relevant, and without errors. Some academic journals only publish about 10 percent of the articles submitted to them, so the standards for publication tend to be quite high.

Each journal issue will contain a number of articles, each of which describes in detail a study or series of studies. Many of them are available online, either through a regular Internet search or through the school library (more on this later). Although academic journal articles are often written in fairly formal language, they tend to use a very specific format, which makes it easier to follow.

The Anatomy of an Academic Journal Article

ABSTRACT
A summary of the research

- Usually includes the variables studied, the hypotheses or research questions, the main findings, and implications of the research
- Will give you an idea of whether the article is relevant to what you're looking for

INTRODUCTION
Also called a literature review, because it reviews the literature on this topic

- Explains the research question, and why it's important
- Covers what is currently known about the question

METHOD
Explains how the study was conducted, and may include the following subsections:

- Participants—how many, where from, age range, gender, what incentive they received for participating in the study, and anything else that might be relevant to the study
- Measures—what tests, scales, or measures were used

- Procedures—describes exactly what the participants did

RESULTS
Explains the results of the data analysis

- If it's a qualitative study, will probably include quotes
- If it's a quantitative study, will include the statistical analyses
- Can be difficult to follow, but don't skip it; the graphs and tables can be helpful

DISCUSSION
A summary and discussion of the findings

- Usually the first paragraph summarizes the findings; if you don't understand the statistics in the results, often this will help clarify
- Points out potential flaws or limitations of the study
- Points out value of study
- Sometimes gives practical applications/implications

REFERENCES/CITATIONS
A list of all sources cited in the paper (but only those cited in the paper)

- Follows a specific style (often APA, but not always)
- A good source for articles on the topic

Books

Academic journal articles are not the only useful types of research to look for when you are searching for references. You will undoubtedly also look for books, whether in hardcopy or digital formats. Books have long been a standard reference for academia and scholarly research, and they can be important sources of information for the social science researcher. However, books offer some challenges when trying to use them as a reference. One problem for social science students is the time that it takes to read them. Students are often busy doing research for many courses at the same time and simply do not have the time to read many books. Another problem is that academic books are typically secondary sources of information. While a book may be very detailed and contain considerable analysis, the social science studies they use for their analysis are typically studies that have already been published elsewhere. The book may be very useful for summarizing and contextualizing these studies for you, but if you use the findings from these studies in your research, you will be expected to cite the original publications for the studies, not the book.

A final problem is the challenge of distinguishing an academic book from a non-academic book. You shouldn't assume that university or college libraries only list scholarly books on their catalogues. For example, you can find comedian Tina Fey's (2013) book *Bossypants* in our university library. This is an entertaining and well-written book, and we're glad our university has a copy of it, but with all due respect to Ms. Fey, it is not a scholarly book.

There are a number of ways to distinguish academic from non-academic books, but many of these distinguishing features are difficult to identify from a catalogue listing. You can sometimes identify a scholarly book, though, by either its title or its publisher. Academic books often have titles or subtitles that seem more scholarly. Academic books are also often published by academic publishers. You can sometimes identify an academic publisher because it has the name of a university as the part of its name (e.g., Oxford University Press). This is not always the case, though, and many academic publishers are not directly affiliated with a university and do not have such a readily identifiable name. In these cases, it is useful to know the names of publishers who specialize in publishing academics in your field. For example, Island Press specializes in publishing scholarly books focused on environmental studies and geography, and the American Psychological Association publishes scholarly books in psychology. Sometimes, though, the best way to determine whether or not a particular book is an academic book is to check it out. Ultimately, books can be very useful and appropriate references for research in the social sciences. It is quite likely that most of your references for a social science paper will be either journal articles or books.

Inappropriate Sources of Social Science Research

Social science research is not only found in academic sources. Social science is interesting and fun, and people like to read about it, so you'll find descriptions of social science research everywhere, from popular books to magazines, to blogs. We encourage you to read everything you find on your topic, because it will help you discover what the biggest issues and unanswered questions are, what types of research are being done, and also perhaps some of the misconceptions about the topic.

As interesting and informative as these non-academic sources are, however, they are not appropriate as sources for your paper. If you have been asked to write about the current literature on a topic within the social sciences, the expectation is that you are using and referring to the original research, not someone else's description of it. Another reason not to use these sources is that you do not know how accurate they are. Magazines and blogs are sometimes more concerned with increasing their number of readers than with the accuracy of their claims. Consider the following headline:

> "A bottle of wine a day is not bad for you and abstaining is worse than drinking, scientist claims" (Jivanda, 2014)

This was published in a British newspaper, and the cheers and clinking glasses could be heard around the world. But wait a minute. Here's another headline, a week later:

> "A bottle of wine a day is harmless? The evidence suggests otherwise" (Gage, 2014)

We knew it was too good to be true! The first article, published in *The Independent*, quoted a retired professor who claimed that decades of research backed up his claims, but there was no link to this research and it's unclear if any of it was ever published. The second article, published in the science section of *The Guardian*, refuted the claims, based on solid, peer-reviewed evidence that they provide links to in the article. Unless you did some digging, you might be tempted to believe the first headline, which is clearly misleading and possibly completely incorrect. The only way to know for sure is to find the original research in an academic source.

We want to mention one other source not considered to be academic: Wikipedia. Wikipedia is a free online encyclopedia created by users. The entries are often long, detailed, and include sources. Anyone can edit an entry, which is great if that person is an expert in the field, or not great if that person has misinformation about the topic or deliberately wants to mislead users with incorrect information. Admittedly, there are protections in place to ensure the entries are as accurate as possible, but you can still not assume the information provided is correct. Even the creators admit it is imperfect and "a work in progress" (Wikipedia, 2017). The scope of this project is admirable, and there is much to like about it, but it is not an academic source and you should never cite Wikipedia in an academic paper.

Age of References

While searching for academic references for a social science paper, you will likely find references from many different years. Do not overlook the publication date too quickly; it can be a very important criterion for evaluating a reference. In general, more recent references are preferred in the social sciences. This is because the social sciences are sciences. You will remember that science is an ongoing process of investigation and knowledge creation. We never really prove things in the sciences. Rather, we find supporting evidence for a theory until the theory is shown to be falsified and/or a better theory is identified. Saying that we know something demands a lot of evidence, and we never cease looking for this evidence. In this never-ending process, it can be assumed that more recent research is based on a better understanding of a theory or a phenomenon than older research. Thus, if you are going to write about our understanding of a theory or phenomenon, it is best if you write about our most recent studies.

Determining what can be defined as recent research can be challenging, though. In some relatively new fields or in highly dynamic fields with rapidly evolving insights, only studies from within the last few years might be considered to be current. In other, more well-established fields or with topics that have been studied for a very long time, a current study might be one from the last decade or two. Be aware, though, that the emphasis on current research should not be seen as justification for excluding much older references. Sometimes, a study or an article is so pivotal that it changed the way scholars think about a topic. Unfortunately, identifying such pivotal references early in a research project can sometimes be very difficult. If this is the case, make sure you keep your mind open that some older references cannot, and should not, be overlooked.

WHERE TO FIND ACADEMIC SOURCES

Now that you have decided on a topic and know what kind of sources to look for, you are ready to starting searching. The success (and ease) of your literature search will depend on many factors, but one important factor is looking in the right places. There are different options for how to search for research articles, and depending on your topic, one may be better than another. Remember you are looking for articles that will help you answer your research question, so quality is more important than quantity. The search that turns up the most results is not necessarily the best search.

What to Search For

Once you have your research idea or question, another decision you will have to make is what search terms (also called keywords) to use in your search. **Search terms** are significant words or phrases related to a topic. A search term may be the topic word you're using, but it may also be a synonym for the topic. It may also be a term that describes a foundational concept relevant to the topic. For example, you may be researching people's attitudes toward pets. Thus, a keyword may be "pets," but it may also be "cats" or "dogs." You may also use the phrase "companion animals" as a search term. By themselves, each of these search terms will undoubtedly return a daunting number of search results, many of which may have little relevance to your topic. Thus, it may be necessary to add another search term. In this case, you might use the search term "attitudes." If you know of a particular author who has done research about this topic or has published this research in a book or a journal, you may wish to use the author's name as one of the search terms. Try different search terms and search term combinations. See how many results you get with each combination of words. You may get thousands, or you may get just a few; either extreme may be problematic, and you may have to broaden or focus your choice of keywords. Check out the titles of the results that you saw. They may not seem quite relevant to your research question. If they do not seem relevant, you may have to modify your keywords.

Using Commercial Search Engines

Students often start their search for scholarly articles with a commercial online search engine such as Google. Such searches are easy—you probably use this method of finding information all the time, and you're likely very good at it. One problem with this method is that it often returns many thousands of results. This can appear quite promising, because it seems to suggest that you are researching a rich topic with lots of information about it. Of course, too many results can be just as problematic as too few or even no search results. The challenge of winnowing out the relevant sources from the less relevant ones can be very time-consuming. You might assume that the first results will be the most relevant, but that's not always the case. Commercial search engines typically have complex algorithms that take hundreds of variables into account when determining relevance, and unfortunately many of these variables have more to do with generating income for the creators of the search engine and less to do with scholarly relevance. Using a commercial search engine also adds complexity to the evaluation process. The search results will not be limited to academic sources—they are designed to give you everything on the topic, and "everything" includes everything anyone ever decided to post on the Internet about it, regardless of how accurate, relevant, or articulate it is. It is not always easy to distinguish between academically appropriate references and non-academic Web references. For example, a document on a college or university website may be a primary research article that has been peer-reviewed and published elsewhere in an academic journal. It may also be an unpublished article that has not passed peer review. It may also be a news story promoting research being done by researchers at the university. Since some colleges and universities allow students to create webpages or websites within the school's website, a university webpage may simply be a student blog. Thus, while it is tempting to use a commercial search engine to find your sources, it is a potentially counterproductive approach and can actually take more time.

A somewhat more desirable approach for finding research articles is to use a commercial search engine focused primarily on academic references, such as Google Scholar. Such a scholarly search engine often offers many of the features of academic library databases, in that they are more focused on academic and scholarly sources. They also have some helpful features. For example, sometimes they link directly to an article so you can download it to your computer. They will also link you to a list of references that have cited a particular reference. This might help you find other related sources that didn't come up in your search. You can also get a formatted reference (for example, in APA style), thereby saving you some time and effort in trying to get every comma and period in the correct place when formatting your reference list. It is also sometimes possible to customize the settings of the search engine so it will check each reference to see if it is in your school's library. Better yet, all of this search capability is available for free, without having to log on to your university library's website. However, there are potential pitfalls to the use of commercial scholarly search engines. First, the search result may list documents that appear to be academic articles but are not truly scholarly. And even if the reference is scholarly, it may not be peer reviewed. Depending on the type of paper you are writing and your instructions for the paper, either of these problems turns a promising source into an unsuitable reference. Second, it may not find all the related articles for you. It's difficult to know how thorough these search engines are, so you may be missing out on some key articles if you only rely on them for your searches. Third, even if you are fortunate enough to find a suitable academic reference using one of these scholarly search engines, you should use the search engine's citation formatting feature with great care. Our experience has been that they are not always accurate, so you should double check any preformatted references to make sure that it exactly follows APA style (or whichever style you are using). In the end, we suggest that scholarly search engines are worth trying. However, you should be aware of their strengths and weaknesses, and do not rely on them as your only approach to finding good academic articles.

Your School Library's Website

A useful place to begin your research in earnest is in the place where generations of academics have begun their research: in the school library or, perhaps, its more contemporary extension, the school library website. When you first arrive at a university or college library website, it may look like many other websites you have visited. It may even resemble the website for your municipal library. However, school libraries are typically designed to meet the sophisticated research needs of scientists, some with very specialized requirements for their research. They are not only catalogues for the libraries' collections; they are also typically the gateways to very comprehensive, and expensive, research databases and online collections. These online resources are not meant to be replacements for the physical resources of university or college libraries, such as hardcopy books and journals, at least not yet. However, they are essential tools for finding both hardcopy and digital resources.

When you first arrive at your school's website, you may be asked to log on with your student card or your school library card. While you may do some relatively simple tasks, such as conducting simple searches of the library's catalogue, you will likely be unable to access many of the library's resources until you have logged on. This is because many of the library's resources are very expensive subscription services, and they purchase them for the exclusive use of members of the school (i.e., students, faculty, and staff). Part of your tuition goes to the library so they can maintain these services. Requiring you to log on first enables them to restrict access to people who have paid for the service. If you are unsure how to log onto your library website, ask a librarian.

Once you are on the school library website, you will likely notice a catalogue search box. This may be a good place to begin your research. The challenge, like any search, is knowing what to search for. By now, you may have your topic and have developed an initial research question. If you do, you will likely try searching the catalogue with your topic word(s). It is quite likely you will be offered a list of hundreds, if not thousands, of library resources that satisfy that search. This list may contain a wide variety of resource types, such as books, journals and journal articles, videos, sound recordings, magazines, newspapers, or microform. The reference may be available online or may be physically stored in one of the libraries on your campus, in a library of another campus, or even at an affiliated school's library. You'll probably realize fairly quickly that a more sophisticated and more focused search for your references is needed.

School library catalogues will typically offer advanced search options. With these advanced searches, you will be able to search with multiple search terms simultaneously. You will also be able to use Boolean operators, like "and," "or," and "not," to combine several search terms. You will be able to limit your search by the types of sources that you want. You may even be able to limit your search by the library, the campus, or the university. Advanced searches add a great many options to your searches. They also require you to make a lot of decisions before you begin searching.

Databases

Library catalogues are very useful places to begin your research. However, they do have their limitations, particularly when looking for academic journal articles. Fortunately, university and college libraries typically subscribe to databases of academic journal articles. These can be much more efficient and powerful when looking for journal articles. These databases are usually accessible through your school's library's website, after you log on. The databases also tend to be highly focused and specialized in the kinds of journals that they catalogue. Therefore, different databases will be most appropriate for different disciplines. If you do not know which databases are most relevant to your discipline, your library will usually have listings of the databases most relevant to your discipline. Searching a database is typically very similar to the ways you search your library catalogue. For every record, though, you will find other useful information, such as the number of academic references that have cited this reference in their publication. This can be useful in helping you get an idea about how important other scholars consider the findings of a study. You will also often find a link to a listing of the references this publication cites. We will see how this information can be useful shortly. If the article seems promising, the database may provide you with a link to that article within your library's collection. If no link is provided, it may mean your library does not have access to this article. This information can be very useful to know early in your research. If your library does not have access to the article, you do not necessarily have to abandon using it in your paper. However, it does mean that you may have to find alternative ways to get a copy of the article. Again, your library can be very helpful for finding alternative places to access an article.

Sometimes you'll come across information for an article that looks promising, but you will be unable to access the entire article until you pay. If you are a student, don't pay for academic articles! There's a good chance you can get it (legitimately) some other way. Ask a librarian for help, as they can often get these articles for you through agreements they have with other schools.

Mining for References

There are a number of other places to find research materials. One place is within the references you have already found for your topic. Even primary research articles will typically provide a brief literature review or introduction at the beginning of the article. They will also often cite relevant references elsewhere within the articles. If you find an article that seems relevant to your topic, you can use these citations as guides to find other articles that might be relevant to your research. This approach is particularly useful for finding those key older research articles that reflect watershed moments in our understanding of the topic you are writing about.

There are also other types of publications that you can "mine" for their reference lists. Textbooks can sometimes be very useful sources for lists of relevant research. Because textbooks are generally secondary sources, they are often not desirable references. However, many textbooks cite the sources for their information, and all textbooks should cite any research used to illustrate a concept. Textbooks can also be useful for understanding concepts you are going to use in your research. Once you have mined the relevant references from the textbook, you will still have to use your library resources to find the article.

Another source for finding research about your topic or research question is literature reviews. As previously mentioned, most primary research articles will include a brief literature review as an introduction. However, some academic journal articles are just literature reviews. Like textbooks, these literature reviews can be very useful for understanding concepts relevant to your research question. In addition, since literature reviews rely on primary research articles for their reviews, they will contain many citations and references. As with textbooks, though, all of the cited references will be older publications than the article itself. This may be a problem if the literature review is not quite current. In general, you will not use the literature review itself as a reference unless you use some of the literature review's analysis as part of your paper.

A final place to look to find useful reference lists is in a master's thesis or doctoral dissertation. These documents tend to be rather large and may contain very sophisticated disciplinary jargon. However, they also typically contain quite comprehensive literature reviews. They also tend to be narrowly focused. Therefore, you may be able to find a thesis or dissertation that is very similar to your research topic. Until relatively recently, getting a copy of a particular thesis or dissertation was sometimes very challenging. There would typically be only one university library with a print copy. If the author of the thesis or dissertation graduated from a different university than the one you were attending, getting a copy could be a long process. Fortunately, most of these documents are now published in digital format. If your library does not have a copy, you can get help from one of your librarians in obtaining a copy from another university. Some countries, like Canada, also maintain central depositaries of graduate students' theses and dissertations. Canada's thesis depositary is called Theses Canada. You will not be able to find every document you want there, but it is very useful to look. The richness of these documents' reference lists certainly makes the effort worthwhile. Because the graduate students must defend their research before committees of other academics, the primary research discussed elsewhere in the theses and dissertations can be cited as an academically acceptable reference.

IN CONCLUSION

Research Takes Time

When you are looking for appropriate references for a social science paper, do not assume it will be a brief activity or one that you can effectively do while you are in the process of writing your paper (or watching Netflix). You must begin the process of finding appropriate references well before the due date for your paper. You need to budget time to read and reread your references. You should then reread them yet again. This is to ensure that you completely understand what the authors are saying.

Be Prepared to Do It Over and Over

You won't find all the relevant sources in one try. Although all researchers wish there was one magical place where they could find all the best articles on their topic, we're sad to say this place does not exist. You'll need to try different databases and different search terms. You will also probably find that you need to conduct additional searches as you start writing your paper. New ideas might come up, or you might find you don't have enough information or research on a particular point you want to make in your paper. We're not going to lie: It can be a frustrating process, but it can also be very rewarding. There may be instances where you have gone on a lengthy quest to find a copy of a particular article that looked promising, only to find that it's not appropriate for your paper. However, there will also be times when you find the perfect article, making you feel like a research superhero.

Ask for Help

If you are uncertain about how to begin looking for appropriate references, or if you simply need a little help during the process, consider contacting your school librarians. At many university and college libraries, there will be librarians who specialize in the needs of different disciplines or different faculties. You may find this very useful. However, no matter which discipline you are in, a librarian can be an essential aide for your research. Do not be embarrassed in asking for their help—even established researchers often seek their help for their research. Be patient when seeking their help, though. Librarians are very busy research professionals with many students and other researchers seeking their help, particularly toward the end of term. This is one further reason to start your research early.

REVIEW IT

1. What is a primary source?
2. Describe the six parts of an academic journal article.
3. Books have long been important sources of academic information. However, there are some challenges in using books as academic references. Identify two of these challenges.
4. References for your papers should generally be recent sources. How can you determine what is recent?

5. When searching for references for your papers, it is best to avoid commercial search engines. Why?
6. What is meant by "mining for references"?

APPLY IT

Let's say you have chosen "bullying through social networking sites" as a research topic. Where would you look for information? What search terms would you use?

Conduct a search, first using Google, then using Google Scholar, and then using your school library's database. What do you notice?

Conduct the same search using different search terms. What happens? Do you get the same sources or different sources?

Using your school library's database (or Google Scholar if you don't have access to a database), first search for "bullying AND social networking," and then search for "bullying OR social networking." What is the difference between these two search terms? How many search results do you get for each? Which might be the more effective search strategy?

4 APA Style: Citing Social Science Research

You may have noticed that academic writing can be a bit dense. Each discipline has its own jargon or specialized vocabulary, and reading it can sometimes feel like you need a secret decoder ring to make any sense of it. Although they may use different terminology, one way the social sciences maintain consistency is to use a common style to communicate their findings. These styles are systems not only of how research is cited but also how research articles are structured, what language is used, and where the research is published. They provide a degree of consistency in the field so that even if you don't understand the language and terminology used, you'll at least understand the structure. In this chapter, we'll show you how to identify and use one style commonly used in the social sciences: APA style. Although you will likely run across other methods of citing sources in the social sciences, this is one of the more common ones. Consider it your secret decoder ring for the social sciences.

LEARNING OBJECTIVES

1. Understand what APA style is and why it's important
2. Learn how to write a research paper using APA style
3. Learn how to cite sources using APA style

WHAT IS APA AND WHY DOES IT HAVE A "STYLE"?

"APA" is the American Psychological Association, an organization that represents psychologists in the United States. Its members include researchers, teachers and professors, clinicians, consultants, and students. Their mission is to "advance the creation, communication, and application of psychological knowledge to benefit society and improve people's lives" (American Psychological Association, 2017). In 1929, they published a seven-page document on how to prepare a scientific article, written by a group of psychologists, anthropologists, and business managers. The goal of the article was to create a standard procedure for presenting scientific information, in order to make it easier for readers to understand. It included recommendations about writing style, the format of the article, and the way to cite sources (Bentley et al., 1929). That seven-page article has since become a 272-page book, now in its sixth edition, called *Publication Manual of the American Psychological Association* (2010).

The book describes many aspects of writing and publishing. Like the original article, it includes sections on writing style, formatting an article, and citing sources properly, but it also covers things like research ethics, presenting statistics, and using bias-free language. The general idea is that if the rules for the communication of scientific information are well established and clearly laid out, then both writers and readers will be able to focus on the research itself and not on the way it is presented. Think of it as a school uniform for social science.

Although APA style was created by a psychological organization, it is not just for psychologists. While not all of the social sciences use it, many of them do. You will come across different citation methods in your academic travels, but chances are much of the research you read will use at least some elements of APA style.

Common Referencing Styles

APA (American Psychological Association; http://www.apastyle.org)—used in the social sciences

ASA (American Sociological Association; http://www.asanet.org/sites/default/files/quick_tips_for_asa_style.pdf)—used in the social sciences

Chicago (Chicago University Press; http://www.chicagomanualofstyle.org)—used in the social sciences and humanities

CSE (Council of Science Editors; http://www.scientificstyleandformat.org/)—used in the sciences

MLA (Modern Languages Association; http://style.mla.org)—used in the humanities

We know what you're thinking: Why don't all the disciplines get their acts together and just use one style? One reason for the variety of styles is that different disciplines use and value different types of resources, and their citation styles reflect those differences. For example, in the social sciences, the emphasis is on original research articles and scholarly books, whereas in history the emphasis may be more on archival data or artifacts. Even the legal field has its own style, as the emphasis there is on legal cases. Another reason for all the different styles is that many of these disciplines have been around for a long time. They have developed their style based on the individual needs and quirks of their fields, and, like many of us who have been around for a long time, they are resistant to change.

So how do you deal with all these different styles, especially if you are taking courses in both the social sciences and the humanities, where the styles are almost sure to be different? First, clarify whether your instructor feels strongly about which style you use. They may not care, as long as you are consistent. If that's the case, then use the style you are most comfortable with. If you are instructed to use a specific style, then be sure to use that style. There are websites that can help you. Your school's library or writing centre probably has materials too; they may even offer workshops.

We're going to suggest that you embrace the opportunity to learn the different styles of the academic disciplines. Remember that if each style is a secret decoder ring that will help you interpret and understand the material you are reading, then more rings equals more knowledge. Plus, you'll be a hit at parties when you are able to cite your sources in multiple styles.

WRITING A PAPER IN APA STYLE

Research Articles

In Chapter 3, we briefly described the components of a journal article. To refresh your memory, most journal articles follow this basic structure:

Title
Abstract
Introduction/Literature Review
Methods
Results
Discussion
References

This structure is recommended by APA (2010). Even if you are reading a social science article that does not use APA style, if the article is describing an original research study it probably has all these elements. This makes finding what you are looking for in a research article much easier. Imagine, for example, you are researching the various ways people measure or assess recycling behaviour. Once you've done a literature search for articles that address recycling behaviour, in order to compare how researchers have measured it, you don't have to read every article from start to finish. If you know that researchers describe the measures they use in the methods section, then you just need to skip to the methods sections of all your articles to find what you are looking for. Similarly, if you are looking for articles that have used a particular statistical test (say, for example, an analysis of variance), you just need to skip to the results section, where the research findings are described. This is one area where knowledge of the particular conventions used in your discipline comes in very handy; it can save you time.

Student Essays and Papers

Chances are you are not writing up original research in your undergraduate social science course, so we are not going to go into the details of APA style for research studies. There is excellent information about this in the *Publication Manual of the American Psychological Association* (2010) and on their website (http://apastyle.org), and we recommend that you consult them if you are conducting original research.

Our focus is on how to write a paper for a course when your instructor asks for APA style. You should check with your instructor to find out what, exactly, they mean when they ask for APA style. They may be simply talking about the referencing style you use, or they may mean the entire paper and its formatting has to conform to APA style. In this section, we'll show you how to do both: first, how to format your paper in APA style, and second, how to credit sources and create a reference list.

Ultimately, since your instructor is likely the one marking your paper, our advice is to follow their instructions for formatting your paper.

General Format

If you are not writing up the results of a research study, your paper will not have as many sections as a typical social science journal article. Here's what you should include:

Title page
Main body
References

Some instructors may also ask for an abstract, which would simply be a summary of the main points you make in your paper.

Your entire paper, including the title page, should be double-spaced, in 12-point font, with 1-inch (2.54 cm) margins and the beginning of each paragraph indented by 0.5 inches (1.27 cm).

Title Page

An official APA-style title page has very little information on it: It includes the title of the paper, the author's name, and the author's affiliation (i.e., the school or institution they are at). These are centred and double-spaced. At the top of the title page, in the header area, there is a running head, which is a short version of the title of your paper on the left, and the page number on the right.

The running head is a bit tricky, as it appears one way on the title page and a slightly different way throughout the rest of your paper, so you'll have to use a feature of your word processing program that allows you to have a different header on your first page. On the title page, the running head should look like this:

Running head: SHORTENED TITLE OF YOUR PAPER

Be sure to match the use of upper and lower case exactly; only the shortened title is in all caps, and "Running head" is lower case except for the initial "R." On subsequent pages you take out the words "Running head," so it looks like this:

SHORTENED TITLE OF YOUR PAPER

This is the official APA-version of a student title page, but individual instructors may have their own preferences. We often ask our students to include their instructor's name on their title page. Be sure to read your assignment instructions or check with the instructor to find out what they want.

Main Body

Unless you have been asked to include an abstract, the main body of your paper will begin on the second page. Include your full title, centred but not bolded or underlined, at the top of the page, and then begin your paper underneath it. Don't leave an extra line after your title.

Running head: ACADEMIC LITERACY AND SOCIAL SCIENCE   1

The Benefits of Academic Literacy in the Social Sciences

Your Name

Your School

Figure 4.1: APA-Style Title Page for Student Papers

ACADEMIC LITERACY AND SOCIAL SCIENCE   2

The Benefits of Academic Literacy in the Social Sciences

Universities face increasing pressure to meet conflicting demands: operate with less government funding while holding tuition constant (Bradshaw, 2013), and maximize the employability of their graduates (Denham, 2013). Some post-secondary institutions have attempted to resolve this conflict by creating literacy courses that all students must complete early in their academic career (Weissman & Boning, 2003). These foundational courses are intended to provide students with specific knowledge and skills that will help them succeed in their upper-level university courses. Although the idea behind literacy courses is theoretically sound, there is very little information on whether they actually do promote student success. The purpose of this paper is to review the effectiveness of these courses, to determine if they do what they set out to do.

Many universities have some form of a core program, either within a department or faculty or across the entire institution...

Figure 4.2: APA-Style Main Body of Paper for Student Papers

ACADEMIC LITERACY AND SOCIAL SCIENCE   10

References

Bradshaw, J. (2013, March 10). Canadian universities feel the squeeze of spending cuts.

    The Globe and Mail. Retrieved from http://www.theglobeandmail.com/news/national/

    education/canadian-universities-feel-the-squeeze-of-spending-cuts/article9582355/

Denham, J. (2013, September 13). Graduates unprepared for employment. *The*

    Independent. Retrieved from http://www.independent.co.uk/student/graduates-

    unprepared-for-employment-8814643.html

Healey, M., Matthews, H., Livingstone, I., & Foster, I. (1996). Learning in small groups in

    university geography courses: Designing a core module around group projects.

    Journal of Geography in Higher Education, 20, 167-180. doi:

    10.1080/03098269608709364

Figure 4.3: APA-Style Reference Section of Paper for Student Papers

---

References

This includes a list of all of the sources you cited in your paper. Do not include sources that you read or looked at but did not cite. The formatting of the references themselves is very picky—we'll get to that later. The entire list should be in alphabetical order by the last name of the first author of each source, double-spaced. The references section should begin on a new page, with the title "References" at the top, centred but not bolded or underlined. Each source should start on a separate line, with the first line flush left but the remaining lines for each source indented by 0.5 inches (1.27 cm). This is called a hanging indent, and your word processing software should have a feature that makes this relatively easy to set up.

CREDITING SOURCES IN YOUR PAPER

If you are writing a literature review, you will read and discuss many different sources in your paper, and it is expected that you will give credit to those sources. We discuss this more in Chapter 8 on writing a literature review, but for now, suffice it to say that when you are writing any kind of academic paper, you need to document where your information came from, whether that information is a research finding, the idea of another scholar, or simply a fact that would not be considered common knowledge.

APA has a good system for crediting sources. First, you document the source in the body of your paper using in-text citations, and second, you provide the full source in your references section. **In-text citations** are not the entire source; they are simply the author's (or authors') last name and the year the work was published. This allows you to give credit to the author(s) within your paper without breaking up the flow of your paper too much. If a reader wants more information about the source, they can easily find it in your references section. In most cases, there is no need to refer to the title of the source you are citing in the main body of your paper. In a literature review or other type of academic essay, never provide the entire citation in the main body of your paper.

In-text citations are pretty straightforward, but they do differ slightly depending on the number of authors there are. We've provided a number of examples below.

General Format

There are two main ways you can refer to a source. You can make the statement, then provide the source in parentheses, using the author's last name and the year of the publication, or you can use the author's last name directly in your sentence, with only the year in parentheses. Here's an example of the difference between the two:

> Students tend to take better notes by hand rather than by computer (Mueller & Oppenheimer, 2014).

> Mueller and Oppenheimer (2014) found that students tend to take better notes by hand rather than by computer.

Both are correct. Note, though, how the first example places emphasis on the research finding, whereas in the second example, because you begin with the author's name, the emphasis is more on the author.

Do not include the author's initials or their first name, regardless of whether you use their name in the sentence or in parentheses at the end of the sentence. When there is more than one author, keep them in the order in which they appear on the publication (i.e., don't be tempted to put them in alphabetical order). Authorship is usually determined by how much each author contributed to the work, and the authors will have decided this before publishing the article.

One Author

When the source has only one author, it's very straightforward to create an in-text citation. Use their last name and the year of the publication.

> Physical activity has been found to have positive effects on anxiety, depression, and sensitivity to stress (Salmon, 2001).

> Salmon (2001) found that physical activity can have positive effects on anxiety, depression, and sensitivity to stress.

Two Authors

When the source has two authors, you need to list both of them, as well as the year of publication. Notice how when you provide the authors' names outside of parentheses, you use the word "and" to connect them, but when you provide their names inside parentheses, you use "&" to connect them.

> Research suggests that expressing gratitude can have a positive effect on subjective well-being (Emmons & McCullough, 2003).

> Emmons and McCullough (2003) found that gratitude can have a positive effect on subjective well-being.

Three to Five Authors

With more than two authors, citing them all begins to get a bit tedious, so APA provides a short-hand method once you have already cited them once. The first time you cite them, list all the authors. Notice how you're still just using the last names of all the authors, with "and" if you're referring to them in the sentence and "&" if you put them in parentheses. Also note that now there is a comma after each name, including right before the "and" or "&".

> Many evidence-based learning techniques come from the fields of cognitive and education psychology (Dunlosky, Rawson, Marsh, Nathan, & Willingham, 2013).

Dunlosky, Rawson, Marsh, Nathan, and Willingham (2013) suggest that many evidence-based learning techniques come from the fields of cognitive and education psychology.

If you refer to this source again in your paper, you don't need to list everyone again. In subsequent mentions of this source, use only the first author's last name, followed by "et al." and the year.

One of the most effective learning techniques is practice testing (Dunlosky et al., 2013).

According to Dunlosky et al. (2013), one of the most effective learning techniques is practice testing.

More than Five Authors

Every now and then you'll come across a publication with more than five authors. In this case, you don't need to list them all. Even the first time you refer to them, just give the first author's last name, followed by "et al." and the year.

Mindfulness meditation has been found to have modest but significant positive effects on chronic pain (Hilton et al., 2017).

Hilton et al. (2017) found that mindfulness meditation can have modest but significant positive effects on chronic pain.

No Author

Some publications are written by groups, such as a corporation, association, or government agency. In this case, use the group's name as the author.

Crime rates in Canada have been steadily decreasing since 1991 (Statistics Canada, 2015).

According to Statistics Canada (2015), crime rates in Canada have been steadily decreasing since 1991.

If the organization's name is a well-known abbreviation or acronym, like "APA" for the American Psychological Association or "PETA" for People for the Ethical Treatment of Animals, then write it in full the first time you refer to it, and use the abbreviation or acronym in subsequent mentions.

First mention:

> Provide enough information so readers can find the source in your reference list (American Psychological Association, 2010).

Second mention:

> Don't put periods between the letters in an acronym (APA, 2010).

Citing More than One Source at a Time

When you are reviewing and synthesizing the academic literature on a particular topic, you'll often find that more than one research study can be used to back up a claim. Citing more than one source can give more weight to your claim, so don't be afraid to do this, within reason (i.e., two or three sources— not ten). When you list more than one source, list them alphabetically, by the first author's last name.

> Disney movies have proven to be a rich source of data for examining how films can influence children's beliefs and attitudes (Hoerrner, 1996; Lawson & Fouts, 2004; Padilla-Walker, Coyne, Fraser, & Stockdale, 2013).

If you are citing more than one publication by the same author(s), give their last name once, followed by the years of the publications.

> Our beliefs and self-theories can have an impact on our motivation, and hence our ability to learn (Dweck, 1986, 2000; Schunk, 1991).

Citing Other Authors' Sources

As you are reading through the research you have found for your paper, you may find that one of your sources has cited an article you haven't read but would fit well in your paper. You should look up this source in the references section of the source and track down the article they are referring to. Then you can cite it yourself. You should not cite works you haven't read for a few reasons. First, if this is for an academic paper or essay, your instructors want to know how well you can review and synthesize the literature, not how well you can lift citations from other sources. Second, if you cannot demonstrate that you actually read the source, it could be considered a form of plagiarism. Third, you don't know that the original author is citing that source correctly. Perhaps the secondary source found the exact opposite of what the person citing it claims—the only way you'll know for sure is to read it yourself.

If you can't track down the original source, either because it's in another language or is out of print, then you can cite it as a secondary source. Use this technique with caution; it's actually pretty rare to see secondary sources cited in academic essays in the social sciences.

> According to Watson (as cited in Peterson, Park, & Seligman, 2005), Aristuppus was one of the earliest philosophers to explore hedonism as the act of maximizing pleasure and minimizing pain.

Quotations

We discuss the use of quotations in Chapter 8, on writing a literature review, so you might want to use that chapter as a resource for deciding when to use quotations. If you decide you are going to quote the words of another source directly, the rules are pretty straightforward: always provide the source, including the page number. However, the format is different, depending on whether you are quoting less than 40 words or more than 40 words.

Quoting Fewer than 40 Words

When you are just quoting a short passage (i.e., less than 40 words), incorporate it into your paragraph.

> One problem with relying on popular media for information is that it "can inadvertently oversimplify, misrepresent, or overdramatize scientific results" (Lewandowsky, Ecker, Seifert, Schwarz, & Cook, 2012, p. 110).

You could also incorporate this quote with the authors mentioned in the sentence:

> According to Lewandowsky, Ecker, Seifert, Schwarz, and Cook (2012), one problem with relying on popular media for information is that it "can inadvertently oversimplify, misrepresent, or overdramatize scientific results" (p. 110).

The page number always immediately follows the quote. Use "p." before the number. If the quote falls on two pages, use "pp." before the number range.

(pp. 10–11)

If you've already mentioned the author(s) name and the year in the sentence, you don't need to restate it at the end of the quote.

Quoting 40 or More Words
If you are quoting a longer passage (which would be very unusual in a short paper), separate the quote from the rest of the paragraph by starting it on a new line and indenting the entire block of text by 0.5 inches (1.27 cm). Don't use quotation marks.

> There can be skepticism about the use of statistics in social science. If they are not presented with integrity, they can be pointless.

>> The secret language of statistics, so appealing in a fact-minded culture, is employed to sensationalize, inflate, confuse, and oversimplify. Statistical methods and statistical terms are necessary in reporting the mass data of social and economic trends, business conditions, "opinion" polls, the census. But without writers who use the words with honesty and understanding and readers who know what they mean, the result can only be semantic nonsense. (Huff, 1954, p. 8)

> There can be skepticism about the use of statistics in social science. As Huff (1954) states, if they are not presented with integrity, they can be pointless.

>> The secret language of statistics, so appealing in a fact-minded culture, is employed to sensationalize, inflate, confuse, and oversimplify. Statistical methods and statistical terms are necessary in reporting the mass data of social and economic trends, business conditions, "opinion" polls, the census. But without writers who use the words with honesty and understanding and readers who know what they mean, the result can only be semantic nonsense. (p. 8)

Notice the following from the two examples above:

- If you use the author's name and date in the sentence introducing the quote, you only need to include the page number at the end.
- There are no quotation marks around block quotes.
- The citation at the end of the block quote (either the author name, date, and page number or just the page number) comes after the period, and there is no period after it.
- If your paper is double-spaced, then double-space the block quote too.
- If the original material you are quoting includes citations, keep them in. You do not need to include them in your reference list unless you have cited them elsewhere in your paper.

FORMATTING THE REFERENCE LIST

The references section goes at the end of your paper, and it should include every source you cite in your paper. Essentially, the reference list provides enough information so that anyone who wants to look up one of your sources can do so.

General Format

The basic elements of a reference include the author name, the date of publication, the title of the work, and information about where it was published. Depending on the type of source you are using (e.g., a book, a journal article, an online source), the formatting of the reference will look a bit different, but all of these elements must be present. The format of the author and date is pretty consistent across different types of sources.

Author Name(s)

The author name is always in the format of last name first, with a comma, followed by the initial(s) of their first name(s) and middle name(s) (if provided). Notice that there is a period and a space after each initial.

Jane Smith → Smith, J.
Jane Denise Smith → Smith, J. D.
Jane D. A. Smith → Smith, J. D. A.

Date

With few exceptions (e.g., when you are citing a newspaper article), the date is just the year of publication. It appears in brackets, followed by a period.

> (2017).

Citing Journal Articles

The general style of a reference for a journal or other periodical is listed by APA (2010) as follows:

> Author, A. A., Author, B. B., & Author, C. C. (year).
> Title of article. *Title of Periodical, xx*, pp–pp. doi:xx.
> xxxxxxxxxxx

There are a few things to take note of, in addition to what we've already covered about the author name and date:

- The title of the article is in sentence case (i.e., all lower-case, except for the first word), followed by a period. If there is a colon in the title, the first word after the colon has an initial capital too, as do proper nouns.
- The name of the journal is in title case (i.e., all words are capitalized, except for articles, prepositions, and conjunctions that are three letters or less), followed by a comma. You can find more detailed information on the use of title case in APA style by searching "APA" and "title case."
- The volume number of the journal follows the title, and is also italicized. It is followed by a comma. See our discussion below of when to include the issue number as well.
- The page range is the range of pages in the journal that the article appears on. It is followed by a period.
- "doi" stands for digital object identifier; it is a unique alphanumeric code linked with the article. Older articles won't necessarily have one, but you should be able to find one for more recent articles. Notice that there is no space after the colon, and no period at the end of the doi.

Volume and Issue Numbers

Journals are periodicals, which means they are published regularly, like magazines. Most journals publish more than one issue per year: some as many as 12, and some as few as two. For this reason, they often are identified with an issue number. For example, for a journal that publishes monthly, it will probably have issue numbers ranging from 1 to 12; for a journal that publishes quarterly, it would have issue numbers ranging from 1 to 4. In addition to an issue number, a journal article will also include a volume number, which refers to the collection of issues for the particular time period, often (but not always) a year. For example, "Volume 35, Issue 4" might refer to the fourth issue published in the thirty-fifth year that the journal has been in existence.

It is necessary to include this information when citing a journal article. However, there is a catch: You only need to include the issue number if the journal begins at page 1 with each new issue. They don't all do this. Most journals in the social sciences start at page 1 for the first issue, and then the second issue begins with the number after the last page of the first issue. If each issue begins with page 1, then obviously the issue number is needed in order to indicate which issue the journal article appeared in. If the pagination is sequential for all issues within a given volume, then you don't need to cite the issue because you can tell which volume it's in by looking at the page number.

You would likely need to check the website of the journal to find out whether they start each issue with page 1 or not. For example, let's say you want to cite an article by Agocs, Langan, and Sanders, published in 2015 in the journal *Gender & Society*, called "Police mothers at home: Police work and protective parenting practices." If you go to the website for the journal (http://journals.sagepub.com/home/gas) and find the list of issues they have published, you'll notice that they list their journals by volume number, and under each volume is a list of issues contained in that volume. For the year 2015, there are six issues under "Volume 29." Most importantly, you'll notice that Issue 1 begins at page 5, and that each issue within that volume carries on the page numbering from the previous issue; Issue 2 begins on page 169. For this reason, when you cite the Agocs et al. article, you only need to include the volume number and not the issue number:

Agocs, T., Langan, D., & Sanders, C. B. (2015). Police mothers at home: Police work and protective parenting practices. *Gender & Society, 29,* 265–289.

Let's say you want to cite an article by McLaren, McGowan, Gerhardt, Diallo, and Saeed, published in 2013 in the *Journal of Leadership Education*, called "Business without the math: Competing discourses and the struggle to develop an undergraduate leadership program." If you go to the website for this journal (http://www.journalofleadershiped.org/index.php/issues) and find the issues published in 2013, with a bit of digging you will find that the first article of each issue begins on page 1. In other words, the pagination is by issue rather than by volume, so you would need to include the issue number:

> McLaren, P., McGowan, R. A., Gerhardt, K., Diallo, L., & Saeed, A. (2013). Business without the math: Competing discourses and the struggle to develop an undergraduate leadership program. *Journal of Leadership Education, 12*(2), 1–17.

As you can imagine, this rule can make things a bit confusing, and many people wish APA would change it and just make the issue number required all the time. However, for now this is the official policy of APA.

Finally, note that the volume number is italicized, but if you do include the issue number, it is not italicized.

Journal Article with One Author

> Welsh, A. (2010). On the perils of living dangerously in the slasher horror film: Gender differences in the association between sexual activity and survival. *Sex Roles, 62,* 762–773. doi:10.1007/s11199-010-9762-x

Journal Article with Two Authors

> Gunson, B. K. P., & Murphy, B. L. (2015). Measuring progress on climate change adaptation: Lessons from the community well-being analogue. *Journal of Integrated Disaster Risk Management, 5,* 115–134. doi:10.5595/idrim.2015.0110

Journal Article with Three to Seven Authors

> Law, D. M., Shapka, J. D., Domene, J. F., & Gagné,
> M. H. (2012). Are cyberbullies really bullies? An
> investigation of reactive and proactive online aggres-
> sion. *Computers in Human Behavior, 28*, 664–672.
> doi:10.1016/j.chb.2011.11.013

Journal Article with More than Seven Authors

> Flicker, S., Danforth, J., Konsmo, E., Wilson, C., Oliver,
> V., Jackson, R., ... Mitchell, C. (2013). "Because
> we are Natives and we stand strong to our pride":
> Decolonizing HIV prevention with Aboriginal
> youth in Canada using the arts. *Canadian Journal of
> Aboriginal Community-Based HIV/AIDS Research, 5*(1),
> 3–23.

Note that every once in a while you will come across a journal that does not assign doi numbers, like the journal above. If there isn't one, it's okay to not include one.

Citing Books

Books are normally pretty straightforward to cite. Use the same format for single and multiple authors as with journal articles. The general style of a reference for a book is listed by APA (2010) as follows:

> Author, A. A. (year). *Title of work*. Location: Publisher.

Here are a few things to note:

- The book title is in italics, but only the first word has an initial capital; everything else is lower case, excepting proper nouns. If there is a colon in the title, the first word after the colon has an initial capital too.
- There is a period after the title.

- The format of the publisher location varies a bit. If it's a Canadian or US publication, you tend to see the city, a comma, and an abbreviation of the province or state (e.g., Vancouver, BC; New York, NY). If it's not North American, you tend to see the city, a comma, and then the country written in full (e.g., Paris, France).
- The publisher location information is followed by a colon, and then the name of the publisher.

Book with No Edition Number

> Cairns, J. (2017). *The myth of the age of entitlement: Millennials, austerity, and hope.* Toronto, ON: University of Toronto Press.

Book with Edition Number

> Hughes, W., & Lavery, J. (2015). *Critical thinking: An introduction to the basic skills* (7th Canadian ed.). Peterborough, ON: Broadview Press.

Citing a Chapter in an Edited Book

Some books are a collection of articles or essays written by different people. In this case, it is considered an edited book, and the citation rules are a bit different. If you are using a particular chapter or article within the book, then you need to specify which chapter it is. You also need to differentiate between the editor(s) of the book and the authors of the individual chapters (also called the contributors). The editor gets their name on the front cover, while the contributors get their names on their individual chapters (and also probably on the contents page).

> Nicholson, S. (2015). A RECIPE for meaningful gamification. In L. Wood & T. Reiners (Eds.), *Gamification in education and business* (pp. 1–20). New York, NY: Springer.

A few things to note:

- The person who wrote the article/chapter is considered the author, so their name goes first.
- Don't italicize the chapter title or put it in quotations.
- Only the first letter of the chapter title is capitalized. However, in the example above, the word "RECIPE" is all caps in the title, so you would leave it that way.
- Notice that the editors' names are listed as initial(s), followed by a period, followed by the last name—they aren't reversed like they are for the author name. Also, there is no comma before the "&".
- Treat the title of the book like you would for a regular book: in italics, with only the first word having an initial capital.
- Include the page range that the chapter falls on. Note there's no period or comma before the parentheses containing the page range.

Citing Magazine and Newspaper Articles

You might find magazine and newspaper articles in print or online, and it's okay to use either form, as long as you cite it properly.

Magazine Article

> Gunson, B. (2015, February/March). Climate change SOS (save our syrup!). *Ontario Arborist*, 17.

Online Magazine Article

> Fridman, A. (2017, September 8). How positive psychology transforms people and organizations—the academic view. *Inc.* Retrieved from https://www.inc.com/adam-fridman/how-positive-psychology-transforms-people-and-orga.html

Newspaper Article

>Dagostino, S. (2014, April 17–30). All in the family: New
>anthology examines queer relationships. *Xtra!*, p. 16.

Note that in APA style, newspaper articles and book chapters are the only references for which you include a "p." (or "pp." if the article appears on multiple pages) before the page number. We don't know why.

Online Newspaper Article

>McLaughlin, J. (2016, September 27). Seasonal agricultural
>workers deserve right to call Canada home. *Huffington
>Post*. Retrieved from http://www.huffingtonpost.ca/
>janet-mclaughlin/seasonal-agricultural-workers_b_
>12159226.html

Citing Technical Reports

The general style of a technical report is listed by APA (2010) as follows:

>Author, A. A. (year). *Title of work* (Report No. xxx).
>Location: Publisher.

If you can't find a report number, just leave it out.

Technical Report

>McLaughlin, J. (2009). *Migration and health: Implications
>for development* (Policy Paper 2). Ottawa, ON: The
>Canadian Foundation for the Americas Labour
>Mobility and Development Project.

Technical Report Retrieved Online

>Hannem, S. (2016). *Let's talk about sex work: Report of the
>REAL working group for Branford, Brant, Haldimand, &*

Norfolk, assessing the needs of sex workers in our community. Brantford, ON: Resources, Education, Advocacy for Local Sex Work (REAL). Retrieved from http://www.sexworkisrealwork.com/about

Citing Doctoral Dissertations and Master's Theses

Long, J. (2011). *Shifting notions of citizenship in the Netherlands: Exploring cultural citizenship and the politics of belonging through neighbourhood spaces in Rotterdam* (Doctoral dissertation). Retrieved from http://ir.lib.uwo.ca/etd/341/

Citing Electronic Media

There are likely many other online sources you will run across that aren't listed here, such as blog posts, message boards, and comments sections. The general format is as follows:

Author, A. A. (year, month day). Title of post [Description of form]. Retrieved from http://www.xxxx

Blog Post

Hoplock, L. (2017, July 3). Infographic: Why do people swipe right (or left) on Tinder? [Web log post]. Retrieved from http://www.scienceofrelationships.com/home/2017/7/3/infographic-why-do-people-swipe-right-or-left-on-tinder.html

Video Blog Post

Potholer 54. (2017, August 27). The scientific method made easy [Video file]. Retrieved from https://www.youtube.com/watch?v=AIgy5JS-QhQ

Message Posted to an Online Forum

> Anvilized. (2017, November 19). Re: My oddly shaped
>   cheese fits my oddly shaped bread [Online forum
>   comment]. Retrieved from https://www.reddit.
>   com/r/mildlyinteresting/comments/7dy5bb/
>   my_oddly_shaped_cheese_fits_on_my_oddly_shaped/

Citing Lecture Notes or Slides

Lecture

If you are citing something your instructor said in class, and there is no written documentation (other than your lecture notes), then cite it as "personal communication" in the body of your paper. You do not need to include it in your reference section.

> Geographers and psychologists may differ in many ways, but they do agree on their passion for social science (D. Morris, personal communication, September 25, 2017).

PowerPoint Slides

In the body of your paper, you would cite the last name of your instructor and the date.

> Some geographers would be considered social scientists, whereas others might not (Morris, 2017).

In your reference section you would cite it like this. If your instructor posts lecture slides on your learning management system, such as Desire2Learn or BlackBoard, then include that in your reference. If you are citing posted lecture notes rather than slides, substitute [Lecture notes] for [PowerPoint slides] in the example below.

> Morris, D. (2017). *What is social science?* [PowerPoint
>   presentation]. Retrieved from MyLearningSpace.

A QUICK COMPARISON OF APA AND ASA STYLE

As we mentioned earlier, APA is not the only style used in the social sciences. Many sociologists use ASA style, which is the official style of the American Sociological Association. The good news is that many of the conventions of citing sources are similar, so once you learn one referencing system, you will pick up the others pretty easily. For example, let's say you were citing a publication by Rashad, which was published in 2009. In APA style it would be cited as "(Rashad, 2009)." In ASA style it would be cited as "(Rashad 2009)." The only difference is the use of a comma in APA style. If you were quoting something by Rashad, and therefore needed to cite a page number too, in APA style it would look like this: (Rashad, 2009, p. 28), whereas in ASA style it would look like this: (Rashad 2009:28). The way they list sources in their references sections is different too. Here's what the source would look like in APA style:

> Rashad, I. (2009). Associations of cycling with urban sprawl and the gasoline price. *American Journal of Health Promotion, 24,* 27–36. doi:10.4278/ ajhp.071121124

And here's what it would look like in ASA style:

> Rashad, Inas. 2009. "Associations of Cycling with Urban Sprawl and the Gasoline Price." *American Journal of Health Promotion* 24:27–36. doi:10.4278/ ajhp.071121124

See if you can spot all the differences between them. As you have probably noticed, they are pretty similar but there are subtle differences, such as the use of commas, the author's first name, and the use of quotation marks. Being detail-oriented is an asset when it comes to proper citation, but don't worry—even if that isn't your strong suit, it does get easier the more you do it.

APA Style Checklist

OVERALL FORMATTING
- Double spaced
- 1-inch (2.54 cm) margins
- 12-point font
- Header should include a shortened version of the title on the left, and the page number on the right

TITLE PAGE
- Include "Running head," and the short title of your paper in all caps
- Include the title of your paper, your name, and your school
- Check with your instructor to see if any other information is required

IN-TEXT CITATIONS
- If there are more than two authors, only list all authors the first time you cite the source
- Use "and" in list of authors outside parentheses, and "&" in list of authors inside parentheses

REFERENCES
- Include all sources cited in your paper
- Don't include any sources not cited in your paper
- List alphabetically, by first author's last name
- Use a hanging indent for each separate entry

REVIEW IT

1. The *Publication Manual of the American Psychological Association* provides standards for citing references. What other style guidelines does it provide?

2. Why don't all of the social sciences use the same referencing style?
3. What size margins are standard in APA style?
4. When providing an in-text citation at the end of a sentence, where should you place the final punctuation?
5. You are referencing a journal article. When should you include the issue number?
6. Which sources do you include in your references section?

APPLY IT

Put the following sources into APA style.

Article title: Prioritizing global conservation efforts
Authors: Kerrie A. Wilson, Marissa F. McBride, Michael Bode, Hugh P. Possingham
Date: 2006
Journal: Nature
Volume number: 440
Pages: 337 to 340

Book title: Beyond Revenge: The Evolution of the Forgiveness Instinct
Author: Michael E. McCullough
Date: 2008
Publisher: Jossey-Bass
Location: San Francisco, California

McCullough, M. E. (2008). *Beyond revenge: The evolution of the forgiveness instinct.* San Francisco, CA: Jossey-Bass.

Wilson, K. A., McBride, M. F., Bode, M., & Possingham, H. P. (2006). Prioritizing global conservation efforts. *Nature, 440,* 337–340.

Answers:

5 Critical Assessment: Evaluating Social Science Research

So you've found some sources that you like the look of. You searched in all the right databases, figured out what was scholarly and what wasn't, and you even know how to cite them using APA style. The next step is to figure out if these sources are as good as you hope they are. Although you'll find a lot of really great social science research out there, you'll also find some not-so-great stuff, and it's not always obvious which is which. In this chapter, we'll show you how to identify the good, the bad, and the ugly when it comes to social science research. We also know that you won't always be relying solely on journal articles and books in your research, so we've got some tips on how to evaluate websites too.

LEARNING OBJECTIVES

1. Learn how to critically assess and evaluate social science research
2. Understand how to evaluate non-academic sources

THINKING CRITICALLY ABOUT SOCIAL SCIENCE RESEARCH

Once you have developed your initial research question and begun looking for appropriate academic references, you will have to begin evaluating these references to see if they address your specific research question. This may seem straightforward. You might assume that if it is a book found in a university or college library, it is a good reference. This can be a perilous assumption: Remember that your school library has more than just academic books! You might also assume that if an article is published in a scholarly journal, then it is a good reference. As we will see, this is not always the case. Furthermore, even if you are confident that a reference is a good one, it may not be the best one for the arguments you are trying to support. Evaluating sources can be time consuming, but if you do it before you start writing your paper, it could actually save you time. By spending the time upfront to ensure that your sources are solid, you can save yourself frustrating rewrites when you realize halfway through that the source isn't as good as you thought. Not only can carefully evaluating your sources save you time, but it can also get you a better grade on your paper.

Evaluating your sources means to think critically about them. You've probably heard a lot about the value and importance of **critical thinking**. William Graham Sumner (1940) defined it as "the examination and test of propositions of any kind which are offered for acceptance, in order to find out whether they correspond to reality or not" (p. 632). In other words, thinking critically means to not accept at face value everything you hear, read, or see. This doesn't mean you should go into your research assuming that all the research you read will be terrible and that your sole job is to uncover the flaws. Critical thinking does not mean being critical; it means you have assessed the merits of the arguments and conclusions that the research is making to determine whether it is appropriate for your purposes.

EVALUATING SOCIAL SCIENCE RESEARCH ARTICLES

In Chapter 2 we covered the basics of social science research methods, so you already have a good sense of how social scientists conduct research. You also know that good research is usually tied to theory in some way, and that research findings do not mean very much until they have some context. The good news is that really poorly done research tends not to get published, so it is unlikely you will come across a study with no theory, no context, or no redeemable features. That being said, there is no such thing as a perfect research study, so any research you find will be flawed in some way. The challenge for you, as a potential consumer of this research, is to think critically about whether those flaws are fatal or not. This involves not only identifying the flaws, but also determining whether those flaws make a difference to the conclusions that are being drawn from the research.

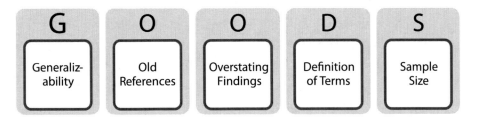

Figure 5.1: The GOODS Test for Evaluating Research Articles

The GOODS Test

In an effort to give you an easy way to remember these potential issues in social science research, we've given them a catchy acronym: GOODS. It's not as good as the acronym used for evaluating websites (you'll have to keep reading if you want to find out what it is), but it may help to think about whether a research article has got the GOODS to be a good source for your paper.

Generalizability

Generalizability refers to the extent to which the findings are applicable to the larger group under study. In other words, how appropriate is the sample? Do the people chosen for the study represent the people to whom the researchers wish to generalize their findings? There are two related issues here: *who* is in the sample, and *how* they are selected for the study.

1. Who Is in the Sample
    Take a look at who the researchers selected as participants in their study. For example, in some fields, a lot of the research is done on university students. This is fine if the research involves an issue specifically related to young adults or if the phenomenon under study is universal, but it would be inappropriate if the study is on, for example, successful aging. In the same way, using senior citizens for a study on adjustment to university would be ridiculous. This may seem obvious, but it's not always easy to find participants for a research study, so it's not uncommon for researchers to use samples that are "good enough" rather than perfect.

2. How the Sample Was Selected
    Also look at how the researchers got their sample. Could it be biased? For example, imagine if a researcher wanted to better understand attitudes toward technology, but decided to collect data using an online survey.

Believe it or not, some people are either afraid of, or have very negative feelings about, technology. Would they be likely to fill out an online survey? Probably not. Therefore, an online survey of attitudes toward technology would be limited, because it would be missing this potentially very interesting group of individuals. The sample would be biased toward people who already have positive attitudes about technology.

Interestingly, the polls for the 2016 US presidential election may have been the victim of bias introduced by the methods used to collect data. Many pollsters predicted that Hillary Clinton would win over Donald Trump and were surprised when this turned out to be inaccurate. A poll conducted by the *Los Angeles Times* was one of the few that accurately predicted that Trump would win; other polls suggested a small positive margin for Clinton (Lauter, 2016). One difference between this poll and many others was that it was conducted online rather than by phone. The *LA Times* did something really interesting: They asked voters whether they were comfortable talking about their vote. This was a contentious election, and the two candidates were very different. As it turned out, people who supported Trump, especially women, reported being less comfortable sharing their voting intentions by phone than those who supported Clinton. This might be one reason why the phone polls underestimated Trump support: Some people didn't want to admit that they were voting for him so they either lied or refused to answer. Because of that, the sample of voters contacted by phone was not representative of the population—it excluded people who intended to vote for Trump but felt uncomfortable sharing that with someone on the phone. Trump supporters reported feeling more comfortable sharing their voting intentions in an online poll, so the *LA Times'* online poll had a better, more representative sample of voters.

Biased samples aren't only found in election polls or in online surveys. Look for possible reasons why a certain group of people might be more likely than others to participate in the study: Maybe the subject matter is overly personal, or maybe the compensation (or lack thereof) for participating in the study is more likely to attract some people. If "four out of five dentists recommend" a particular brand of toothpaste, did that poll happen to be conducted on the five dentists who were just given a free sample?

Old References

Science is an unending journey toward a goal we can never truly reach. Our knowledge is always changing as new theories supplement or supplant older ones. This can be frustrating for social science students and researchers who are attempting to decide if a reference is too old to be either relevant or useful. Because science is an ongoing process in which even mistakes are seen as valuable and informative, few studies can be said to be completely irrelevant. This adds little clarity for the social science student who has limited time and resources; it would often be impractical, if not impossible, to cite every study about a topic. A decision must be made about which studies are too old to use as supporting references in a social science paper.

The general assumption about the acceptable age for references is that more recent references are more desirable than older references. This assumption comes with many qualifications, though. For example, what is "recent" can vary with the topic or phenomenon being investigated. Some topics or phenomena have long histories of investigation. In the studies of these topics, progress may be slow and new insights may be relatively infrequent. Thus, when examining the study of these topics, a 20-year-old reference may be considered "recent." Conversely, when studying a relatively recent phenomenon, such as online social media, a five-year-old study might be considered out of date. Thus, in deciding which references are "too old" to use as sources, a broad understanding of the evolution of knowledge about the topic is needed. It would be very difficult to discern if a study is too old simply by reading the article about that study. An appreciation of the context of the study is needed.

There are important exceptions to the "more recent is better" assumption about the best ages of references. As knowledge about a topic grows, there are sometimes key studies or articles that reflect critical steps in our changing understanding about the topic. As you research your topic, you will often be able to identify these key studies because many articles about the topic will make reference to them. It is recognized that these key, foundational studies provide critical context for understanding the later studies. Thus, if you are planning to discuss this topic, it will likely be important to provide similar context by also citing them.

Overstating the Findings

Researchers get very excited about their research, and sometimes they go a bit overboard on how important their findings are. Remember that science is cumulative, and no single study will tell us everything about a topic, so it would be highly unlikely that any study you read will "prove" the existence of some phenomenon. Be cautiously skeptical when researchers claim that their study "proves" anything.

One way that research findings can be overstated is to exaggerate small, non-significant differences. It's natural to look at the means of two groups and assume that because one mean is higher than the other, the groups must be different. When researchers or media reports speak of differences, look for this magical term: "statistically significant." If it's not statistically significant, it's not meaningful, and you should not put much stock in their claims.

Another way that findings can be overstated is to place too much emphasis on one aspect of the study results. For example, imagine that a researcher interviews ten people about their experiences with the public school system. Let's say that, out of those ten interviewees, nine say they felt they got a pretty good education, and one says they hated it and wished they had gone to a private school. If the researcher chooses to focus on this one person's opinion because it is more interesting or because it confirms popular beliefs about differences between public and private schools, then they are not accurately presenting their findings. It can be tempting for a researcher to want to present the most counterintuitive or unexpected finding, and it's perfectly acceptable to do this, but if the researcher focuses only on this one person's experience without placing it in context (in other words, without mentioning that most people were happy with their school experiences), then they are overstating their findings.

Definition of Terms

It may seem obvious, but if you find that the results of two studies seem to contradict each other, take a look at how they define the concept they are studying. In science there is often only one definition of a concept—for example, scientists all agree on what "gravity" is—but in the social sciences, where the concepts can be a bit fuzzier, there can sometimes be different definitions. Think about the concept of "forgiveness." What does it mean to you? Some people think that to forgive is to forget, so if you haven't forgotten a hurtful thing someone did to you, you haven't forgiven them for it. Others, however, believe that forgiveness is not about forgetting. In fact, they believe that forgiveness is about letting go of hurt and anger despite being very aware that the transgression happened (in other words, not forgetting it). If you have two research studies on forgiveness and one of them concludes that people generally do not forgive and the other one concludes that people are generally very forgiving, it may be because they are using very different definitions of forgiveness. Keep this in mind as you are critically assessing the literature. Two studies may have wildly different results simply because they are measuring different things.

Sample Size

It's a little-known fact that 50 percent of social scientists are geographers. Actually, it's a little-known fact because it's not true. But if your sample included only the two social scientists who have written this book, you would find that, indeed, half of them actually are geographers and half are psychologists. With a sample size of two, it's very easy to misrepresent reality. Although the scientific method gives us the tools to conduct research on smaller samples and then generalize those findings to the larger population, as a general rule, larger samples are better than smaller ones.

Research studies differ a lot in terms of how many participants they use in their studies. Some types of studies do not need many participants. For example, qualitative studies using interviews tend not to have a high number of participants, because they are more interested in better understanding the experience of a few people than in generalizing their findings to the entire population. A case study, which is an in-depth qualitative exploration of the experience of just one person or event, can further our understanding of a particular social science phenomenon with a sample size of one. Quantitative studies tend to require more participants, but even they vary in terms of how many. For example, experiments, where one or more groups of participants are compared to other groups, require only 15 to 20 participants in each group. In a simple study comparing two groups, a sample size of 30 to 40 would be fine (but any less than this would be suspect). In a regression study, where researchers are looking at the extent to which a set of variables predicts a given outcome, a sample of less than 100 participants would be considered small.

As a general rule, large samples are usually better than small samples, but they can also be expensive and time consuming to study. Imagine how long it would take to interview 1,000 people about their health behaviours, or to have 500 people in an experimental group that receives a specific type of treatment for depression and another 500 people in a control group. Large samples are simply unrealistic for often underfunded social science research, so don't be too critical of smaller samples.

A Final Word on the GOODS

Above we outlined some, but by no means all, of the things you should keep in mind when assessing research studies as sources for your paper. We want to stress, however, that if you do find any of these flaws in a research article, it does not mean the article does not have merits. Rather than throwing it out as a source, identifying these kinds of issues can help explain why the findings of one research study are not consistent with another, even though they are studying the same thing. If you notice and assess these issues in your paper, you will demonstrate that you can think critically about research, and that usually will get you a better grade.

EVALUATING WEBSITES

For most of your social science papers, you will want to limit your references to academic books and scholarly journal articles. However, there are many other tempting sources of information that are not only easier to find but may also be easier to read and understand. We're going to talk about the easiest, but also one of the most contentious, sources: websites. We completely understand the appeal of websites, and in some cases they can be incredibly valuable sources of information. The key is to know whether they are appropriate for your research or not. Your instructor may solve the problem of determining the appropriateness of Internet sources by simply not allowing you to use them in your paper. However, if you are allowed to use websites as resources in your paper, make sure you know that the information is accurate.

To Use Websites or Not to Use Websites in Your Research?

There are a number of convincing reasons to be cautious about using websites as references in a scholarly paper. First, you often do not know the qualifications of the authors of these websites. Although this may also be true, to some extent, of the authors of scholarly journal articles and books, at least with those sources you have some assurance that the peer-review and editorial processes will catch authors that lack expertise on the topic about which they are writing. With websites, you have no such assurance. Second, websites also often fail to support their claims with citations and reference lists. This can be problematic because, if the websites plagiarize their claims and you use these claims, you can be accused of committing plagiarism (Loui, 2002). Third, the information you find on websites can be just plain wrong. Therefore, as you can see, it can be rather risky to use websites as academic references.

Despite these reasons to be cautious about using websites for your research, there are times when they can be pretty useful. We mentioned in Chapter 3 that websites can be helpful when you are trying to narrow down your research question because they can provide background on the topic. Even looking at the menu of a website can give you an idea of some of the subtopics within the main topic. Websites can also give you a sense of public opinion on a topic, which is something that scholarly articles are less likely to do. Also, reputable websites often list (and sometimes even link to) related resources on the topic, some of which are scholarly articles. Finally, in cases where there is little scholarship about the topic you are researching, websites may be the only option for providing background information.

The CRAAP Test for Evaluating Websites

Our general advice about using websites for your research is to proceed with caution. What does that mean? It means if you are going to use them, make sure they are reliable, and if they look sketchy, don't use them. Fortunately, there is a way to separate good websites from not-so-good ones. And even more fortunately, it has an awesomely appropriate acronym. The CRAAP test, developed by Blakeslee (2004), uses six evaluation criteria to help you determine if a website should be trusted or not: currency, relevance, authority, accuracy, and purpose.

Currency

How old is the webpage? The age of the information it provides is an important consideration in evaluating its usefulness. Most trustworthy websites will provide dates when the webpage was created and/or last updated. If these dates are not posted, it may be difficult to evaluate the currency of the information. You

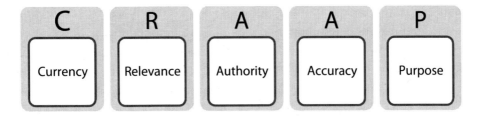

Figure 5.2: The CRAAP Test for Evaluating Websites

may be able to test the currency of the webpage by trying some of the links on the page, if there are any. A page that has many broken links may not have been updated in quite some time. Keep in mind that currency is more important to some topics than to others. For example, social science research can barely keep up with the rapid development (and subsequent decline) of various social media tools. If you come across a website on research about social media that hasn't been updated in a couple of years, you should consider it to be hopelessly out of date. However, if you are studying a topic like the history of psychoanalysis, a method of therapy developed by Sigmund Freud in the early 1890s, then you probably aren't missing too much current research if the website hasn't been updated in a while.

Relevance

Is the information on this website relevant to both your research question and the intended audience of the paper you are using it for? As we have already discussed, the use of a website as a reference should be an extraordinary occurrence. Therefore, using a webpage whose information does not add something relevant and substantial to your discussion is not a good idea. If you can't find the same information elsewhere and you decide to use information from a website, be sure the information is suitable for a university-level audience. If you think you might be embarrassed if your instructor notices you are using this website as a reference, perhaps you should not use it in the first place. You should always assume that your instructor will check out any websites you cite when they are marking your paper.

Authority

Who is the author of the webpage? The Internet can provide a global voice for almost anyone with access to a computer and an Internet connection. This is one of the great strengths of the Internet. It is also one of its great challenges, at least for someone who is looking for trustworthy information. On the Internet, spurious information and untested theories often compete on an equal footing with careful studies and supported claims. Indeed, pseudoscientific information may even seem more plausible than rigorous research if it is presented on a skillfully constructed website. Therefore, it is useful to try to determine a little bit about the author or the sponsoring organization of the webpage. What are the credentials of the author? A trustworthy webpage does not necessarily have to be written by somebody with a PhD. Perhaps you can even think of one or two celebrities with PhDs who have their own websites but whose opinions you may not entirely trust. However, demonstrated expertise in the topic being discussed on the websites can be a useful factor in determining the trustworthiness of the site. Sometimes, it is not easy to identify the name of the author of the website. In these instances, find out a little bit about the sponsoring organization of the website. Have you ever heard of them before? Can you find a little about the organization elsewhere on the Internet? If the identity or reputation of the sponsoring organization is indiscernible, you may want to look for a different reference.

Accuracy

Many websites are created by their authors to share their opinions. Opinions are not necessarily undesirable in social science research; however, they should be supported by evidence. Ideally, this evidence should come in the form of peer-reviewed scientific studies. Without these supporting studies, opinions will likely be of little value to your research. The accuracy of a website can also be reflected in its attention to detail. Is the webpage well-written? Is the grammar correct? Are there any typos? Is there any evidence that the information on the website has been reviewed by someone other than the author? If there are problems in the details, there may be more substantial problems with the content of the page.

Purpose

Why was the website created and maintained? Was it created to persuade its readers of something or to simply inform? Is it a commercial site or a site seeking donations? Are advertisements visible on the page and, if so, how many? None of these considerations would, in themselves, necessarily suggest that a website is untrustworthy. However, depending on the answer to these questions, you may want to investigate the website further or continue searching for other references. For instance, a website that claims smoking does not cause cancer is less convincing if it is full of advertisements for cigarettes. You can assume a website full of advertisements is making money, and although for-profit sites are not necessarily less reliable than non-profit sites, it should raise a flag for you to dig a little deeper into their motives.

A Final Word on CRAAP

The CRAAP test will not guarantee that the information you find will be 100 percent reliable, but it will help you evaluate it more critically. The social sciences are changing, as are the ways we share and search for information.

While the Internet will undoubtedly become an evermore important source of information for social science researchers, care must still be taken to ensure that the information is trustworthy and academically appropriate.

A Checklist for Evaluating Your Sources

RESEARCH STUDIES

- Did they define their terms?
- How many participants are there? Is the number appropriate for the type of study?
- How were participants selected? Do they represent the population under study?
- How old is this study?
- Are the findings meaningful?

WEBSITES

- How old is the website?
- Does this source provide information that is not available any-where else?
- Does the author of the website have the authority to speak on this topic?
- Does it have errors?
- Does it have a hidden (or not so hidden) motive that might suggest the content is biased?

REVIEW IT

1. Are all scholarly sources good sources? Why or why not?
2. What is the difference between critical thinking and being critical when it comes to evaluating sources?
3. Describe the different components of the GOODS test.
4. In general, recent references are preferable to older references. When might it be important to include an older reference?

5. How can websites help you in your research? When should you not use them?
6. Describe the different components of the CRAAP test.

APPLY IT

Evaluate the Wikipedia entry for "social science" according to the CRAAP test. Does it pass?

Now do a Web search for "bias in Wikipedia." Does this change your evaluation of the website? Why or why not?

6 Doing the Right Thing: Ethics and Integrity in the Social Sciences

You might be wondering why we've included a chapter on ethics in this book. What does this have to do with you, you might ask, especially if you have no intention of ever conducting your own social science research? The first goal of this chapter is to help you understand and appreciate the rights of the people who give their time, their energy, and sometimes even their lives for scientific research. All of the research findings we benefit from, such as medical treatments and cures, effective therapies for mental illness, and even many of the policies that protect us from harm, have been the result of research carried out on humans. In this chapter we'll talk about what happens when those participants aren't treated with respect, and how social science has evolved to make sure that researchers conduct their research in an ethical and responsible way.

The second goal of this chapter is to help you conduct your academic work with ethics and integrity. You may not be dealing with human participants, but you will be faced with choices. Just as researchers have ethical guidelines to help them make good choices, as a student, you do too. And just as entire communities can be affected when social scientists make poor choices, your choices in your academic work can affect not only you but also your fellow students, your instructors, and your school.

Most of us don't think about our values and moral codes on a daily basis. As you are reading this chapter, think about your own ethical principles. Do you always act according to your principles? Is there a line you wouldn't cross? In other words, what are your limits? What would it take for you to step over that line? Our hope is that by getting you to think about ethics and integrity in the social sciences, it will also get you to think about it in your own life.

RESEARCH INTEGRITY

The Reason for Research Ethics

Imagine you have been asked to be in a research study for a psychologist. When you arrive at the lab, the researcher explains that it is a study on the use of punishment on memory, and you will be training another participant, the "learner," to remember lists of words. You meet the learner, and see that he is hooked up to a machine. The researcher explains that you will be administering electric shocks to this person whenever they do not remember a list of words properly. The learner looks a bit nervous, and explains that he has a heart condition. The researcher says not to worry about it, and takes you to another room where you can hear, but not see, the learner.

Your task is simple: Read lists of words to the learner and have him recite them back to you. If the learner gets a word wrong, you are to flip a switch on a machine in front of you that will administer a small electric shock to the learner. Each time he gets a word wrong, you are to administer progressively stronger shocks. After a few correct passes, the learner gets a word wrong. You reluctantly flip the switch, and hear him say "Ouch!" You pause, but the researcher asks you to carry on with the experiment. After a few more passes, the learner gets another word wrong. You flip the next switch, and he yells a bit louder. As he makes more mistakes and your electric shocks get stronger, the learner sounds more distressed. He starts yelling louder and begging for the study to stop. The researcher insists that you keep going. Eventually, the learner stops responding at all. You keep reading the list of words and increasing the shocks when he doesn't answer, until you get all the way to the highest level of shock (labeled "extreme").

After a while, the researcher tells you to stop and takes you next door to the learner's room. To your great relief, the learner is just fine. The researcher explains that he is an actor pretending to be in distress, and the shocks you thought you were giving him were fake. You learn that it wasn't a study of memory after all. It was really an experiment to see how far you would go when a person in authority tells you to harm another human being. Phew, you didn't hurt him after all! But wait, you just spent the last 30 minutes or so being incredibly stressed about the situation in which you found yourself. You have been sweating, shaking, and stuttering, in a state of heightened anxiety because of the choices you were making even though you felt you had no choice. In addition, you just demonstrated that you would, if instructed to by someone in a lab coat, shock another human until you believed they were unconscious. In all likelihood, that's not something you wanted to know about yourself, was it?

This experiment actually took place, in a lab at Harvard University in the 1960s. The researcher was Stanley Milgram, and his research, which he described in an article called "Behavioral Study of Obedience" in 1963 and later in a book called *Obedience to Authority: An Experimental View* (1974), demonstrated that approximately two-thirds of us would obey a person in authority if they told us to administer the maximum amount of electric shocks to another person. His research has also become the poster child for unethical research. It's impossible to talk about the evolution of research ethics in social science without talking about this study. Milgram wasn't the first researcher to treat his participants unethically—during the Second World War, the Nazis conducted inhumane experiments on prisoners, many of which resulted in death—but this study was one of the first to get social scientists thinking about ethics.

It's important to keep in mind that Stanley Milgram wasn't a terrible person. He believed that since he explained the real purpose of the research to his participants afterwards, deceiving them at the beginning of the study was okay. Plus, in his defense, the results of his research helped us better understand how good people can be led to do terrible things. He said his goal in conducting the research was to examine how people in Nazi Germany, especially those working in the concentration camps, could have done such cruel and merciless things to other humans. The story of Milgram's studies on obedience demonstrate that ethics are important, but they can also be complicated.

Ethics and Research Participants

Because social science research focuses heavily on humans and how they think, behave, and interact with each other, it follows that much social science research uses humans as participants or research subjects. Unfortunately, history has shown us that, if left to their own devices, some scientists will mistreat, abuse, and/or ignore the basic human rights of research participants. Therefore, universal ethical guidelines for how to treat research participants seem like a really good idea, right? Surprisingly, it took a long time for these guidelines to be developed.

It wasn't until 1948, after criminal proceedings found a number of German physicians guilty of crimes against humanity for conducting painful and often fatal experiments on concentration camp prisoners, that the Nuremberg Code was established. The Nuremberg Code didn't really focus on what you could or couldn't do to research participants; it only required that their participation be voluntary, and that they provide informed consent. It took another 18 years for more prescriptive recommendations to be put in place. The Declaration of Helsinki was established by the World Medical Association in 1964, and it was intended to guide medical research on humans. Not only did it specify that participants must give their consent, it also covered things like minimizing risk, making sure the research is conducted by qualified individuals, and having the research protocol reviewed by an independent committee.

Unfortunately, the Nuremberg Code and the Declaration of Helsinki weren't enough to stop unethical studies from happening. In the end, it took public outcry against a particularly egregious study, known as the "Tuskegee Study of Untreated Syphilis in the Negro Male," to force policy-makers to actually set some rules for research. In this study, researchers wanted to follow the natural progression of syphilis, so they collected a sample of Black men, tested them for the disease, and then observed them to see how the disease runs its course if left untreated. There are many ethical concerns with this study, but the most pressing issues are that the researchers didn't inform the men that they had syphilis, and they didn't offer them treatment for it. When left untreated, syphilis can cause blindness, dementia, damage to the internal organs, and eventually death, so not giving them appropriate treatment was a major violation of their human rights. When the general public found out about the Tuskegee study, a commission was formed to recommend guidelines for the ethical treatment of humans in both biomedical and behavioural research. The resulting document, the Belmont Report, was published in 1979 and became the foundation of all subsequent policies on how to treat human research participants.

Three Basic Ethical Principles

The recommendations set out in the Belmont Report (Department of Health, Education, and Welfare, 1979) come from three basic ethical principles:

Continued

1. **Respect for persons**—This covers two important considerations. First, it should be recognized that people are autonomous agents and can make their own decisions. This is related to informed consent, in that you have to give people enough information to make their own decisions about whether to participate in the research. Second, it should also be recognized that some people are less capable of making their own decisions. People with diminished autonomy should be protected, and special consideration should be given to whether they can give truly informed consent.

2. **Beneficence**—This principle is concerned with both protecting people from harm and ensuring their well-being. Researchers must first ensure that participants are not harmed, emotionally, socially, or physically, in the course of the research. However, research may come with risks, and it is the role of the researcher to consider whether the risks are justifiable or not, given the potential benefits of the research. The consideration of well-being may come with exposing some research participants to minimal risk in order to maximize the long-term benefits of the research.

3. **Justice**—This principle requires that the risks and benefits of research should be distributed equally. In other words, the burden of being a research participant should not fall disproportionally on one group while another group benefits from the research, especially when it comes to research that has some risks associated with it. Historically, many unethical research studies have been guilty of violating this principle by using poor, sick, or cognitively impaired research participants who would never be able to benefit from the findings of the study.

Nowadays, there are a number of ethics policies in place. Many disciplines within the social sciences have their own policies. For example, the American Psychological Association and the Canadian Psychological Association both have their own Code of Ethics, as do the American and Canadian sociology associations. However, these codes are all pretty much based on the guiding principles set out in the Belmont Report.

Canada's Tri-Council Policy Statement

In Canada, the federal government provides very clear rules on research with humans. All researchers conducting research with humans must follow the guidelines set out in the *Tri-Council Policy Statement: Ethical Conduct for Research Involving Humans*, also known as the TCPS 2 (Canadian Institutes of Health

Research, Natural Sciences and Engineering Research Council of Canada, & Social Sciences and Humanities Research Council of Canada, 2014). It's called the "Tri-Council" policy because it is a joint partnership with the three major funding agencies in Canada: the Social Sciences and Humanities Research Council (SSHRC), the Natural Sciences and Engineering Research Council (NSERC), and the Canadian Institute for Health Research (CIHR). These agencies fund much of the research conducted in Canadian universities, using money from the federal government (in other words, Canadian tax dollars). Because the researchers are using public funds, the government has a vested interest in making sure that their research is conducted ethically. Any researcher in Canada who conducts research on humans must follow the policy, and if they don't, their funding will be pulled. So, it's serious business.

The TCPS 2 contains the same three core principles as the Belmont Report, although instead of beneficence, the TCPS outlines "concern for welfare." What this means is that whether you are conducting or participating in research in Canada or the United States, and mostly likely many other countries, your experience will be similar.

Basic Rights of Research Participants

Because this book is not intended to be a comprehensive review of the research process, we're not going to cover all the intricacies of the ethics of research involving human participants. However, since you are a human, and most likely you will be invited to be a research participant at some point in your life, we're going to briefly talk about what you should expect.

1. **Voluntary participation**. First and foremost, you cannot be forced to participate in a research study. This may sound like an easy requirement—if you don't want to do the study, just say no, right? Well, it's not always that easy. Imagine that you are in a class where the instructor asks for volunteers to participate in a research study. She assures you that declining to participate will have no effect on your grade. But, it's a small class, and it will be obvious if you don't participate. You are worried that, even if she promises that lack of participation won't affect your grade, the instructor may remember that you didn't participate and be a bit less generous in her grading of your final essay. How comfortable do you feel saying no? Is your participation truly voluntary? If the instructor really wants students to feel free to not participate, she could leave the room and have someone unconnected to the course do the data collection and hold onto the data until all the essays are graded and the final marks submitted. This would help make participation truly voluntary.

Sometimes researchers offer compensation for participating in research studies, and this too can affect whether participation is voluntary. Especially with biomedical research studies (often testing new drugs), the higher the risk of the study, the higher the compensation. Researchers know that if you are asking someone to risk unknown side effects, you need to pay them for it. But who might be more willing to take on this risk? If you have a job, a place to live, and food in your fridge, you might be more likely than someone who really needs the money to take a pass on a high-risk study that could cause strange, unpleasant things to happen to you. If you are in a dire financial situation and have limited options, could you really turn down the chance to make some money, even if it meant potentially severe side effects? So is participation really voluntary?

2. **Informed consent**. After you agree to participate in a study, the researcher must clearly outline what will be expected of you. "Informed" means you know what you are getting into before you agree to anything. Often this information comes in the form of a letter or information sheet that you are given right before the study. The researcher will give you the form to read, answer any questions you might have, and then ask you to sign it. It's often referred to as an informed consent form, and while these consent forms will look different depending on who is conducting the research, there are some common elements to look for.

Elements of the Informed Consent Form

Information about the study—This will be a brief description of the purpose of the study and what participants will be expected to do.

Risks—This section will explain any risks or harms you might experience as a result of participating in the study. Potential risks may be physical, but in social science research they are more likely to be psychological or emotional (e.g., if the study raises issues that you find upsetting, or if you disclose information that you later regret revealing) or social (e.g., if your privacy or status is threatened because of your involvement in the study). If there are any risks, this section should also provide a list of resources to help you with any adverse effects of participating in the study, such as a counsellor or hotline.

Benefits—This section will explain if there are any benefits to participating in the study. Normally the benefits are to society in the form of advancing scientific knowledge rather than to you as an individual.

Confidentiality—This section will specify that all information you provide will be kept anonymous and confidential. It should also explain how anonymity and confidentiality will be ensured by the researcher. Often this is done by not storing your name with your data, limiting who has access to the data, storing the data in a secure facility, and destroying the data after a specified amount of time.

Compensation—This section will explain whether, and how much, you will be compensated for participating in the study. If you're doing the study as part of a course requirement, it should also state how much course credit you will receive, and if there are alternate ways to earn this course credit. If there's no compensation section on the informed consent form, it probably means you are doing the study for free.

Voluntary participation—This section should reassure you that your participation is voluntary. It should also state that there will be no penalty if you choose not to participate. In addition, if you begin a study and decide partway through that you'd rather not participate, you have the right to withdraw without losing your compensation.

Feedback and publication—You have a right to know what the researchers are going to do with the study results. They may not know exactly where they will present or publish their findings, but they should specify whether it will be at academic conferences, in scholarly publications, in government reports, and so on. They should also tell you how you can get access to the findings once the study is over.

Contact information—In addition to providing contact information for the researcher, this section should also include contact information for the ethics board who approved the research.

3. **Confidentiality and anonymity.** Social science research is based on trust between the researcher and the research participant. You are giving up your time, your energy, and your personal information, and the researcher has the moral and ethical obligation to keep this information safe. On the informed consent form, they will explain how they will ensure that the data you provide to them, and your identity, will be protected. However, there are limits to what they can promise, and you should be aware of these limits before you reveal any personal information.

One limitation concerns studies conducted online. Under the US *Patriot Act*, the United States government can gain access to information stored online as part of their anti-terrorism initiatives. This means that if you participate in a study for which the data are stored online on a US server, the US government theoretically can access your data. You may not care if the US government knows your name and how old you are, but if the study you participated in asked you to reveal personal information about, for example, any illegal activity or risky behaviours you have engaged in, this might be a bit more of a concern for you. And don't assume that a study conducted by a Canadian researcher will make your data more secure. Anything stored on cloud servers, including those used by Google, Apple, and Facebook, is fair game. Many Canadian researchers take great pains not to store their data on US servers, but since they have no control over how data is transferred online and much of it is routed through the US, it still isn't 100 percent secure.

The other limitation to confidentiality concerns any admission of illegal behaviour, whether you disclose this online or in person to an interviewer. Researchers may be subpoenaed to provide their data to the courts if it is believed that their data could contain information pertinent to a court case. This happened to Russel Ogden, who was a master's student in the School of Criminology at Simon Fraser University in the 1990s. His research included interviews with people who had participated in assisted suicides. When the Vancouver coroner began an inquest into the assisted suicide of one of the people Ogden had studied, they contacted him to get the name of one of the people who had helped with the procedure (which was illegal). Ogden cooperated as much as he could, but he refused to disclose the name because he had promised his participants confidentiality. Eventually, Ogden was able to keep his data confidential, but it was not without a court battle and the associated legal costs. Ogden was willing to defend his participants, in part because it was the right thing to do, but also because he could not continue to conduct this kind of research if participants did not trust him to maintain confidentiality. As with journalists who refuse to reveal their sources, the consequences of refusing to cooperate with the courts can be high and can even include jail time, and not all researchers might be as willing to take the risk that Russel Ogden did.

Research Involving the First Nations, Inuit, and Métis Peoples of Canada

In Canada, there are special considerations for those wishing to study members of our Indigenous population, which includes First Nations, Inuit, and Métis peoples. There are a number of reasons for these special considerations. First,

Indigenous communities have cultures and traditions that are unique, and traditional Western research methods may not be appropriate to study them. Second, members of these communities should have more of a say in how and whether they are studied. Traditionally, much of the research conducted in (and on) Indigenous communities has been done by non-Indigenous researchers, and that research often has not accurately reflected the reality of those communities. Third, it is important to ensure that the research conducted in Indigenous communities actually benefits the individuals being studied; historically, this has not always been the case. Fourth, new knowledge may be uncovered through collaborations between researchers using both Indigenous and Western research methods.

The key phrase used throughout the various guidelines on conducting research in Indigenous communities is that it should be "culturally competent and mutually beneficial." The fact that so much prior research has not met these two criteria has led to a need to build trust and create respectful relationships between researchers and participants.

The TCPS 2 (Canadian Institute of Health Research et al., 2014) has a separate chapter on research with First Nations, Inuit, and Métis people. Although the core principles are the same (i.e., respect for persons, concern for welfare, and justice), they are expanded to ensure that researchers:

1. seek engagement with the entire community,
2. consult with and receive approval from leaders of the community before speaking with individual participants,
3. become informed about and respect the customs of the community affected by their research,
4. use a collaborative approach whenever possible,
5. ensure that the communities they are studying benefit from the research,
6. include and recognize community Elders in their research, and
7. ensure that the communities have a say in how the results of the research are shared.

These recommendations are framed as a starting point in the conversation about how best to ethically and respectfully conduct research with Indigenous communities. Although the Canadian Tri-Council Policy specifically mentions research with members of Indigenous communities, these guidelines would be essential for research with any culturally distinct and/ or marginalized group.

ETHICS AND THE RESEARCH PROCESS

No research study on its own will change the way we see the world. Instead, knowledge comes from the accumulation of research findings of multiple studies, conducted by different researchers over a long period of time. In this way, each new study contributes to what we know about a topic by building on the studies that came before it. This means that new research depends on the reliability of previous research. Imagine a human pyramid, where the structure of the pyramid (and the safety of the person at the top) depends on each participant reliably staying in place. If one person is a flake and doesn't hold up their part of the pyramid, the entire thing could collapse. In the same way, one unreliable or fraudulent research study could cause an entire field of knowledge to collapse. That's why social science researchers not only have an ethical responsibility to their research participants—they also have an ethical responsibility to the field of social science.

Research fraud can also erode public trust in scientific research. When people start being skeptical of all research findings, how does science move forward? And how do consumers of this research know what is legitimate and what isn't? Fortunately, cases like that of Michael LaCour, described in the box that follows, are rare, but they do happen.

A Case of Research Fraud

In December 2014, the journal *Science* published a study by Michael LaCour, a PhD student in political science at the University of California, Los Angeles, and Donald Green, a well-respected political science professor at Columbia University. The study, entitled "When Contact Changes Minds: An Experiment on Transmission of Support for Gay Equality," claimed to have found that having a 20-minute phone conversation with a gay canvasser made people more positive toward same-sex marriage, and that those new attitudes persisted even nine months later. How to get people to change their attitudes is sort of a holy grail for social science researchers—if we knew how to successfully change attitudes, we could get people to stop being racist, sexist, and homophobic, and that's just a start. So, this research finding was of interest to a lot of researchers who study attitudes. In addition, *Science* is a very prestigious journal, and it's very selective about the research it publishes. As a result, this research study got lots of attention, being mentioned in newspapers like the *New York Times* and the *Wall Street Journal*, and on the podcast *This American Life*.

Five months later, in May 2015, *Science* issued a retraction of the article, at the request of Donald Green, the second author. A retraction is a formal method of withdrawing the study from the field, and it usually indicates that the research was flawed and should not be cited, used, or paid attention to. Apparently, some researchers had tried to replicate the findings of the study, and when their study didn't work out, they noticed some sketchy things about LaCour and Green's results. When Green confronted LaCour and asked him to provide the original data so it could be double-checked, LaCour claimed to have accidentally deleted the file. Then he changed his story and claimed that the Ethics Review Board at his university had asked him to delete it to protect his participants' confidentiality. The problem was, he never submitted his study to the Ethics Review Board in the first place, and besides, it would be highly unusual for a board to request this—participant confidentiality can easily be ensured by removing their personal information from the data file. Ultimately, LaCour couldn't provide any evidence that he had actually conducted the study or collected any data—in other words, it was entirely fabricated. He wrote the article published in *Science* based on made-up data and lied about his methodology. After being accused of research fraud, he also falsified some documents to try to make it look like he had conducted the study. Green, his co-author, had been relying on LaCour to take care of the data collection and analysis, and as soon as he found out what had happened, he asked that the article be retracted.

If the research fraud wasn't bad enough, it was later found that LaCour misrepresented his credentials on his CV (his academic resume): He made up a bunch of research grants he never actually received, and he lied about having received a teaching award. As soon as this scandal came to light, LaCour lost an academic job at Princeton University that he had recently been offered.

Source: LaCour, M. J. & Green, D. P. (2014). When contact changes minds: An experiment on transmission of support for gay equality. *Science, 346* (6215), 1366-1369. doi:10.1126/science.1256151

Types of Research Misconduct

Making Up Data

Way back in Chapter 2, we talked about the research process. If you recall, there are seven steps in doing research: (1) select a topic, (2) develop a research question, (3) design the study, (4) collect the data, (5) analyze the data, (6) give meaning to the findings, and (7) inform others. None of these steps are optional. If a researcher makes up their data, they are completely missing two steps in the research process (collecting and analyzing the data) and replacing them with a completely bogus step (making up a bunch of data that fits their hypothesis). Data collection can be time-consuming and expensive for sure, but data is evidence and without it, all that is left is an untested theory.

Misrepresenting Results

Sometimes a researcher may collect data, but then the data do not give them the results they were expecting. The temptation might be not to completely make up data but to remove any data that do not "fit" instead. This data could be in the form of a study participant whose numbers are far off anyone else in their group, or even an interview that revealed information that was inconsistent with all the other interviews. There are instances where it's okay to remove data from the analysis, but this has to be disclosed in the study description, and it must be with good reason.

Lying about Credentials

Not all research fraud consists of faulty research findings; sometimes it consists of faulty researchers. When a research article is published, it lists the name and credentials of those who conducted the research. Credentials, which usually only include the researcher's academic degree and where they conducted their research, are often used as a shortcut in determining whether the research is legitimate. You don't know these people, but if you know they have an advanced degree in their area of research, you can normally assume they know their stuff. The problem is, it's actually pretty easy to lie about credentials, because people rarely check them.

Lying about credentials might not just mean making up a degree or two; it could also mean having a degree but representing yourself as an expert in an area in which you are not qualified. Someone with a degree in sociology would not be qualified to speak as an expert on theoretical physics, just as someone with a degree in theoretical physics would not be qualified to speak as an expert on sociology. They both may be experts, but in very different areas. A degree or certification is only legitimate if it is in the area in which the person is claiming expertise; otherwise, they are misrepresenting their credentials.

Conflict of Interest

If you read a study in which the researcher claimed that their research proves that smoking does not cause cancer, what's the first thing you would do? Go out and buy some cigarettes, or look to see who funded that research? Hopefully you chose the second option. Conflict of interest can happen when researchers receive funding or other resources from parties who have a vested interest in the research results turning out a specific way. For example, if a pharmaceutical company hired a scientist to test whether their new drug works, they probably would prefer that the results show that their drug is effective. The scientist might feel pressured by the funders to not report negative findings or to downplay the severity of side effects, especially if the pharmaceutical company had set them up with a fancy new lab in which they could conduct their other non-funded research too. Labs are expensive, and research funding to pay for them is hard to come by.

Plagiarism

Plagiarism involves using the work of someone else and claiming it as your own. You've likely been warned about this in your own academic work. Plagiarism is considered to be fraud because it does not represent the work of the author; in effect, it's stolen from someone else. Like lying about your credentials, presenting the work of others as your own means you are claiming credit for something you did not do. Academic journals take plagiarism pretty seriously. Most of them use plagiarism detection software to check research articles for plagiarism in the same way that teachers check students' essays, so if a researcher were to plagiarize, their research study would not be published.

The Implications of Research Fraud

The implications of research misconduct can be huge: It's not hard to imagine the damage that could be done if a pharmaceutical company fudged the data on the effectiveness of their drugs. In the social sciences, this is less likely to happen, since we're not developing potentially life-saving drugs, but often public policy is based on research. If that research is not valid, then the policies based on it can be misguided or completely wrong. Also, as we'll see in Chapter 10, it's difficult to undo the damage of a convincing fake research finding.

ACADEMIC INTEGRITY

When we talk about cases of research misconduct or fraud, we are talking about cases in which individuals made a conscious decision to act unethically. In that sense, misconduct is the opposite of integrity. We all face situations in which we have a choice as to whether to act with integrity or not. If you notice someone leave their wallet behind in a store and you run after them to return it, despite the fact that no one would notice if you took it, you are choosing to act with integrity. For the record, your integrity would be a bit more questionable if the reason you returned the wallet to its rightful owner was because you were afraid of getting caught. As the saying goes, "Integrity is doing the right thing even when no one is watching" (ironically, we have no source for this quote; it has been misattributed to C. S. Lewis, but the truth is, no one really knows where it came from; O'Flaherty, 2015).

If you are a student, you too face these kinds of decisions in your academic life. Whether you are writing an essay, taking a test, or studying with friends, you are faced with many opportunities to act with integrity or not. In this section, we'll talk about what actions are considered to be academic misconduct, we'll review some of the social science research that has attempted to better understand this issue, and, finally, we'll go over some practical tips so that you can make sure you always approach your academic work with integrity.

An Early Example of Academic Misconduct

We don't really have a good way to know when people started cheating in school, but one of the earliest descriptions of academic misconduct comes from China (Crozier, 2002; Lang, 2013). From the early seventh century and continuing on to the twentieth century, if you wanted to get a job in the civil service in China, you had to pass a series of very difficult exams. The subject of the exams was Confucianism, a system of thought proposed by Chinese philosopher Confucius. To pass the exams, test-takers needed to have intricate knowledge of the original works of Confucianism. In addition, they were required to memorize and reproduce, in writing, entire sections of the work. And, if that wasn't hard enough, they even had to compose Confucianism-based poetry!

The test actually consisted of a series of exams that got progressively harder, and you had to pass one to move on to the next one. There were no rewrites, so if you failed one, you were out. People studied for years to take these exams, and writing the entire series could take months. In addition, they were only offered in specific places, so often test-takers would have to travel long distances to write the test. Why would anyone subject themselves to this? It's because the reward was very high. If you were successful, you would be given a high-ranking government position for life. In a time and place when stable employment was hard to come by, this was a very appealing prospect. Many, many people attempted the test, despite the fact that it was gruelling and the chances of success were pretty low.

Whenever you combine a difficult task with a high-value outcome, some people will look for ways to gain unfair advantage. They didn't have cellphones back then to text each other the answers, but they still found creative ways to try to cheat on the tests. There are reports that people would buy pre-written essays to memorize for the exams. Archaeologists have uncovered some evidence of ancient unauthorized exam aids that were used for these tests. Not only have they found tiny ancient cheat sheets, small enough to hide inside a writing implement, but in an example of a really impressive combination of cheekiness and lack of integrity, they have even uncovered an item of clothing—let's call it a "cheat shirt"—on which someone wrote out the original Confucian texts. Of course, the penalties for being caught cheating were high—not only did it mean failing the exam, but it would bring disgrace to your family and could even result in the death penalty—but that didn't stop people from trying.

What Is Academic Integrity?

You likely won't be faced with any tests as strenuous or soul-destroying as the Chinese civil service exams, but that doesn't mean that you won't be faced with difficult courses and a heavy workload at times. You might even be tempted to find some shortcuts that will help to lighten your load a bit. Some of those shortcuts will be perfectly reasonable and helpful (reread Chapter 1 for a review of effective and time-saving study techniques), but some might not be.

In the following section we list and define some common types of academic misconduct. We feel it's important to define these types of misconduct because students often are unaware of the more subtle forms of misconduct. So, you need to know what is allowed and what is not so you can make better choices. We have seen countless students be surprised at an allegation of academic misconduct because they honestly did not understand that what they did was wrong. Although some types of academic misconduct are very obvious in their disregard for integrity (for example, spending hours making a cheat shirt with the clear intention of using it during your exam), others may be a bit more surprising to you. Although each school may have its own policies regarding academic integrity, many of them clearly state that ignorance of the rules is not an adequate excuse for misconduct. In other words, the "I didn't know I wasn't allowed to do that" argument won't get you out of trouble. Therefore, the better you understand what is and is not allowed, the more confident you will be that you are acting with integrity.

Types of Academic Misconduct

Plagiarism—Plagiarizing involves presenting the work or ideas of others as your own. This could involve copying text or images from someone else without citing them properly, but it could also involve using their ideas without giving them credit.

Cheating—The most obvious type of cheating is copying answers from someone else during a test or exam. Cheating is a broad term, though, and could include any number of other dishonest actions.

Lying or forgery—Lying about your dog eating your homework or having to attend your grandmother's funeral is considered academic misconduct, as would any other instance in which you misrepresent the reasons for missing an exam or not handing in an assignment. Faking or forging a doctor's note is even more serious, as it constitutes fraud, which could get you kicked out of school.

Submitting work that is not your own—This could include handing in an essay that someone gave you (maybe a student who had taken the course previously), or purchasing a paper from an essay-writing service. Basically, if you did not write the entire paper, it is not your own work and is considered to be academic misconduct.

Self-plagiarism—You may not realize this, but submitting the same piece of work for credit in more than one course is considered self-plagiarism, and it is considered to be academic misconduct.

Helping others engage in academic misconduct—Even if you don't benefit directly from it, helping others cheat is still considered to be academic misconduct. This might include telling a student from a different section of your course what questions were on the test, sharing your assignments from a course you took the year before with someone taking the course now, or posting test questions or assignment answers on social media.

Unauthorized collaboration—Many students find it helpful to have study groups where they work with friends on an assignment, but if your instructor hasn't given you permission to collaborate, it could be considered misconduct. This can be tricky, as students don't always know they aren't supposed to work together because instructors don't always make their expectations clear. Some instructors permit working together as long as everyone hands in their own work, but it's always safer to ask if you aren't sure.

Using unauthorized aids during exams—The point of tests and exams is to assess your knowledge, so if you use items during the test that give you unfair advantage on the test, the test is no longer an assessment of your understanding of the material. If you are caught, your instructor would be justified in giving you a zero on the test. As we noted above, students have been trying to sneak some form of cheat sheet (or shirt!) into exams since the seventh century, and new technology brings even more opportunities for cheating during exams. Regardless of how you do it, it is considered to be academic misconduct.

You should become familiar with the policies of your school. If you aren't sure, ask. Remember that what you may think is fine may not be considered fine by the person marking your paper or exam. McCabe, Butterfield, and Treviño (2012) conducted an extensive survey of student and faculty experiences of cheating in schools across North America, and one very telling finding was that although students and instructors generally agree that things like significant plagiarism, copying from someone else during a test, and being caught with crib notes during a test would be considered moderate or serious cheating, there are also "grey" areas when it comes to what is considered cheating. The survey revealed fairly large discrepancies between student and instructor perceptions on two actions in particular. The first is sharing information about a test that others haven't taken yet: Only 71 percent of students, but 93 percent of instructors, consider this to be moderate or serious cheating. The second is collaborating on assignments that are supposed to be done individually: Just 37 percent of students, but a whopping 84 percent of instructors, consider this to be moderate or serious cheating.

You can see the importance of making sure you know what is allowed and what isn't. You may have a very persuasive argument about the benefits of working with other students on assignments (and there are good arguments to be made), but the fact is, if your instructor considers it to be misconduct, then regardless of what you believe and how eloquently you can argue your case, you could be disciplined for doing it.

The Social Science of Cheating in School

How Often Does It Happen?

Cheating is a social issue: It can affect not only the perpetrators but also those around them. It has been of great interest to social scientists, partly because they are interested in what motivates students to act unethically and partly because they are interested in finding ways to stop it from happening.

One of the pioneers of the study of academic integrity is Donald McCabe, who was a researcher and professor in the Management and Global Business department at Rutgers Business School. McCabe, also known as "Dr. Ethics," was one of the first social scientists to take a scientific approach to academic integrity. Using the scientific method to study integrity is important, because without evidence we would not really know much about academic integrity, or even whether it was a problem. McCabe and his colleagues (2012) point out that published reports of the incidence rate of academic misconduct in higher education (i.e., colleges and universities) range anywhere from 3 to 98 percent. This is not very helpful information; is academic misconduct a problem or not? If only 3 percent of students engage in it, then we could probably eliminate this section of the textbook entirely and call it a day. If it's 98 percent, then we should probably think about expanding this chapter into an entire book.

Upon closer examination, it appears that the large discrepancy in esti-mated rates of misconduct is mostly due to differences in the methods used to study it. One notable difference between studies is how misconduct is defined. It's easy to see how this could make a difference. For example, you would probably get very different answers if you asked the question, "Did you cheat during university?" compared to "Did you ever collaborate with other students on assignments when you were supposed to work individually?" As we noted earlier, given the differences in the degree of severity of the various forms of academic misconduct, different people may have different definitions of what misconduct (or cheating) actually is. Without an agreed-upon definition, you won't really know what you're measuring. Another difference in methodology is whether you ask students to self-report on their misconduct. Not surprisingly, people tend to be reluctant to disclose risky or unethical behaviour, so if you ask students to tell you, even if you promise them anonymity, they may not be entirely truthful.

For these reasons, it's difficult to know what the incidence rates of academic misconduct actually are. If you ask students after they have graduated, when they arguably would be less inclined to lie because they could no longer be punished for it, 81.7 percent report having engaged in some form of academic misconduct in their university careers (Yardley, Rodríguez, Bates, & Nelson, 2009). If you consider that some students probably still didn't want to admit to cheating, that estimate is likely higher. However, the researchers asked about 19 different, specific behaviours and their incidence rate includes anyone who admitted to even one of those behaviours. Sharing assignments was listed as the most common form of cheating. So, while 81.7 percent (or more) have engaged in misconduct, much of it was of the milder form.

Why Does It Happen?

In addition to being interested in *how often* academic misconduct happens, social scientists are also interested in *why* it happens. Are students who cheat bad people? Most researchers agree that this is not the case. Although there are some dispositional (i.e., personality) factors that might influence whether a person is likely to cheat, environmental or situational factors play a much larger role. Researchers who conduct experiments on cheating have demonstrated that it's possible to get almost anyone to act in a dishonest way if you structure the environment just right. So, if most people have the potential to act dishonestly, the reason why some people cheat and others don't must be due to with situational or environmental factors.

What are these factors? Lang (2013) proposes that there are four conditions within academia that encourage dishonest behaviour.

1. **An emphasis on performance**. What motivates you in the classes that you take, or have taken in the past? Did you work hard solely in order to get high grades? Or did you work hard so you could master the course content? Maybe it was a bit of both. When the primary goal of the learning environment is on doing well or getting high grades, the focus is on performance; when the primary goal is to learn the material and develop new skills, the focus is on mastery. When the emphasis is on performance rather than mastery, students are more likely to engage in academic misconduct.

   Think about your approach to your classes. Do you try to actually learn and remember the material in your classes? Do you practice the new skills you are learning in other contexts? Do you try to focus on the process of learning rather than on your grade? If your goal is to master the material, then you are less likely to cheat because you know that if you did cheat, you would miss out on a learning opportunity—as your parents might say, you're only hurting yourself. However, if your goal is strictly to get the best grade you can, cheating will not affect your goal (unless, of course, you get caught). You can see how the approach you take could influence your behaviour when it comes to academic misconduct.

Unfortunately, our academic system tends to encourage a performance-based approach. Awarding grades for performance shifts the focus to the grade rather than the learning. When good performance is rewarded with high grades, students will inevitably focus on grades over learning. This is especially true for students wishing to earn scholarships or go on to graduate or professional programs. Because these tend to be awarded to those with the highest grades, they promote a performance-based approach.

There's no easy solution for this. The traditional grading system is not going to change, and the realities of the current economy mean that students often come to university because they feel they need to in order to get a job, not simply because they love learning. Just be aware of the approach you are taking to your studies, and try to find a balance between performance and mastery.

2. **High stakes riding on the outcome.** The potential rewards can play a large role in whether people are more or less likely to cheat. Not surprisingly, when the stakes are high and there is more to lose, cheating is more likely to happen. You can see this with the civil service exams in China: If you did well, you were rewarded with a good job and would be set for life, but if you didn't, you would return to your life of poverty with little hope of escaping it. It's no wonder people cheated.

Some of your courses in university may be set up to inadvertently increase the likelihood of academic misconduct. When you have a course in which a majority of your grade comes from just a few large tests or assignments, the focus, naturally, is on performing as well as you can on these assessments. If you don't do well on one of them, the consequences can be huge—it could mean the difference between passing and failing the course. You'll recall from Chapter 1, however, that failing can have many benefits, and it actually helps us learn new things. With only one or two high-stakes assignments in a course, you are unlikely to take chances that might help you learn the material better because the consequences of failing are too high. Courses like this may unintentionally encourage cheating because they place students in a position where they have to focus too much on performance over mastery because so much is riding on the outcome.

Statistics show that your employment prospects are better if you have a university or college degree. Although the stress of university does not compare to the stress of the civil service exams in China, the stakes may seem pretty high to you. And the stakes may not be just the tangible rewards of a degree. You may face other significant pressures to do well, from your family, your friends, and even yourself.

We're not going to suggest that you try not to care so much about the potential rewards of your university degree so you will be less likely to act unethically. However, we are going to suggest that you try to make realistic assessments of the individual outcomes leading to that degree. Your degree is made up of many different courses and many, many, different tests and assignments. Will one test make or break your degree? Likely not. Even one course can be retaken. In other words, although each test and assignment is important, when you are stressing out about them, try to take a broad look at all you are trying to accomplish (i.e., earn your degree and get a job). Are the stakes really as high as you think they are for this one task?

3. **An extrinsic motivation for success.** Take a moment to think about the reasons you are in school. To what extent are you doing it because someone else wants or expects you to, and to what extent are you doing it because you want to? The distinction here is whether you are motivated by external factors (extrinsic motivation) or by internal factors (intrinsic motivation). As you might be able to guess, when your motivation is extrinsic—maybe your parents expect you to get a degree, or maybe your company won't promote you unless you have a degree—you are more likely to engage in academic misconduct. Why? Because when you aren't doing it for yourself, you are doing it for someone else. When you are doing something because you really want to do it, it increases your enjoyment of it and it makes you care about it more. When you are in school because you want to learn and develop new skills, you will be less likely to take unethical shortcuts because you know that those actions won't actually help you reach your goals.

In reality, we are all motivated by many different things. You may feel the pressure of family expectations to get your degree, but it's likely that you want it too. Even if your motivations are multidimensional, try to focus on your own goals.

4. **A low expectation of success**. It probably comes as no surprise that when people feel like they can't succeed, they are more likely to resort to desperate measures like cheating. Whether the low expectation of success is warranted or not, it can drive people to do things they wouldn't normally do. Sometimes people just have a low opinion of their own abilities, and this causes them to cut corners. Sometimes the situation is set up so that failure is almost inevitable. For the civil service exams in China, the chances of success were something like one in a million. With odds like those, it's no wonder people tried to find unethical ways to gain advantage.

    You may find yourself in situations where you don't feel optimistic about your chances of success—this is an inevitable fact of life, and you can't always control it. What you can control, however, is your approach to the difficult task. Does the upcoming test seem impossible? Is that because you didn't go to class, or because you really don't understand the material? Can you get help before the test, either from your instructor or a study group? Can you use some of the study techniques in Chapter 1 to help you study more effectively? Usually situations like this are either (a) not as bad as they seem, or (b) resolvable, with some effort. Try to take a step back from the situation to make sure you are assessing it accurately.

Acting with Integrity: What Schools Can Do

The responsibility for academic integrity lies with everyone: students, instructors, and schools. However, since you're the one reading this textbook and not your instructors or the university administration, we're going to focus more on what you, as a student, can do to make sure you are acting with integrity in your courses. Your school probably is making efforts to promote academic integrity, though. In 2014, the Education Advisory Board released a report listing five policy recommendations for schools regarding how to promote integrity and reduce academic misconduct. It's likely that your school is doing at least some of them.

1. **Make sure students have access to academic tutors and writing support services.**
    Remember that when students have low expectations for success, they are more likely to resort to cheating. If a student is struggling with writing a paper and has nowhere to turn for help, it creates a situation where they might be tempted to resort to less ethical strategies to finish the paper, like

copying from someone else or paying someone to write it for them. Writing support services and peer tutors offer an alternative to these more desperate measures. Having a range of options is also important because, as nice and friendly and willing to help as your instructors may be, some students do not feel comfortable asking them for help.

2. **Integrate academic integrity programming into new student orientation and continue programming throughout the academic year.**
   Many schools lay out the rules regarding academic integrity as soon as students arrive on campus. Obviously, it's important to know the rules about what is and is not allowed, and also the penalties for breaking these rules. The problem is, how much do you remember about your first few weeks at school? It was probably pretty overwhelming, with lots of information competing for your attention. We doubt that the rules on academic integrity make it into the long-term memory of many brand-new undergraduates. For many reasons, new student orientation (i.e., Orientation Week) is not the best place to make a lasting impression about academic integrity. That's why this policy recommendation suggests that the rules must be restated and reinforced throughout the academic year. We would also suggest going a bit further and reinforcing academic integrity in every academic year—it doesn't hurt to have a refresher every year and, like any skill, practice makes perfect!

3. **Design courses and assignments to discourage academic misconduct.**
   Unfortunately, instructors don't always do their part in preventing academic misconduct. In a perfect world, students would not share old exams or homework assignments, but the fact is, this sometimes happens. As we know, when a student is struggling, they will search for alternative ways to succeed. And when they are under time pressure, they may pick the easiest way, even if it is not the most ethical way. By switching up exam questions and assignments and generally being more creative in their methods of assessment, instructors can remove this temptation. This, in turn, may encourage students to seek out more acceptable forms of help, like writing support services or peer supports.

4. **Integrate academic integrity programming into the classroom.**
   As we stated above, academic integrity is everyone's responsibility. Individual instructors can be instrumental in helping students in their courses be better

equipped to act with integrity. This could be something as simple as taking a few moments at the beginning of the course to explain what misconduct is (beyond the short blurb that is usually included on the syllabus) and going over what his or her expectations are regarding academic integrity. Considering that students and instructors do not always agree on what is "cheating," especially when it comes to areas like collaboration on assignments, making this explicit can save everyone a lot of grief.

5. **Allow for an informal resolution process between instructors and students for minor cases of misconduct.**
    Schools vary widely in their approach to academic integrity. Some schools have a very rigid, legal-based process, while others are more informal. Although major cases of misconduct such as fraud or impersonation require formal sanctions, this recommendation recognizes that sometimes students mess up in minor ways that can be better handled by a meeting in which the instructor explains what the student did wrong and provides advice on how to fix it. For example, if your essay is flagged because you improperly cited your sources, a lesson on how to cite properly will help you more than getting a zero on your paper, a scary meeting with the dean, and no instruction on how to cite properly in your next paper. You can't control what policies your school has, but you can make sure you are aware of them.

Acting with Integrity: What You Can Do

Even though there are certainly things your instructors and your school can do to promote a culture of integrity, the ultimate responsibility for your personal integrity lies solely with you. Whether or not the learning environment you find yourself in is a perfect fit for you and your unique abilities, one of the things you can control is how you respond to that environment. You may be faced with situations in which performance is valued over mastery or the stakes are really high or you feel that you aren't doing it for you but for someone else or you don't think you will succeed—in other words, situations that have been known to promote unethical behaviour. Every student will face these challenges at some point. But just because the environment may be a minefield of stressors doesn't mean it's out of your hands. You always have control over your actions, and you will be held accountable if you make the wrong choice.

Acting with Integrity

Here are some strategies for getting through your degree with your integrity intact.

GENERAL ADVICE

- Know the rules. Make sure you know your school's policies about academic misconduct.
- If you aren't sure, ask. If assignment instructions are not clear or if you aren't sure whether something is allowed or not, get clarification.
- Be organized. Don't leave things until the last minute—this is the most common reason students give for their academic misconduct.
- Be true to yourself. Don't let yourself be pressured by friends to act against your principles.
- Ask for help. If you are struggling, speak to someone—anyone—before you get to the point where you feel you have no option but to cheat. There are lots of resources on campus: your instructors, teaching assistants, the student support centre, friends, private tutors, study groups, and the campus wellness or counselling centre. Don't be afraid to ask.

WRITING PAPERS

- Learn how to paraphrase well. See Chapter 8 on writing a literature review for tips on how to paraphrase.
- Learn how to quote properly. Chapter 8 covers this too!
- Don't cut and paste. Never cut and paste sections from other sources into your notes or essay, even if you intend to rewrite them later. You may forget to do it, and it will look like you deliberately copied it.
- Keep careful notes while you are researching your paper. Keep a research log, research notes, and a list of all your sources, so you can go back and double-check things before handing in your paper. It can also serve as proof that you actually did the work in case you are ever questioned.
- Become familiar with the plagiarism detection software your school uses. This software will compare your essay to any sources on the

Continued

Internet, including academic sources and other students' papers—if you cut and paste anything from the Internet, it will be flagged.

- Always back up your work. Losing your essay the night before it's due because your computer crashed might tempt you to cut corners.

TAKING EXAMS

- Know the rules. Make sure you understand and follow all the rules during the exam. Even if your phone is turned off, if you are not allowed to have it with you, you could get in trouble if you are caught with it.
- Protect yourself. If you are concerned about someone looking at your work during an exam, ask to be moved.
- Online tests are still tests. Even if you are taking a test in the privacy of your own home, working with others or using your textbook if the instructor has instructed you not to is still considered cheating. Remember that integrity means doing the right thing even if no one is watching.

WORKING WITH OTHERS

- Don't lend your essays to friends. Even if they promise not to copy it, both of you will get in trouble if they do. Protect yourself and your friendship, and don't share your work.
- Know the rules. Find out if collaboration is allowed. Instructors and courses differ in what they allow, so don't assume that because it is allowed in one course, it will be allowed in another.
- Talk to your group mates. At some point you'll be faced with group work. Especially if you don't know them well, have a discussion about integrity with the group. Your grade and reputation depends on everyone being on the same page.

IF THE WORST HAPPENS

You're human, and humans sometimes make mistakes. Hopefully this will never happen to you, but if you do find yourself being accused of academic misconduct, there are a few things to keep in mind.

- Know your rights. Read the school's policy on academic misconduct. Find out what the process is, what your rights as a student are, and what resources and supports are available to you.
- Know the potential penalties. Students often think that if they get caught for any kind of academic misconduct, they will be thrown out of school. In our experience, academic suspension or expulsion only happens in very rare cases. It's more likely that you'll get a zero or grade reduction on the assignment or test, which is still not a nice outcome, but it's not the end of the world.
- Be honest. If you get busted for severe plagiarism, and the instructor shows you evidence that most of your essay has been copied from another source, own up to it. Lying and excuses will not help your case.
- First-timers often get a break. Many schools realize that one mistake should not tarnish a student's record forever, so if you've never been caught committing academic misconduct before, the penalties might be lighter, especially if you are in your first or second year. Keep in mind, however, that the most you'll get is one free pass. If you get caught again, or if you get caught in your third of fourth year when you would be expected to know better, you cannot expect any leniency.

REVIEW IT

1. Who was Stanley Milgram? Why is he important to our understanding of research ethics?
2. Describe the three basic ethical principles for research as recommended by the Belmont Report (1979).
3. Describe the elements of informed consent as outlined in the Tri-Council Policy Statement: Ethical Conduct for Research Involving Humans.
4. The US *Patriot Act* has important implications for confidentiality and anonymity in an online study. What are these implications?
5. What is meant when a journal article is retracted?
6. What are the four factors that encourage dishonest behaviour in schools?

APPLY IT

Are the following studies ethical? Why or why not? How would you make them more ethical?

A researcher is interested in how illness and stress impact grades in undergraduate students. Unbeknownst to the students, the researcher gets information about their visits to the campus wellness centre, including the doctor, the nurse, and the counsellor, and their grades in all their courses.

You are testing out a new drug but are aware that it has some pretty severe side effects. You are offering $100 in return for trying out the drug for a month. In order to recruit participants for your study, you only put up signs in the part of town where people with lower incomes tend to live.

7 Presentations: Talking about Social Science Research

There is no secret formula for giving a good presentation. While there are general guidelines for giving effective presentations, each presentation is a unique experience. The expectations for your presentation will vary, the venue will likely vary, your audience will vary, and your topic will likely vary. Your comfort with any or all of these variables will also likely vary. Thus, if there were a secret to giving a good presentation, it would be that you need to be prepared, at least as much as possible, for all these variables. The closest we can offer to a secret formula is a set of guidelines for giving a good presentation. Some of these guidelines are so well established that they can almost be thought of as rules. Many are the product of social science research. Others are more like conventions. Some have universal applicability, while others will vary somewhat between disciplines. However, all are designed to help you give presentations that are memorable for all of the right reasons.

LEARNING OBJECTIVES

1. Understand why presentation skills are important
2. Learn how to share social science research in a presentation format
3. Learn how to create effective slides to accompany your presentation
4. Learn how to provide feedback that is effective

THE IMPORTANCE OF EFFECTIVE ORAL COMMUNICATION SKILLS

You are probably reading this chapter because you have to give a presentation in class. Despite what you might think, your instructor has not included an oral presentation in the course requirements to punish you. Your instructor knows that it has been widely recognized that effective presentation skills are essential for all university graduates and educated professionals (De Grez, 2009; Fallows & Steven, 2000), and is giving you an opportunity to develop and refine your skills. You should thank them!

Being able to speak clearly and effectively in front of other people is an important life skill. You'll probably need to give a presentation, either by yourself or in a group, in other courses that you take. This chapter is mostly intended to help you with in-class presentations. However, you will likely be faced with many situations in your life outside of school where oral communication skills will come in handy. It may be in the career you choose or in the hobbies or interests you have outside of work, such as volunteering as a youth leader, engaging in community activism or politics, or even giving a toast at a wedding. Many of the tips and techniques in this chapter can help you with those as well.

Social scientists need to have effective oral presentation skills too. If you think back to Chapter 2, where we talked about the steps in the research process, you'll remember that the final step is to inform others of your findings. This step is essential; it is both an obligation and an honour for social scientists to share the results of their research. One way that social scientists share their research is through publishing it, in journals or in books. However, most do not simply hide behind their computers writing articles all day. Social scientists often present their work at academic conferences, in which they are required to give a clear, succinct talk about their research. Many of them teach in universities, where they need to be able to present information in a clear and engaging way. Some of them even share their research with industry or governments, where it may be necessary for them to present a convincing case to their audience about the implications of their research for policy and practice. In other words, social scientists must have effective oral presentation skills and, like every skill, it takes time and practice to develop them.

A Note on Performance Anxiety

How are you feeling? Are you excited about giving a presentation on social science research, or is the thought of this assignment causing you some anxiety? If you are feeling more dread than excitement about it, you have a great deal of company: Fear of public speaking is the most common social fear and social phobia (Kessler, Stein, & Berglund, 1998; Ruscio et al., 2008). Believe it or not, some of your instructors probably share this fear, even if you are unable to perceive it in their lectures. Think about it: The kind of person who chooses to spend endless years in school doggedly pursuing a graduate degree because they love doing research is not necessarily the kind of person who is comfortable speaking in front of groups of people. Many (but not all) scientists are actually introverts (Berry, 1981); they are happier in small groups and draw their energy from quiet introspection rather than being the life of the party. So how do they manage to get up in front of sometimes large groups of students to teach? They have learned to manage their fear. Some may have even conquered their fear. With practice and a few effective strategies, you can learn to manage your fear as well. You can do this while you are learning to give more effective presentations.

PREPARING YOUR PRESENTATION

Before You Get Started

When preparing to give a talk, there are several basic questions you need to ask. Getting the answers to these questions will allow you to establish the context and the goals of your presentation.

1. **What is the purpose of this presentation?** This question is, perhaps, the most fundamental question you should ask when preparing for your presentation. If you are a student, it is possible that this question is answered in the course syllabus. If this is the case, make sure you read the course syllabus! If it has been a while since you last read the syllabus, read it again. Sometimes, only the most basic details about the purpose of the presentation are provided. If this is the case, you may want to check with your instructor to find out more details. If your presentation is not for a class, you still need to ask this question. What purpose is your presentation meant to serve? What are the expectations of the group you will be presenting to?

2. **Who is the audience?** This question is closely linked to the first question. However, this question addresses more than just the interests and expectations of the audience; it also addresses the level of expertise of your audience. If you are a student, you may assume that your instructor is your audience. This may be understandable because your instructor is likely the person who is grading your presentation. However, you are also presenting to your peers (i.e., other students)—don't forget them. Your instructor is aware of the qualities of an effective presentation, and effectively ignoring the majority of your audience is not one of these qualities.

3. **Where will the presentation be held?** If all of your presentations have been given in your course classrooms, this may seem like a silly question. However, you should check to make sure that the class presentations will be held in the same room that you use for class. For non-course-related presentations, this is an even more important question to ask. Maybe you've been asked to speak at a meeting of a group on campus or maybe a community group has invited you to speak. As social scientists, we are often called on to give presentations in distant locations and/or locations that we have never visited before. What will the room be like? Will it be a large lecture theatre or a small room? Will there be a lectern? What kind of media equipment will be available? If you are not given this information beforehand, who can you ask to find out about it? Thus, this question about where the presentation will be held is really a "catch-all" question for many other important questions.

4. **How long will the presentation be?** The time provided for scholarly presentations is often strictly enforced. Make sure you stick to this time limit when you are preparing and rehearsing your talk. A presentation that is longer than the time allowed will either be rushed or truncated. Your instructor may not cut you off if you go over, but you may be taking time away from other presenters if you exceed your time limit. Try not to go under the time limit either. If your presentation is significantly shorter than the time allowed, it may appear to be inadequate. In either case, the result will likely be that you give a presentation that is not as effective as you want it to be.

Structuring Your Talk

An effective presentation is, in many ways, like a good story. Like any good story, a presentation must flow logically, from the beginning or introduction to the concluding remarks. To achieve this, it must have a well-planned structure. Rushing through the introduction and omitting key background information may leave your audience wondering what you are talking about. A weak main section may mean that they miss the key arguments and relevance of your presentation. A hasty conclusion may make your presentation seem rushed and leave the audience with many unanswered questions. Thus, taking the time to structure your presentation before you fill in the details can play an important role in determining its success.

Introduction

The introduction is a critical part of any presentation. It can also be one of the most challenging for the speaker. During this time, you will likely be feeling a combination of fear and excitement. Thus, there is a natural tendency to want to rush into the more substantive parts of your presentation. However, do not be overly hasty. The introduction serves important functions for both the presenter and the audience. For the presenter, it allows a transition into the intellectual and physical rigours of making a presentation. It also allows you to gain the audience's full attention before beginning the most substantive parts of the presentation. It also allows the audience time to transition from whatever activities they were doing before the presentation. This section also allows the audience an opportunity to be introduced to the speaker(s) and the subject before the detailed discussion begins. Thus, while as a speaker you may want to get past the introduction as quickly as possible, do not ignore its important role in creating an effective presentation.

While it may seem self-evident, one of the first things you should do in an introduction is greet your audience and introduce yourself. Unfortunately, some presenters miss this step. We get it: You're nervous; you want to get to the point quickly. However, first impressions are important, and this is your first chance to show your audience how awesome you are. Taking five or ten seconds to say hello and give your name can go a long way toward presenting a professional and polished image.

Once you have greeted the audience and introduced yourself to them, provide your audience with a framework for your presentation. Within this framework, you should state the topic of your presentation; provide a brief description of why this is an important topic, why they should care, and/or your motivation for choosing this topic; and provide an outline or agenda for the presentation. It is also sometimes useful to include a short anecdote or interesting fact to gain the audience's attention. This approach must be done with care, though, because a short anecdote can easily become a long story that distracts from the purpose of the presentation. Even greater care must be taken if you try to gain the audience's interest by including a joke. While a joke can be an attractive way to introduce a public presentation, the subjective nature of humour and the formal nature of academic presentations make this a risky strategy. A failed or distasteful joke may cause great offence and doom a presentation from its opening, no matter how wonderful the rest of the presentation may be.

The length of the introduction is important. Despite the many things to be introduced, the introduction should be brief and concise. The combined lengths of the introduction and the conclusion should be no more than 25 percent of the total length of a presentation; most (i.e., 75%) of the total time of a presentation should be reserved for the main section of your presentation. Thus, for a ten-minute presentation, the combined times for the introduction and conclusion should be two-and-a-half minutes. If this time is divided equally between the introduction and the conclusion, each should be no more than one minute and fifteen seconds. Thus, if you are going to include a short anecdote in your introduction, it must truly be short.

Main Section

The main section is the body of your presentation. In this section, you will present your findings and/or provide your key arguments. Often, a great deal of information is presented in a relatively short time. Thus, many of the key concerns for the main section deal with ensuring that this information is offered in an orderly, logical, and coherent manner. It is rare for a presenter of an academic presentation to have all of the time they need to present all of the information that they want. Instead of covering a little bit about everything, it is far better to highlight only the key findings or main points. This means that you may have to exclude some relatively unimportant information, even if you find it personally interesting. This is frequently a necessary compromise. Because these main points may sometimes appear to be disparate and unrelated facts, greater care must often be taken to highlight their connections and show their connections to the broader subject. While this may take extra time, time that you may want to use to expand your talk, creating these connections will help create a more coherent message.

Graphs and charts can be very useful aides in creating a concise and coherent presentation. They must be used with care, though, and they must be presented in a size that is easily read, even from the back of the room in which you are presenting. Your charts and graphs should also be well labelled, have an appropriate title, and not be overly complex. Also, if you use graphs and charts, do not simply put them up on the screen and begin talking about them. Give your audience a moment to "digest" the details of the graph. It is also very useful to point out these details. Once the audience has adjusted to the details of the graph or chart, take a moment to point out the important features or trends on the graph. All of this may negate some of the savings in time that a graph provides. However, for some kinds of information, a chart or graph may still be the best choice for ensuring conciseness and coherence.

Conclusion

Like the introduction, the conclusion plays critical functions in a presentation. In the conclusion, the speaker is able to summarize the key elements of the main section of their presentation and tie them together. The speaker is also able to illustrate how these elements relate back to the subject of the presentation. It also allows the speaker to thank the audience for listening. The end of the conclusion also usually signals the beginning of the question period, if time has been scheduled for questions.

While the arrival at the conclusion is often a time for silent relief for presenters, it should not be treated with any less planning or thoughtfulness than the introduction or main section. As you approach the beginning of the conclusion, cue the transition to your audience. This cue may be verbal, as in using the phrase "in conclusion." You may also change your position, such as moving from a position behind the lectern to a position closer to the audience. Even though the conclusion should be as concise as the introduction, you should briefly summarize your main points and illustrate how they relate to the subject of the presentation. You may also take the opportunity to illustrate how these points and the subject relate to broader topics or concepts. Once you have done this, it is time for your concluding statements. These statements may simply reinforce your main points, they may highlight opportunities for future research, and/or they may be a call for further action. Try not to lose focus at the end of the presentation, though. The most important part about these concluding remarks is that they must be presented with at least as much enthusiasm and strength as the rest of the presentation. Do not allow your concluding remarks to simply fade away.

The final part of the conclusion must be the thanking of the audience and, if it is allowed, the call for questions. If you are asked questions, answer them to the best of your ability. If you do not know the answer, say so. If there are no questions, do not be offended.

A Checklist for Structuring Your Talk

INTRODUCTION
- Introduce yourself
- State your topic
- Explain why your topic is important/why your audience should care
- Provide an outline or agenda for your presentation
- Give a short anecdote (optional)

MAIN SECTION
- Present your key arguments/findings
- Don't try to include too much—it's better to spend more time talking about less
- Use graphics/charts to enhance, not detract from, your presentation

CONCLUSION
- Briefly summarize your main points
- State how they relate to your presentation topic
- Highlight opportunities for future research or further action
- Thank the audience, and ask if there are any questions (if time for questions is allowed)

Preparing Presentation Slides

Over the past decade and a half, presentations have been transformed by the near ubiquitous use of presentation software to create slides that accompany talks. Way back when we were undergraduate students, professors either wrote everything on the chalkboard or had transparencies projected by an ancient machine that more often than not had a burnt out bulb. Good times! Nowadays, there are many more options for including visuals with a presentation, including many different types of software. There is evidence that, when used properly, this software can enhance learning and understanding (Mayer, 2009). The key to the effective use of presentation software is to use it in a way that enhances learning and does not distract. You can probably think of presentations or classes that you have attended where the slides were either unclear or unreadable. Although there is some variation as to what is considered to be the best practice when it comes to creating presentation slides, here are some general recommendations.

How Much to Include on a Slide
1. Do not put too much information on one slide. A mistake new presenters often make is to try to include everything on their slides. Keep in mind that they are meant to supplement what you are saying, not restate it word-for-word.
2. Keep individual points short.
3. Do not use more than three main bullet points on a slide.

Font
1. The minimum size is usually considered to be 24-point font. However, it depends on the size of the screen and also the size of the room. If you're in doubt, it's best to err on the side of caution, so go larger than you think you'll need.
2. Sans-serif fonts, like Calibri or Arial, are best. Avoid goofy fonts (Comic Sans, we're looking at you!) or overly fancy script fonts.
3. If you need to emphasize a word or point, do it with boldface or underlining, but not both—using both is like wearing a belt and suspenders (i.e., it's overkill).

Colours
1. High-contrast colours are preferable, as they are easier to read, especially from a distance.
2. Dark text on light background is generally preferable. Don't be afraid to use black text on a white background. It may look old-school, but it's actually easiest to read, and can look more professional than a busy background or one that is not contrasting enough.

Animations
1. Use animation and slide transitions with caution, as they can be distracting.

2. In general, if animations must be used, limit them to appear or disappear (and not be spinning or continuing to animate as you are speaking). If you do use animations, double-check before your presentation that they do what you want them to do.

Images
1. Sometimes a picture can say a thousand words (or at least save you a few seconds in your presentation). The right picture can be very effective in helping you make a strong point or to explain something complicated in your presentation. However, some disciplines are more open to using pictures in presentations than others; check with your instructor about their preference if you aren't sure.
2. Do not use unnecessary images that may clutter the slide.
3. Don't overlay text on a picture unless you are absolutely sure that it is readable from the back of the room. If the contrast between the text and the image is not high enough, your audience won't be able to read it.
4. Avoid busy graphics and clip art.

Proofread
1. Check your slides for spelling errors and faulty transitions.

Citations and References
One of the important ways that scholarly presentations differ from other presentations, including those you may have done in high school, is that all the claims you make must be cited. Determining what must be cited is similar to the ways you determine what to cite in an essay. However, there are a few more options for satisfying this requirement than in your academic papers. For example, you may use formal written citations with each claim that you make on a slide, similar to how you would cite in an essay. Alternatively, you could limit discussions about a reference's claims to a slide. Thus, your citation would be part of the title and all information on that slide can be assumed to be from that reference. Some skillful presenters can do their citations orally, thus eliminating the need to include citations on their slides. This is the riskiest way to cite, though, because there is always a chance you will forget to cite the authors during the presentation, thereby plagiarizing the information. Whichever approach to citing you use, you must still include a slide with your list of references at the end of the presentation. See Chapter 4 for how to present references in APA style.

DELIVERING YOUR PRESENTATION

Before

It is very important for you to have your presentation ready well before the date of your presentation. As a busy student with many competing assignments, this may be difficult to do. However, by taking the time to plan ahead, you'll reduce the anxiety that comes with feeling unprepared. The better you prepare for your talk, the better it will go.

Scripts and Cue Cards

In preparing for a presentation, some people will decide to write their presentation out in full, as one would write an essay. Some people prefer to simply create an outline of their presentation, sometimes placing this outline on cue cards for study and rehearsal. There are advantages and challenges to both approaches and the effectiveness of each is often little more than a matter of personal preference and available time. However, if you do write a formal script for your presentation, remember that a spoken presentation is structured in a different way from a written essay. Your presentation should also be written in a somewhat less formal voice than the one you typically use for written essays. Thus, if you write a typical essay as a script for your presentation, you will have to make some important adjustments in style and structure. As a general rule, it takes about two minutes to read aloud a 250-word page of text. Keep this in mind as you are writing your script.

Once you have a script, there are important questions about how can you use it. Can you simply stand at the front and read your script? Is it preferable to use the script to practise and only use lecture notes when you are presenting? Is it better to use no notes at all? The acceptance of reading scripts while presenting varies considerably between disciplines, sub-disciplines, and instructors. If you are required to present as part of a course, it is important to find out what your instructor prefers or requires. You should also get to know what is considered to be acceptable in your discipline and sub-discipline. Just like instructors' preferences, these can vary considerably. For example, in cultural geography, it is often acceptable to read a script verbatim, as one might read an essay. However, in many other sub-disciplines of geography, the use of any kind of script, including lecture notes or cue cards, is generally frowned upon. Psychology is the same: Presenters do not read from scripts. In general, if there is any doubt about the acceptability of scripts during a presentation, it is best to assume that they are not acceptable.

Think about the talks and lectures you have attended. Did the speaker read from a script or use no notes at all or something in between? Often a speaker comes across as more engaging when they do not appear to be reading from a script—think about how awkward some of the presenters at awards ceremonies seem when they are obviously reading from a teleprompter. Giving a talk while appearing to be speaking off the cuff is challenging, and requires practice (see below), but it's a skill worth aiming for.

Practice, Practice, Practice!

Once you have completed your presentation, the most important thing to do is rehearse it. It is easy to imagine that, having done all of this preparation work, the words will come naturally to you on the "big day." We can tell you from experience that this is rarely the case. Even experienced presenters need to practise before getting in front of an audience. People who can get up and speak clearly, coherently, and confidently about a topic without first practising it are few and far between. We recommend that you rehearse your presentation, out loud, *at least ten times*, and at least one of those times should be in front of another person. This may not be realistic if you are giving an hour-long seminar, but if you are giving a talk that is anywhere between five and fifteen minutes long, finding the time to practise it ten times should not be a problem.

Practice has a number of benefits. The first time you give your presentation out loud (whether it's to yourself, your dog, or another human), you will most likely notice parts that either don't flow right or don't make sense. It's easier to detect these problems when you are speaking than when you are reading. Also, without a great deal of practice, it is easy to forget important parts of your presentation, speak too fast or too slow, or spend the entire presentation talking into your script or the screen. Rehearsal, and lots of it, can help you to learn your presentation until you know it by heart, so that you aren't depending on your notes. In addition, practising your presentation in front of others gives you the opportunity to get feedback on it. You may be an expert on your topic, but your presentation should be clear and interesting enough to make sense to a non-expert. Your practice audience will be able to let you know if any of it is unclear. Finally, practice will let you know how long your presentation is, so you can add to it or cut it to make sure it is as close as possible to the amount of time you have been given.

When you practice, be sure to use your presentation slides and any presentation aides you plan to use on the day of the presentation. This will help you make sure all your transitions work well, and that you know which slide is coming up next.

Check the Venue

Unless you are very familiar with the room in which you will be presenting, try to go there before the day of your presentation. Check out what equipment is available. You may have to obtain permission to check this, so make sure you follow the required procedures. If any of the equipment or software you will need for your presentation is unavailable or inoperative, make arrangements for replacements or backups. Obtaining replacement equipment can sometimes take time, so make sure you have done this check at least a week before the date of your presentation. While you are visiting this place, see what it is like to stand in the location from which you will be presenting. Even a lecture room that you are in almost every day can seem strange and a little intimidating from the front. Try speaking as if you are giving a presentation. Have a friend see if they can hear you from the back of the room. All of this can provide important information to you for your presentation.

Look after Yourself

This is one of those things that should seem self-evident, but we can't stress it enough. When we are busy or stressed, we tend to ignore the lessons we learned about healthy living. Simple things like getting enough sleep the night before your presentation, eating healthy, and trying some stress-reduction techniques like yoga, exercise, or mindfulness meditation can go a long way toward helping you perform your best when you give your presentation.

During

As you wait to begin your presentation, there are a few things to remember. One of these is that nervousness while doing public speaking is almost universal; most of your colleagues and almost everyone in your audience share your fears about presenting. While it may not be readily apparent, your classmates and your instructor are silently rooting for you to succeed. Find confidence in the knowledge that they are on your side. Considering that you are about to do something you do not normally do, it would be surprising if you weren't a bit nervous. And keep in mind that you are in good company. Some pretty famous people have experienced what you are experiencing now, including Barbra Streisand, Thomas Jefferson, and even Mahatma Ghandi, all of whom admitted to suffering from performance anxiety to some degree (Stossel, 2014).

As you begin your presentation, here are a few strategies to make your talk more effective.

Speak Loud and Clear

Project your voice so that people in the back row can hear you. This is easy to remember at the start of your presentation but many people's voices become softer and harder to hear as the presentation progresses. With practice and experience, though, you will be able to project your voice to the back of the room for hours without a break.

Look at the Audience

Making eye contact is a good way to connect with your audience. Try to remember to scan the room with your eyes rather than just look at one person. It can be very comforting to fix your eyes on a familiar person who is sitting near the front of the room and speak almost entirely to them; however, by doing this, you may "lose" the rest of the audience and, perhaps, reduce the effectiveness of your presentation. By scanning your eyes around the room, you can not only engage all of the audience with your eyes, you'll also be able to spot any signs of confusion that signal the need for further explanation. Do not turn your back to the audience or read from your slides.

Be Enthusiastic

Although it is sometimes difficult to appear enthusiastic while you are nervous, try to appear and sound interested in your topic. If you do not seem interested in your presentation, it will be difficult to get the audience interested.

Watch Your Body Language

Doing a presentation, even a scholarly presentation, has many similarities to acting. While you may read the lines and seem convincing in your part by simply standing in one place, by introducing some movement, you can seem much more "natural." There is a fine line here: You don't want to flap your arms around like you are about to fly away or appear to be pacing menacingly around the room. For some people, the most movement they feel comfortable doing during a presentation is simple hand gestures. Others are comfortable moving around the room. With experience, though, this will be just as natural as the gestures you make when talking to your friends.

Try to Avoid Nervous Habits

Many of us exhibit unconscious nervous "twitches," such as shaking a leg, fiddling with a pen, or excessive use of the word "um" while talking. It may be helpful to take a video of yourself while you are practising to get a sense of what your nervous habits are. When you are aware of them, you will have much more control over them.

Remember to Breathe

No matter what happens, keep breathing. In the overall scheme of things, this presentation is pretty small, so try to keep some perspective. Try to take it all in stride, no matter what happens.

After

After you have finished your presentation, you may be tempted to focus on all the things that went wrong. Even if you have followed all of the hints in this chapter, it is almost guaranteed that you will be able to think of things you could have done better. This is not surprising: No presentation ever goes perfectly. There is certainly a benefit to identifying what went wrong so you can try to improve your next presentation. However, many of the problems encountered by inexperienced speakers will be resolved with more practice. Therefore, rather than focusing on those things that didn't work as well as you hoped, it is just as useful—and much more uplifting—to identify all the things that worked well. Therefore, after the fear and excitement of the presentation has passed, take a moment and identify five things in your presentation that went well. Write them down. Keep the list. Over time, see how many more things you can add to your list of presentation accomplishments.

BEING A GOOD AUDIENCE MEMBER

If you have a class in which you are required to give a presentation, chances are you'll be listening to a lot of presentations too. You may even have the opportunity (or be required) to give feedback and/or ask questions after the presentation. Just like there are things you can do to make sure that your own presentation goes well, there are also things you can do to help other people's presentations go well. Much of our advice here can be summed up in one maxim: Put yourself in the speaker's shoes. Treat them in the same way you would like to be treated if you were giving a presentation.

During the Presentation

If you have ever given a presentation before, you know how much of an impact the audience can have on how you feel. Standing before a sea of smiling, encouraging faces is much nicer than seeing a bunch of scowling, bored faces. You may feel grumpy or bored or tired, but try not to show it. Watch your body language: Try not to cross your arms, as it tends to make you look defensive even if that isn't how you are feeling. Put your phone away, avoid talking to your neighbour, and pay attention to the speaker. Not only might you learn something interesting, but you might also be asked to provide feedback on their talk or think up questions for them.

Asking Questions

Sometimes you'll have the opportunity to ask questions after a presentation. This can be difficult, especially if you are shy, you tend to process information slowly, or you just didn't understand what the presentation was about. We encourage you to try it. The speaker will probably appreciate it (as long as it's a fair question), and it can actually be fun to have an intellectual conversation with your peers. While there are any number of good questions to ask (e.g., you could ask for clarification on a particular issue, or you could ask if they know of any research on a particular topic related to their talk), there are a few approaches to avoid. Do not, for example, publicly point out mistakes in their talk, especially if they are inexperienced, nervous, or being graded on their presentation. Leave it to the instructor to correct them. Also, avoid putting them on the spot. It's okay to ask challenging questions, but not if you're only doing it to show how smart you are. Finally, be nice. That could (and most likely will) be you up there soon!

Giving Feedback

Often, an instructor will ask you to provide feedback to your peers on their presentations. This is a good learning experience for them and also for you. Being able to evaluate the presentation skills of others will help you think more critically about your own skills. Sometimes you will be asked just to say what you liked most and what you felt could have been improved. No matter how weak a presentation is, there is always something to like about it or how it was presented. Challenge yourself to find something that you liked; never leave this question blank. Again, imagine how you would feel if you received feedback like this. It's also okay to point out flaws, as long as they are specific and helpful. Feedback is meant to be instructive for the receiver so that they can improve, so give them some tips on how. For instance, "The presentation was boring" is not a helpful comment. "I felt the presentation took a bit too long to get to the main point" is more helpful. Regardless of

Table 7.1: Sample Presentation Grading Rubric

Your instructor may or may not use a rubric like this to evaluate your presentation. Nevertheless, it's a good guide to follow. As you are practicing your presentation, try grading yourself on these items. How did you do?

	Needs improve- ment	Satis- factory	Good
First Impressions			
Speaker arrived on time			
Speaker introduced self to audience			
Introduction			
Topic made clear			
Purpose of the presentation clear			
Presented an outline or agenda			
All terms were defined (if necessary)			
Main Part of Presentation			
Main points stated clearly			
Provided sufficient information and detail			
Did not try to cover too much			
Discussion flowed logically			
All sources were cited properly			
Conclusion			
Ending of presentation signalled adequately			
Main points summarized adequately			
Final message clear and easy to remember			
Delivery			
Spoke clearly and audibly			
Talk given with enthusiasm and engagement			
Did not rely too much on notes			
Looked at audience			
Kept to time limit			
Kept a good pace (not too rushed or too slow)			

Continued

Answered questions well			
Visual Aids			
Clear and visually appealing			
Clearly visible to entire audience			
A good amount of text on slides			
Effective use of graphics on slides			
No typos or grammatical errors			
Comments			

whether your feedback is anonymous or not, take care with what you say. If you would feel uncomfortable attaching your name to a comment, reconsider making that comment.

IN CONCLUSION

Keep in mind that every time you give a presentation, it will get easier. Not only will this help you in your other courses, but you are also developing valuable skills for your life. These skills are transferrable to job interviews, work presentations, and wedding toasts. The more effort you put into it, the better (and more marketable) your skills will be.

REVIEW IT

1. Is beginning your presentation with a joke a good idea? Why or why not?
2. If you are giving a 40-minute presentation, what proportion of your time should you spend on your introduction? Your main section? Your conclusion?
3. You have written a 15-page paper and are asked to give a five-minute talk on it. Should you try to say a little bit about everything you covered in your paper, or just focus on a few interesting things?
4. Should you read from a script during your presentation? Why or why not?
5. Why is practising your presentation beforehand so important?

6. Is it better to use flashy, entertaining slides with your presentation or simple, clear slides?

APPLY IT

There are lots of examples of inspiring public speakers: Martin Luther King, Jr., Winston Churchill, and Emma Goldman, for example. Below are two of the most-watched TED talks (with both having over 10 million views), one by novelist Chimamanda Ngozi Adichie and one by global health expert Hans Rosling. What do you think makes them such popular talks? Do they follow the tips used in this chapter?

Chimamanda Ngozi Adichie (novelist): The danger of a single story.
https://www.ted.com/talks/chimamanda_adichie_the_danger_of_a_
single_story

Hans Rosling (global health expert): The best stats you've ever seen.
https://www.ted.com/talks/hans_rosling_shows_the_best_stats_
you_ve_ever_seen

8 The Literature Review: Writing about Social Science Research

In our experience, one of the first things students say when they realize they have to write a literature review is, "What's a literature review?" Don't worry; we're here to help. It's likely that your experience with writing assignments has mainly been with traditional essays, in which you make a thesis statement and then spend the rest of the essay explaining and supporting it. Literature reviews are a bit different. Although many of the elements and strategies are the same (for example, clear and concise writing, properly citing sources, avoiding plagiarism, and following a logical structure), literature reviews are less about sharing your personal opinion or your ability to make a rational argument and more about successfully summarizing and synthesizing the existing research on a topic and presenting it in a clear, condensed report.

If you've been reading the chapters before this one (and hopefully you have), you may have noticed that this book is set up to help you gradually build the skills required to write a literature review. From understanding social science research to finding it, evaluating it, and using APA style to reference it, you've already done a lot of the work in creating a literature review. In this chapter, we're going to show you how to put it all together so you can show off all your great skills.

LEARNING OBJECTIVES

1. Understand the purpose of a literature review
2. Learn the steps in writing a literature review
3. Practise synthesizing sources

4. Learn techniques for writing a literature review
5. Learn the proper way to use sources, including paraphrasing, quoting, and citation

THE LITERATURE REVIEW

What Is a Literature Review?

If you've ever done a literature search on a research topic, you will probably have noticed that there's a lot of research out there. Each journal article you find will address one small part of a larger topic, but no single article will cover the entire topic. Remember that social science knowledge is built in small increments, and each research study builds on the research that came before it. That's great, but it means that there may be a huge number of individual research articles on a particular topic, each contributing one small piece to a larger puzzle. Even for fairly specific or niche topics, this could result in a lot of background reading before you can get a sense of what's going on in that field of study. Let's say, for example, you are interested in learning more about the use of pets to help people with psychiatric and emotional problems. This is a fairly narrow topic, and not widely studied compared to some topics in social science. Using Google Scholar, do a search for "therapy pets" (go ahead; we'll wait).

Wow, that's a lot of results! Each of those studies addresses one smaller subtopic within the area of therapy pets. For example, one article is about the use of pets with children who are in the hospital, another one is about pets as family members, and another one is about using pets as companions for people with dementia. If you wanted to know, generally, what kinds of things therapy pets are used for, and whether they are effective in helping promote mental wellness, would you want to read all of those articles? Wouldn't it be easier if there were something that summarized and synthesized all of those research findings into one comprehensive overview? Fortunately, there is: It's called a literature review.

Literature reviews are very common in the social sciences. Essentially, a **literature review** is an overview of what is known about a particular topic. It synthesizes the published research on a topic, identifying themes, common findings, areas where the research findings do not agree, and any gaps in the research (i.e., unanswered questions). It does the work of providing background information and a summary of key research findings on a given topic so you don't have to go back and read each individual research study. As Baumeister and Leary (1997) put it, "literature reviews serve a scientific field by providing a much-needed bridge between the vast and scattered assortment of articles on a topic and the reader who does not have time or resources to track them down" (p. 311).

Why Write a Literature Review?

If you are working toward a social science degree, you'll probably have to write a literature review at some point. In fact, if you're reading this chapter, chances are your instructor has assigned a literature review as a requirement of your course. Why the focus on a literature review and not a traditional essay? Writing a literature review allows you to demonstrate your credibility as a social scientist. Overall, it shows the breadth and depth of knowledge you have about a topic. It also shows that you have very specific skills that are highly valued in the social sciences (and beyond):

- the ability to ask a research question,
- the ability to find and critically assess research findings,
- the ability to synthesize research findings into a coherent and cohesive report, and
- the ability to use the language and style of social science (e.g., APA style).

Even if you aren't a social science student, you still need to understand social science research. Maybe you'll use social science research to supplement an essay you are writing for another course, or maybe you'll use it to gain a better understanding of something in which you have a general interest. You might even need to dig into social science research to assess some wacky claim made about something you care about. By writing a literature review, you will become much better at interpreting and assessing social science literature.

STEPS IN WRITING A LITERATURE REVIEW

As we mentioned at the beginning of this chapter, if you've been reading the chapters of this book in order, you will already be familiar with (and hopefully practised at) the early stages of writing a literature review. Steps 1 and 2 are covered in Chapter 3, and Step 3 is covered in Chapter 5. As you can see, the actual writing part comes late in the process; much of the hard work is done upfront.

Steps in Writing a Literature Review

1. **Ask a question.** Choose a topic and narrow it down to an answerable question.
2. **Conduct a literature search.** Find scholarly research related to your topic.
3. **Evaluate the literature.** Critically assess the research you found.
4. **Synthesize the literature.** Organize the research into themes and subthemes.
5. **Write.** Write a draft of the literature review.
6. **Rewrite.** Revise, edit, and proofread your literature review.

Even though we've presented it as a series of steps, it's more of an iterative process, meaning that you might return to previous steps at any time in the process. For example, once you have thought about a question, you will probably do a quick literature search to find out how much research there is on that question. If there's too much research, you might need to narrow down your question and make it more specific. Conversely, if there's not enough research, you might need to broaden your question. Later, you may think you have completed your search of the relevant literature, but then something you read suggests a new avenue of exploration that you hadn't thought of, sending you back to your literature search. Be prepared to do this multiple times. The process probably looks more like what's presented in Figure 8.1.

We're going to assume that if you have made it as far as this chapter, you have already completed Steps 1 through 3, and we'll jump in at Step 4.

Synthesizing the Literature

So, you've got a stack of articles. Now what? Hopefully your literature search was successful, and you have a number of good research articles you can use for your literature review. You may have been instructed to use a specific number of sources, or a minimum or maximum number, in your literature review. Don't be too tied to this number at this stage, though. If you've been asked to review the research on a topic, you will likely find more sources than

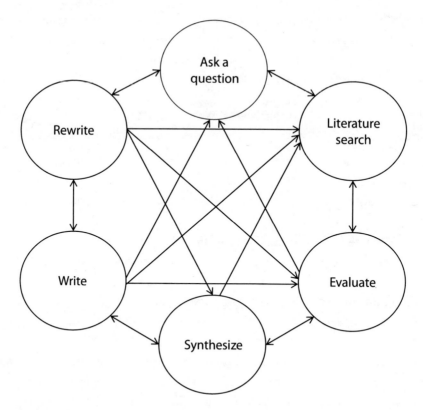

Figure 8.1: Steps in Writing a Literature Review

you think you will use. Part of the process is choosing the best articles to include in your review, and if you stop researching as soon as you have your minimum number of articles, you may miss a really great one. Plus, as you are synthesizing the literature that you found, you may realize that some of it doesn't really fit with the rest. It's okay, and quite common, at this point to toss out an article that you found and replace it with another one. So it's good to have some backups.

A literature review is not simply a summation of a bunch of research articles. It should weave all of the research together into core themes, telling an interesting and hopefully original story about the research topic. **Synthesizing** your research involves organizing it into coherent themes and subthemes. This process is different from summarizing the research because you are not just restating the findings of each research article. Instead, you are looking for ways that the findings fit together to tell a new, cohesive story. For example, let's say you are writing a literature review on why people use Facebook; specifically, you want to look at how people's personalities might be related to the type of posts they make on Facebook. Take a look at the examples below. They show the differences between summarizing and synthesizing.

Summarizing

> Marshall, Lefringhausen, and Ferenczi (2015) did a study of personality and how people use Facebook, and found that extraverts tended to post about their social lives, conscientious people tended to post about their children, people with low self-esteem tended to post about their romantic relationships, and people high in narcissism tended to post about their accomplishments. Seidman (2013) did a study of the Big Five personality traits and Facebook use, and found differences between the five traits. Extraverts tended to use Facebook more frequently than other personality types, and people high in neuroticism or narcissism were more likely to use Facebook for self-presentation purposes. Those high in conscientiousness tended to be more cautious in their use of Facebook.

Synthesizing

> Research has shown that personality is related to Facebook usage (e.g., Marshall, Lefringhausen, & Ferenczi, 2015; Seidman, 2013). For example, extraversion has been found to be related to posting more frequently (Seidman, 2013) and to posting about one's social life (Marshall et al., 2015). Conscientiousness has been linked with more cautious use of Facebook (Seidman, 2013) and posting about one's children (Marshall et al., 2015). Although for most people presentation of the self in a positive way appears to be an underlying motive for posting personal information on Facebook, the personality trait of neuroticism best predicts self-presentation-related posts (Marshall et al., 2015; Seidman, 2013).

Probably one of the biggest mistakes students make in writing literature reviews is to summarize rather than synthesize. When you synthesize, you are making connections between different research articles. You are showing that you have thought about the research at a higher level, and can make suggestions about how it all fits together. A good literature review will add to what we know about a topic because it organizes possibly disparate findings into one cohesive report on the current state of the literature.

Here are some tips for how to organize your sources so that you can effectively synthesize the findings.

1. Read all your sources carefully, and either make notes on or highlight the key findings. We strongly advise against cutting and pasting text directly from electronic sources into your notes, as it can lead to inadvertent plagiarism. Try not to highlight too much—just the important findings.

2. Think about how each source relates to your topic/research question. It might help to draw this out, organize it into a table, or use index cards or some other system that works for you. You may have already thought about how the sources fit with your topic or you wouldn't have selected this source for your literature review, so this step shouldn't be too difficult.

3. Think about whether the research findings fall into themes. You can use these themes as an organizing structure in your literature review. A single source could inform more than one of your themes. If you don't see distinct subgroups, think about whether your sources can be organized by something other than content themes; maybe they can be grouped by the methodology they use, their theoretical perspective, or demographic characteristics of the participants they studied.

    As you read through your articles, either as you find them or once you have a number of them, think about the key concepts or themes that seem to arise about your topic. For example, if you were researching therapy pets, you would find that one theme of the literature is the different groups of people that have benefited from using therapy pets. Another theme might be the kind of pet used. Another theme might be the specific benefits of therapy pets (e.g., emotional, physical).

4. Create a table to keep track of your themes and which of your articles address each of these themes. One article may address more than one theme, so this strategy is more effective than just dividing your articles into piles or folders because it lets you list one particular article under different concepts. Here's what your table might look like:

Table 8.1: Sample Summary Table of Themes and Sources

Key concepts/themes	Article
Who uses therapy pets	Incarcerated women (Walsh & Mertin, 1994)
	Hospitalized children (Kaminski, Pellino, & Wish, 2002)
	People with dementia (Stasi et al., 2004; Walsh, Mertin, Verlander, & Pollard, 1995)
	Undergraduates (Daltry & Mehr, 2015)
Types of pets used	Dogs (Daltry & Mehr, 2015; Walsh & Mertin, 1994; Walsh et al., 1995)
	Cats (Greer, Pustay, Zaun, & Coppens, 2001; Stasi et al., 2002)
Effectiveness of therapy pets	Physical (Creagan, Bauer, Thomley, & Borg, 2015; Kaminski et al., 2002)
	Emotional (Creagan, Bauer, Thomley, & Borg, 2015; Daltry & Mehr, 2015; Kaminski et al., 2002; Walsh et al., 1995)

If you were writing a comprehensive literature review on everything that is known about therapy pets, you would keep going with this list until you had covered all of the articles you could find. A number of themes would come up.

If you have been tasked with writing a shorter literature review, you will need to narrow down your topic quite a bit. It might make sense, depending on your topic, to choose one key concept or theme and break that down into subthemes. For example, perhaps you discovered that there is quite a bit of literature on the use of therapy pets with seniors. You would then start this process over, identifying the key concepts and themes within the articles focusing on therapy pets with seniors.

Table 8.2: More Focused Summary Table of Themes and Sources

Key concepts/themes	Article
Types of pets that are used	Dogs (Walsh et al., 1995)
	Cats (Greer et al., 2001; Stasi et al., 2002)

Continued

Reasons why therapy pets are used	Loneliness (Banks & Banks, 2002)
	Physical benefits (Roth, 2000)
	Psychological benefits (Roth, 2000; Walsh et al., 1995)

Writing Your Literature Review

Once you have identified your key themes, you can start thinking about how you will present the information you have found. Here are some things to keep in mind as you are writing your literature review.

Audience and Voice

As with any type of writing you do, it's important to keep your intended audience in mind. Your audience, if you are writing a literature review as part of a course requirement, will be the person marking it. More broadly, however, literature reviews are most often read by scholars who are interested in learning more about the research on a particular topic. Your language should be clear and relatively formal. Now, by "formal," we do not mean "use as many big and complicated words as you can"; we mean you should write clearly and concisely, and avoid slang or colloquial or casual language.

One thing that can be tricky is knowing which terms need to be defined. You can assume that your audience has a basic understanding of the area of research you are discussing, but you should still define important terms related to your topic. Be sure to include sources for those definitions. Whenever possible, get your definitions from the actual research articles rather than from a dictionary, because researchers often have very specific ways of defining the terms they are studying. For example,

> Animal-assisted therapy is defined as "a goal-directed intervention in which an animal that meets specific criteria is an integral part of the treatment process. AAT is directed and/or delivered by a health/human service professional with specialized expertise and within the scope of practice of his/her profession" (Kruger & Serpell, 2006, p. 23).

Don't refer to yourself (in other words, don't use "I"). Keep in mind that the literature review is not a statement of your opinion; it is a review and synthesis of the literature. Rather than talking about yourself, you should be talking about the research that has been done.

Structure

Even if your literature review is short, it is important to make sure it has a logical, cohesive structure. Don't make your reader work too hard to figure out what you are saying—you don't want to make the person grading your paper cranky! Here are some structural issues to keep in mind while writing your literature review.

- Have a strong introduction. By the end of the first paragraph, the reader should know what your topic is and why it is important. In the example below, notice how it only takes three sentences to present what the issue is (with supporting evidence) and why it is important and worthy of study. Your introductory paragraph can be longer than this, of course, but it should be direct enough to engage your reader right away.

The population in Canada is getting older (Statistics Canada, 2018b). As they age, many individuals experience cognitive decline, increased physical decline, and even loneliness (Banks & Banks, 2002). Thus, finding strategies to improve both the physical and emotional quality of life for seniors is becoming increasingly important.

- Use subheadings. If it makes sense for your topic, use subheadings to separate different sections of your literature review. Subheadings are especially useful if you are speaking about different themes or concepts.
- Conclude on a strong note. Especially if your page limit is relatively small for your literature review assignment, you don't want to spend time at the end restating what you have already said. Your conclusion should not simply repeat the main findings of the studies you found; it should bring them all together to express something in a new way or with a new perspective. The reader should be left with a good understanding of your topic, and also an appreciation for how important your topic is.

Critical Assessment

Remember that the task of the literature review is not just to summarize the existing literature; it should also provide a critical assessment of that literature. This isn't as difficult as it may sound. If you have synthesized the articles well, you should be able to find something that came out of that synthesis. It may be that one area has not been studied enough (in other words, there are "gaps" in the literature); or it may be that two or more studies give conflicting results. You may want to go back and review Chapter 5, which covers how to critically evaluate social science research.

There isn't one correct way to critically assess the literature. You can do it throughout your literature review, perhaps at the end of each subsection. For example, if you have reviewed different types of therapy pets and presented each type of animal and their effectiveness as a separate subsection, you might end each subsection with an analysis of whether the existing literature has adequately demonstrated the benefits of that particular animal as a therapy pet. At the end of your paper, you would have a concluding paragraph that sums up the points you made at the end of each subsection, ending with an evaluation of which therapy pets might be most beneficial for various situations.

This may not work, depending on how you have set up your paper. Another strategy is to present the literature, and then do a critical assessment of it all at once near the end of your paper. You would still synthesize the research findings throughout your paper (i.e., don't just present one study after another), but you would leave your analysis of the research until after you have presented it all.

No one is expecting you to come up with the one missing link that will answer *all* the questions about your topic. Your instructor will just want to know that you have understood the material and are able to think critically about it.

Revising and Editing Your Literature Review

The final step in writing a literature review is one of the most important: revise, edit, and proofread. Ultimately, the goal of the literature review is to inform your readers, but it can't do that if they can't understand what you've written. Very few people can write an amazing, clear, brilliant paper in one draft. That's why going back over what you have written to revise and edit it is so important. Machi and McEvoy (2009) suggest that the first draft of a paper should be considered "writing to understand," while the revised and edited version is "writing to be understood." In other words, in your first draft, you are writing what you know, getting your ideas onto the paper. In order for others to understand your ideas, however, you must polish up your writing so that it is clear.

Unfortunately, this step often gets skipped when you are finishing your paper the night before it is due. When you finish your paper at 4 am and it's due at 10 am, and you still need to get a bit of sleep before class, there isn't time for you to put your paper aside, then pick it up and go through it with a clear mind to identify sections that don't make sense or that could be worded better. So, our best piece of advice here is to start your paper early, and give yourself enough time to revise and edit it once you are finished. A polished paper will almost always get you a better grade than one you wrote in a panic the night before.

When you are reviewing your paper, put yourself in your reader's place. Will they understand what you meant? Does the structure of your paper make sense? Is it logical? Once you feel that the overall structure is good, go back over your sentences. Are they complete sentences? Are they clear? One way to do this is to read the paper aloud as you are reviewing it. It may feel a bit silly, but many people find that it helps them take the reader's perspective. Even better, get a roommate or friend to read it out loud so you hear it in someone else's voice. This will catch problems that your eye is used to skipping over. Finally, check your spelling and grammar. Your software can help with this (although it's not perfect), which is why instructors will not be happy to find typos in your paper.

Don't be afraid to ask for help at this stage. It's often difficult to identify weaknesses in our own writing. Just like all parents think their kids are perfect, you may think your literature review is the most brilliant thing ever written. It may be, but it doesn't hurt to get a second opinion. Make an appointment at the writing centre to get feedback, or ask someone you trust, like a parent or friend, to read it over for you. Just make sure they're reading for clarity, not changing your ideas or adding insights.

USING YOUR SOURCES

One of the key features of a literature review is that you are writing about the work done by others, and so your sources are an important part of your paper. By now you have assembled a pile of good sources, critically assessed them, and thought about how they fit together. This section explains how to actually incorporate them in your paper. You may want to review Chapter 4 on APA style first, because this is where all that information will come in handy. As you are integrating your sources into your literature review, you want to ensure that you are citing them properly. This is an important part of communicating within the social sciences: giving credit where credit is due. You can choose to reproduce the author's original language exactly (quotation) or to rephrase the idea using your own language (paraphrase). Using consistent and correct citation methods not only helps your readers understand where your information came from but it also protects you from inadvertently presenting the ideas of others as your own (also known as plagiarism).

Remember that you are telling a story with the information you have found and not simply summarizing each source separately. For this reason, you should weave your sources into your literature review. Here are some tips on how to do this effectively.

DO begin a paragraph with a statement that you can support with evidence from your sources.

> Therapy pets have been found to be effective in helping seniors deal with their loneliness (Banks & Banks, 2002).

DON'T begin a paragraph with the source, and then spend the paragraph talking about that one source.

> Banks and Banks (2002) did a study on how therapy pets can help seniors deal with their loneliness.

DO cite more than one source to back up your claims, if possible.

> The benefits of therapy pets for seniors have been shown to be both physical (Roth, 2000) and emotional (Roth, 2000; Walsh et al., 1995).

DON'T cite too many sources at once. There is no set rule about how many is "too many," and it varies from discipline to discipline. Keep an eye on how scholars in your discipline handle this aspect of their writing to get a feel for what's appropriate in your field.

> The benefits of therapy pets for seniors have been shown to be both physical (Greer et al., 2001; Roth, 2000) and emotional (Churchill, Safaoui, McCabe, & Baun, 1999; Cohen-Mansfield, 1986; Eachus, 2001; Fick, 1993; Kongable, Buckwalter, & Stolley, 1989; Roth, 2000; Walsh et al., 1995).

DO provide a source if you are making a claim about the relevance, recent focus on, or timeliness of a topic.

With the baby boom generation approaching their retirement years, it is estimated that the number of seniors living in Canada will grow significantly over the coming years (Bohnert, Chagnon, & Dion, 2015).

DON'T make vague claims without supporting evidence.

With an increasingly large aging population, it is important to find new ways to combat loneliness in the elderly.

To Quote or Not to Quote?

In our experience, there are a number of reasons why students tend to use quotations in their papers:

1. They do not understand the point well enough to put it into their own words.
2. They do not feel they can phrase the point better than the original writer.
3. They are afraid of inadvertently plagiarizing, so they quote and cite everything.
4. They believe the more they quote, the less original content they will have to write.

None of these are good reasons to use quotations. First, if you don't understand the point an author is making well enough to rephrase it, then you need to find a way to understand the point better. Maybe you can look at another source that makes a similar point, or maybe you can ask your instructor, a writing consultant, a librarian, or even a friend for help. The better you understand the point, the more effectively you will be able write about it. If you don't understand it, it will likely be apparent to the person grading your paper.

Second, students often feel that they cannot rephrase something better than the original author. This may be true (to be fair, the author is an expert on the topic, and you are at the learning stage), but keep in mind that the person grading your paper will understand this challenge. In addition, try not to simply rephrase what an author has said. Try to capture the essence of their point rather than constructing a similar sentence with different words. You may be surprised at how well you can rephrase it if you spend some time working on it, and as an added bonus we bet you'll understand it better too.

Third, the fear of being caught plagiarizing can cause students to go overboard and just quote everything. While we understand this fear, it can work against you. By quoting everything, you may protect yourself from committing academic misconduct, but you probably will not get a very good grade on your paper. You will have demonstrated that you know how to cite properly, but you will not have demonstrated that you can write coherently on a topic or that you even understand what you are writing about, because you haven't used your own words. By understanding how to properly use sources without plagiarizing, you can feel more confident in your ability to write in your own words.

Fourth, sometimes quotes are used to "pad" an essay, to make it longer. You may feel that the more quotes you use, especially block quotes that take up a lot of space in an essay, the less you have to actually write. Just like using larger fonts or margins, the person marking your paper has seen this kind of thing before, and it won't work. Remember that you are being graded on how well you can communicate about social science research, and if your literature review consists mainly of other people's words, you won't have shown that you can actually do this.

We recommend that you try not to use quotes at all in your literature review, unless your instructor specifically asks you to. Trust us; you'll get a better grade. Your writing will flow better, and you will come across as more knowledgeable about your topic. Now, having said this, there are instances where a quotation may be appropriate. When there is an accepted definition that everyone uses, it's okay to quote it, along with the original source (in other words, the person who actually created the definition, and not someone who quoted them). Also, when you are using specific technical terms, it's better to quote them than to try to rephrase them.

If you are going to quote something, do it properly. Anything that isn't your own words must be in quotation marks or styled as a block quote, and you must provide a source and page number. Refer to Chapter 4 to learn how to quote using APA style.

How to Paraphrase

Even though the bulk of your literature review will be your interpretation and synthesis of a number of sources, there will be times when you need to restate a point from one of your sources. Rather than quote, it's often better to rephrase the point in your own words. This is called **paraphrasing**. Note that paraphrasing does not mean replacing a few words of the original source; it means completely rewriting it, keeping the meaning and intent of the original, but using your own words.

Take a look at this sentence and the two attempts to paraphrase it. Can you see the difference?

Original source:

> AAT most commonly involves interaction between a client and a trained animal, facilitated by a human handler, with a therapeutic goal such as providing relaxation and pleasure, or incorporating activities into physical therapy or rehabilitation (e.g. brushing a dog with a stroke-affected limb). The therapeutic effect may depend on the interaction with the animal as well as with the handler. (Filan & Llewellyn-Jones, 2006, p. 598)

Effective paraphrase:

> Animal-assisted therapy (AAT), which may be practised for emotional benefits such as relaxation or for physical benefits such as increasing range of motion, typically involves a client, a trained animal, and a facilitator (Filan & Llewellyn-Jones, 2006).

Ineffective paraphrase:

> AAT most often involves interaction between a patient and an animal that is trained. The goals of the therapy include relaxation and pleasure or physical therapy or rehabilitation (Filan & Llewellyn-Jones, 2006).

The first attempt at paraphrasing is good because it effectively captures the intent and meaning of the original source but does not look or sound like the original. It paraphrases the idea rather than the sentences themselves. Good paraphrasing shows your "voice" rather than the voice of the source. In other words, as you develop your writing skills, you will also develop your own style of writing. When you paraphrase well, you use your own style rather than the style of the source.

Why is the second attempt at paraphrasing so ineffective? Even though it is not exactly the same as the original, it is very close. Too close. It copies too much of the original writer's sentence structure and simply plugs in similar words. Not only would this be considered a light form of plagiarism, but it doesn't read as well as the original. The original author likely spent time choosing the right words for that sentence. If you take out those carefully chosen words and substitute them with other words, you may be making the sentence less clear.

Good paraphrasing takes work, but it is worth it because it will ensure that you are not unintentionally plagiarizing the original work. Also, when you paraphrase properly, you show that you know what you are talking about, and an essay or paper that is written clearly in your own words will get you a better grade than one pieced together from other people's words.

Here is a handy guide for paraphrasing.

1. Read the original work, and then reread it until you really understand it.
2. Put the original work aside.
3. Make a "reverse outline" by writing down the key concepts of the original work in point form.
4. Using your own words, describe and elaborate on these key concepts.
5. Compare your work to the original source. Check for two things:
    a) Did you keep the original intent and meaning?
    b) Is your wording too similar to the original? If yes, then rewrite it.

The First Rule of Thesaurus Club

The first rule of thesaurus club: You don't talk about, discuss, mention, bring up, speak of, chat about, yak about, or have a dialogue about thesaurus club. In addition to being one of our favourite thesaurus jokes, this demonstrates the potential pitfalls of focusing too much on substituting words when you are paraphrasing. You might be tempted to use a thesaurus to find alternate words, either to make your wording different from the original, or to try to make your own writing sound more sophisticated. Although a thesaurus can be a useful tool in helping to find just the right word, it can also turn a logical, clear sentence into a ridiculous one. Look at what can happen to an innocent sentence when it is attacked by a rampaging thesaurus:

Original sentence: Social science is fun.

"Thesaurusized" sentence: Convivial science is frolicsome.

We're big fans of social science, but even we don't believe that it's actually frolicsome. Misguided use of a thesaurus can alter the meaning of a sentence, so use it with caution. In fact, we recommend trying not to use a thesaurus at all, especially when you are first drafting your paper. If, when you are editing your paper, you notice that you have used the same word over and over, a thesaurus may help you find a synonym, but try to think of an alternate word yourself before looking it up. Clear, simple writing is always better than complex, convoluted writing. The person grading your paper will know if you have tried to sound smarter by using big words, especially if you aren't using them properly. Never use a big word just for the sake of it; in most cases a small word will more effectively get your point across.

CITING YOUR SOURCES

Knowing What to Cite

Often students are unsure of exactly how much they need to cite. Usually it's obvious as to whether you need to cite a particular research article—if you are discussing it in your paper, cite it! However, there are some areas where the decision of whether to cite or not is not as clear. We discuss two of them below. Our general advice is that if you are in doubt, you should cite it. That being said, try not to go overboard with your citations. Just try to keep in mind why we cite in the first place: to give credit where credit is due. As long as you aren't taking credit for someone else's work in your paper, then you have no need to worry.

Common Knowledge

Often when students ask exactly how much they need to cite, the answer they get is that if the statement is not common knowledge, then it needs to be cited. But what is common knowledge? **Common knowledge** is information that people can reasonably be expected to know. For example, we all know that Canada is part of North America, that water freezes at 0°C, and that the sides of a square are equal in length.

Be careful not to mistake common knowledge with common opinion. Just because people may think it's true doesn't mean that it is. For example:

The sky is blue.

This is common knowledge. You don't need to provide a source for this.

Social networking sites like Facebook combat loneliness, making people feel more connected.

This may be a common opinion, but it is not common knowledge. In fact, it might not even be true. There is empirical evidence to suggest that social networking can make people feel more connected to each other (e.g., Deters & Mehl, 2013), but there is also evidence that it can actually make people feel more isolated (e.g., Morahan-Martin & Schumacher, 2003). If you're making a claim like this, you need to provide evidence. Just because it makes sense to you doesn't mean it's true.

You don't necessarily have to cite a scholarly journal article; sometimes you can back up a claim with statistics from Statistics Canada or a similar source. For example:

Crime rates in Canada have been steadily decreasing since 1991 (Statistics Canada, 2015).

Alcohol harm is a growing concern in Canada. In 2015–16, hospitals saw more people for alcohol-related incidents than for heart attacks (Canadian Institute for Health Information, 2017).

Citing Your Instructor

You may find that something your instructor said in class is relevant for your paper. Just because this information doesn't come from a printed source doesn't mean you don't have to provide a source. There are two ways you can incorporate this into your paper. First, you could try to find a printed source for what your instructor said (they tend not to just make stuff up, so there probably is a source somewhere). Second, you can cite the lecture or their lecture notes or slides, using APA style.

You would probably be less likely to run into this issue when you are writing a literature review because your focus will be on reviewing and synthesizing research findings on your topic, in which case you would cite that original research rather than what your instructor may have said about them. In your other courses, where the instructor may be lecturing on the topic you will be writing about, just be aware that lectures and slides are sources too, and if you do use them you need to cite them (and paraphrase them) properly.

If in doubt, cite it! Just remember that citing too much blocks the person grading your paper from seeing which ideas are your own. Use other scholars' work to help your own ideas shine!

A Note on Plagiarism

We talked about plagiarism, which is a type of academic misconduct, in Chapter 6, and provided some general strategies for acting with integrity when you are writing papers. Plagiarism means using the words or ideas of someone else without giving them credit. When writing your literature review, there are three ways that plagiarism can become an issue:

1. When you use the exact wording of the source without quotation marks or citation.
2. When you don't paraphrase effectively: You change a few words, but keep the same sentence structure without fresh expression. Or, you don't provide the citation.
3. When you use someone else's ideas and make no effort to give them credit in the sentence or in a citation.

Proper citation and practising the paraphrasing technique we discussed above will help you avoid inadvertently plagiarizing in your paper. Acting with integrity will help you avoid deliberately plagiarizing. Even if you feel that the work isn't your absolute best effort and you're tempted to plagiarize, just remember that any grade—*any* grade—is better than a zero and a mark on your transcript. And remember that your instructor likely uses software that can easily detect overlapping content between your paper and other sources (including other student papers). No professor wants to play "idea police." So when a professor feels the need to call in a student for a one-on-one conversation about plagiarism, it tends to be uncomfortable for everybody.

It's worth putting in the effort to submit original work. That way, you can feel good about yourself and the grades you get *because* you earned them.

Literature Review Checklist

Before you hand in your literature review, give it one final read to make sure you've covered all of the following:

Format/APA Style

- Double-spaced, one-inch margins, 12-point font
- Includes an APA-formatted title page
- All sources are cited properly using in-text citations (no titles, just author last name and date)
- If you have quoted, page numbers are included in the in-text citation
- All sources cited in the text are included in the references section

Using Sources

- Key terms are defined (preferably not with dictionary definitions)
- All claims are backed up with scholarly sources
- No paragraph is simply a summary of a single source
- Claims are supported by multiple sources, when appropriate
- Quotations are only used when absolutely necessary

Critical Assessment

- Avenues for future research are suggested
- "Gaps" in the literature are identified
- Inconsistencies between studies are identified, if any
- Methodological flaws are identified

General

- Length/number of pages matches that specified in the assignment instructions
- Correct number of sources has been used
- No typographical or grammatical errors

ONE MORE GREAT THING ABOUT LITERATURE REVIEWS

At the beginning of this chapter we gave you a number of reasons as to why being able to write a literature review is a useful skill. If you still aren't convinced, here's one more reason: It's a marketable skill. In other words, employers love people who have the skills that you have just worked on developing. Think about all the things you did to create your literature review: You developed a topic, searched for information on the topic, critically assessed that information, and then presented that research in an informative way. The box below breaks down those steps into transferrable skills you can use to impress potential employers. Don't underestimate the value of these skills. Also don't underestimate the number of organizations that actually create literature reviews (although they may call them reports). Often they do not have the time, skills, or resources to write their own reports. You can now fill that gap for them.

What You Are Actually Doing When You Write a Literature Review

These are some of the skills you develop and practice when you write a literature review. Don't underestimate the value of these skills to employers.

Research	Attention to detail
Time management	Accuracy
Meeting deadlines	Decision making
Critical thinking	Problem solving
Written communication	Creativity
Independent work	Digital/technological fluency
Data analysis	Analytic skills

REVIEW IT

1. How does a literature review differ from a traditional essay?
2. Who is the typical audience for a literature review? In other words, who reads them?
3. Explain, in your own words, the difference between synthesizing and summarizing.
4. Why is quoting large passages of text in your literature review not a good idea?

5. Describe the five steps listed in the chapter on how to paraphrase.

6. Machi and McEvoy (2009) suggest that the first draft of a paper should be considered "writing to understand," while the revised and edited version is "writing to be understood." Explain what this means, in your own words.

APPLY IT

1. Which of the following would be considered summarizing, and which would be considered synthesizing? Why?

> Johnson (2006) found that student use of online quizzes was associated with increase academic achievement. They studied students' use of optional quizzes and found that students who did the optional quizzes performed better in the course than those who did not do the optional quizzes. However, they conclude that this may be due to pre-existing motivational factors, in that students who choose to do extra work in a course are higher-achieving regardless of the quizzes. Derouza and Fleming (2003) found that online quizzes resulted in higher grades than paper-and-pencil quizzes, but suggest that this might be due to the immediate feedback in online quizzes.
>
> While online quizzes may be more convenient than pencil-and-paper quizzes, the issue of relative effect on student achievement is the subject of research interest and speculation. Derouza and Fleming (2003), for example, reported that students who took online practice tests academically outperformed students who took the same tests in pencil-and-paper format; immediate feedback may account for the learning advantage of students who use automated quizzes. Further, student attention may increase in response to the interface of online quizzes, which are typically more visually stimulating than pencil-and-paper formats (EdTech, 2005). Additionally, students may be more motivated to take online quizzes rather than pencil-and-paper quizzes because contemporary youth associate digital formats with recreation and leisure (Rotermann, 2001; Statistics Canada, 2004).

Source: Johnson, G. M. (2006). Optional online quizzes: College student use and relationship to achievement. *Canadian Journal of Learning and Technology/La revue canadienne de l'apprentissage et de la technologie, 32*(1).

2. Using the steps outlined in the chapter, paraphrase the information in the section on "One More Great Thing about Literature Reviews" at the end of this chapter.

9 The Numbers: Understanding Statistics in the Social Sciences

Of all the words in the English language, "statistics" is one that seems to strike fear into a disproportionately large number of people. Not sports fans or actuaries; they love statistics. But for the rest of us, when we hear the word "statistics" we may think of long formulas with symbols we have never seen before, or complicated proofs that make no sense to us. In other words, math. This chapter has two main purposes: to convince you that statistics is not math, and to help you learn how to understand the statistics you will come across in social science research. To be a smart consumer of quantitative social science research (i.e., research that attempts to quantify behaviour in order to better understand it), you don't need to be able to calculate statistics, but you do need to understand where the numbers come from and what they mean. Our focus will be on interpreting the numbers rather than working with complicated formulas. Don't be afraid. Embrace your inner geek, and join us on this "significant" journey (that's a statistics joke; unfortunately, that's about as funny as they get).

LEARNING OBJECTIVES

1. Understand the use of statistics in quantitative social science research studies
2. Be able to tell the difference between descriptive and inferential statistics
3. Learn how to understand when statistics are being used to misrepresent research findings

DESCRIPTIVE STATISTICS

Did you know that the average Canadian over the age of 15 drinks the equivalent of 8 litres of pure alcohol per year, compared to 8.9 litres for those in the United States and 11.5 litres for those in France (Organisation for Economic Co-operation and Development, 2016)? Or that approximately 23 percent of service calls for broken photocopiers during the holiday season are from people photocopying their butts at the office party (Haines, 2005)? See? Statistics are fun!

These fun facts are called **descriptive statistics**, in that they describe something using numbers. They tell us something about a group that we wouldn't necessarily know just by looking at it (and perhaps more than we want to know about what goes on at office parties). They are used in many different contexts. For example, the statistics used to describe the performance of a baseball player (e.g., batting average, home runs, runs batted in), which tell you something about how good the player is, or at least how good a season they are having, are descriptive statistics. So is your grade point average (GPA)—it describes how you performed in your courses.

You may also think of statistics as the odds of something happening or not happening. For example, researchers can look at your health habits, your family history, and your environment and make a very rough estimate of how long you will live. That type of statistics, in which the numbers are used to make predictions or inferences, is called **inferential statistics**. Social scientists use them to make predictions about whether the results they find in studies using a small group of people can be generalized to larger groups of people. More on that later.

You'll run across both types of statistics in social science research, so we're going to talk about them both here. We'll start with descriptive statistics. There are many different kinds of descriptive statistics, but we'll just cover the three most common types: measures of central tendency, measures of variability, and correlations. If you've taken a data management course or something like it in high school, some of the content in this section will be familiar to you. Even if you haven't, you probably already know more of this than you think.

Measures of Central Tendency

A simple way to summarize data is to use a **measure of central tendency**, which is a single number that best represents the group. If you are trying to express, say, how old you and your two closest friends are, you can probably do

Table 9.1: Hypothetical Data on Binge-Watching *Game of Thrones*

Participant number	Number of episodes watched
1	3
2	2
3	6
4	2
5	4
6	3
7	7
8	10
9	4
10	3

that by just listing their ages. However, often when we want to describe what a group is like on some variable, we're looking at a much larger group than three people. That's why having one number to describe the group is helpful.

Let's say that researchers wanted to know how many episodes of *Game of Thrones* people typically binge-watch in one sitting. Table 9.1 contains completely made-up, hypothetical numbers from ten participants. Below we describe three different measures of central tendency that will give the researchers information about how many episodes they can expect people to watch in one sitting.

Mean

The **mean** is the average of all the numbers in a group or sample. People often refer to it as the "average," but in official statistics language it's called the mean. There is math involved in calculating the mean, but it's pretty simple: You add up all the scores and then divide by the number of scores. Statisticians, not being content to use basic language that everyone understands, have a fancy formula for the mean. It looks like this:

$$M = \frac{\Sigma x}{N}$$

Don't let it scare you; it's completely harmless. Let's break it down:

M is for "mean." You'll see this in research articles—it's APA style. When researchers provide the mean of their sample, they will say something like "*M* = 3.24."

Σ is a Greek symbol used to refer to summation. It means to sum, or add, the numbers.

x refers to each score in your sample. If you have ten scores in your sample, then you have ten different values of *x*. Therefore, Σ*x* means to sum, or add, all the values of *x* (i.e., all the scores).

N refers to the number of scores in the group. That's the number you divide by once you have added up all your scores.

If we plug the numbers from the *Game of Thrones* data into the formula, we get:

$$M = \frac{\Sigma x}{N}$$

$$= \frac{44}{10} \quad \begin{array}{l} \text{the sum of all the scores} \\ \text{the number of people in the group} \end{array}$$

$$= 4.4$$

So the mean, or average, number of *Game of Thrones* episodes that people tend to binge-watch is 4.4.

What does the mean actually tell us? It is a single number that helps us better understand the nature of this sample. In this case, it helps us know how many hours of *Game of Thrones* people typically watch in one sitting. Note the use of the word "typically." In reality, no one in our sample actually reported watching 4.4 episodes, just as families do not actually have 1.6 children, which is the mean number of children reported in the 2016 Canadian census.

Median

The **median** is the exact midpoint of the scores in the group. It is simply the score that falls in the middle of the group when you line all the scores up from lowest to highest.

Here are the scores from our made-up data regarding *Game of Thrones* binge-watching:

3   2   6   2   4   3   7   10   4   3

The first thing we need to do is reorder the scores from lowest to highest:

2   2   3   3   3   4   4   6   7   10

Now look for the score that falls in the exact middle. You'll notice there is no score in the exact middle, because there is an even number of scores. In this case we would take the mean, or average, of the two middles scores. This gives us the exact midpoint of the group. The middle two scores are 3 and 4. So,

$$\text{Median} = \frac{3+4}{2} = 3.5$$

The median of this sample or group of scores is 3.5. It is the number that falls in the exact middle of the distribution. Although there is no score of 3.5, you can see that it represents the exact middle.

Mode

The **mode** is the number that occurs most frequently in the sample. It's even easier to figure out than the median; all you need to do is look at the frequencies of each score. Take a look at the scores in the *Game of Thrones* data. There are a couple of 2s, a couple of 4s, but there are three people with a score of 3, and no score appears more than three times in the distribution. The mode is the most common number in the distribution, so in this case the mode is 3.

$$\text{Mode} = 3$$

Sometimes you'll see a distribution with no number appearing any more than any other number. In that case, you would report that there is no mode. For example, the following set of data has no mode:

1   2   3   4   5   6   7   8   9   10

Sometimes you will have a distribution where there is more than one number that appears many times. In that case, you would report more than one mode. If you have two numbers that appear most often, you would say that your distribution is bimodal. If there are three numbers that appear most often you would say that your distribution is trimodal.

For example, if your data looked like this:

| 1 | 3 | 3 | 3 | 4 | 5 | 6 | 6 | 6 | 9 |

You would say that your distribution is bimodal, with modes of 3 and 6.

Mean, Median, or Mode? Which One to Use?

In a perfect world, with perfectly distributed data that does exactly what it's supposed to do, the mean, median, and mode will be pretty close to each other. Unfortunately, social science involves the study of humans, and humans often don't do what they're "supposed" to do. Notice that in our fictitious *Game of Thrones* example, the mean = 4.4, the median = 3.5, and the mode = 3. Clearly our sample is not perfectly distributed. Here's where it pays to be a knowledgeable consumer of social science research. The most commonly used measure of central tendency is the mean, which is why it's probably the one most familiar to you. However, the mean is not *always* the best measure of central tendency to report. The mean can be especially misleading when there is one score that is significantly higher or lower than the rest; these scores are called **outliers**. Go back and take a look at the original scores. There is one score of ten, but the rest are all under seven. When the mean is calculated, this higher score artificially inflates the mean, making it higher than it should be. Because the score of ten is an outlier, the median is actually a more accurate descriptor of the group. So, if you wanted to report how many episodes people typically watch, the more accurate measure of central tendency is the median (3.5) or the mode (3.0). The general rule is that if there are no extreme scores, or outliers, in the sample, then the mean is usually the best choice of a measure of central tendency. However, when there are outliers, it is better to use the median or mode.

Measures of Variability

Measures of central tendency can be very useful in describing what a typical score in the sample might be but, on their own, they don't provide much information about what the entire sample looks like. Consider the grades you got in high school. Your mean grade, which is an average of the grades you got in all your classes, is an indicator of how well you typically did in high school. It's a useful statistic for sure, but it's limited in what it actually says about you as a student. If someone only knew your average grade, they would not be able to tell whether you did equally well in all your classes or whether you tended to

Table 9.2: Grade 12 Grades for Two Students

	Alexis (%)	Jackson (%)
Grade 12 average	**77**	**77**
History	77	92
English	75	53
Art	79	84
Biology	76	89
Algebra	78	67

do really well in some but not so well in others. Consider two students, Alexis and Jackson, whose Grade 12 grades are summarized in Table 9.2.

Notice that Alexis and Jackson both have a Grade 12 average of 77 percent. They are both good students, but are they really all that similar? According to their mean grade they are, but when you look closer at their individual grades, they are quite different. Alexis is very consistent—all her grades are between 75 and 79 percent, so it's safe to say that she performs equally well in all her courses. Jackson's grades are much more spread out—he does very well in some, but not so well in others, and is much less consistent than Alexis. If you had to predict how well these two students would do in college or university, which student would it be easier to make a prediction for? Since Alexis's grades don't vary much, you could probably more accurately predict her future grades.

When we talk about consistency and how much scores differ from each other, we are referring to their variability. **Measures of variability** indicate how spread out, or variable, the scores in a distribution are. These statistics provide valuable information that measures of central tendency on their own do not. There are two common measures of variability that you'll run across in social science research: range and standard deviation.

Range

The measure of variability that you may be the most familiar with is range. The **range** of a distribution is the distance between the lowest score and the highest score. The range can tell you how spread out the scores are. The higher the range, the more spread out the scores are, and the lower the range, the less spread out the scores are. Take a look at Alexis and Jackson's grades again. Alexis's lowest grade is 75 percent, and her highest grade is 79 percent. Jackson's lowest grade is 53 percent, and his highest grade is 92 percent. In social science research you might see the range mentioned in a sentence like this:

"Alexis's scores ranged from 75 to 79 percent, and Jackson's grades ranged from 53 to 92 percent."

But you might also see it expressed as a single number. To calculate the range, simply take the highest score and subtract the lowest score.

Range = highest score – lowest score

Range for Alexis = 79 – 75 = 4

Range for Jackson = 92 – 53 = 39

You might see this written as something like this:

"Alexis's grades had a range of 4, while Jackson's grades had a range of 39."

You can use the range to compare two distributions on the basis of how spread out the scores are. In this case, you can compare Alexis to Jackson, and you would conclude that even though they had the same average in Grade 12, Jackson's grades are more spread out, or variable. This tells you that Alexis was a bit more predictable in her classes—she tended to do well in everything with not much difference between her highest and lowest score. If Alexis was taking a new Grade 12 course and you had to predict how she would do in that course, you'd probably be safe to guess that she'd get around 77 percent, which was the mean grade in her other Grade 12 courses. Jackson was less predictable—with a low score of 53 and high score of 92 percent, it would be harder to predict how well Jackson would do in another course; he might either get an extremely high grade or just enough to pass.

The range can be useful in determining the variability of a distribution, but there are times when it is not the best measure. We know that in Grade 12, the range of the two students' grades were very different—Alexis's range of grades was small, while Jackson's range of grades was high. But all the range tells you is the distance between the lowest and the highest score. It doesn't tell you anything about the grades in between. If all you had was the range of their scores, you would know that Jackson had a 53 and a 92 percent, but you don't know whether the rest of his grades were also really spread out or if they were all 77 percent. Perhaps Jackson really was very similar to Alexis in terms of his abilities, except he just happened to do exceptionally well in one course and not so well in another. The limitation of the range is that it only takes two scores into account to describe the variability of the distribution, and if those two scores are not representative of the scores in the distribution (for example, if they are outliers), then the range will not very accurately describe the distribution.

Standard Deviation

A better measure of variability, and one that is more commonly used in social science research, is the **standard deviation**. The standard deviation is a measure of how much, on average, all the scores in a distribution differ from the mean of the distribution. Whereas the range only tells you how much the lowest score and the highest score differ from each other, the standard deviation takes all the scores into consideration as a measure of how variable the distribution is.

You don't need to know how to calculate the standard deviation in order to understand how to interpret it in social science research, so we're going to spare you thrill of calculating it yourself (but we would highly recommend a statistics course if you are interested in learning more about it!). Think of the standard deviation as an average, or mean, but instead of being the average of the *scores* in a distribution, it's the average of the *difference between each score and the mean*. Going back to our friends Alexis and Jackson, who do you think would have the smallest standard deviation in their grades? Remember that Alexis's grades were all pretty close together, whereas Jackson's were more spread out. If Alexis had an average of 77 percent and all her grades were close to 77 percent, then each of her scores would not differ much. If you took the mean, or average, of those difference scores, it would be a pretty small number, right? As it turns out, her standard deviation is 1.58. Jackson, however, also had a mean of 77 percent, but his scores tended to be pretty far away from 77 percent. If you took the mean of his difference scores, it would be higher than Alexis's. In fact, his standard deviation is 16.43. A standard deviation of 16.43 is much higher than a standard deviation of 1.58, and clearly indicates that Jackson's grades are more spread out, or variable.

Why do we care about variability? It matters first of all because it helps us make predictions. If a student's grades over time show very low variability (i.e., the standard deviation is small), then you can more accurately predict how they will do in future courses, because they are very consistent in their academic performance. A large amount of variability (i.e., a large standard deviation) means less consistency in their academic performance, making it harder to accurately predict how they will do in the future.

Descriptive statistics like the measures of central tendency and the measures of variability can tell you what a distribution looks like, and they can even give you some sense of whether two distributions are similar. They cannot tell you how two groups are related to each other or whether those groups differ enough for us to consider them meaningfully different. For that, we need more complicated statistics.

Correlations (Measuring Relationships)

Back in Chapter 2, we introduced you to the fascinating yet completely bogus relationship between the number of Nick Cage movies released in a year and the number of accidental deaths by drowning. That correlation was created by taking the data on how many Nick Cage's movies were released in a year and the data on how many deaths by drowning there were, and linking them together to see if there was a relationship. Real researchers don't worry too much about Nick Cage movies and drowning (well, they may care about them, but separately), but they often do care whether two variables are related to each other or not. Health researchers, for example, care whether there is a relationship between the amount of sugar you consume and your risk of Type II diabetes. Criminologists care whether there is a relationship between prison sentences and recidivism rates. Psychologists care whether there is a relationship between social support and depression.

Notice how we use the word *relationship* a lot here. Correlation is about measuring relationships between variables, or how connected or associated they are. Although knowing whether two variables are correlated does not tell you whether one variable caused the other one (because correlation does not equal causation), it is an important statistical technique in the social sciences.

When you see correlations reported in research reports, you'll notice the statistic used is *r*, and it will be a number between –1.0 and +1.0 (so, for example, it could be –.58 or +.02 or –.99, etc.). This may seem pretty simple, but that one number can tell you two important things about the relationship between the variables: the direction and the strength of the relationship.

Direction

The direction of the association between two variables refers to how each variable varies in relation to the other. When two variables are positively correlated, it means they both move in the same direction. In other words, when one variable increases, the other one does too, and when one variable decreases, so does the other. For example, there is a positive relationship between the amount you study for a test and the grade you will get on that test. What that means is that if you study a lot, your grade will likely be higher, and if you do not study much, your grade will likely be lower.

When two variables are negatively correlated, they move in opposite directions. When one variable increases, the other variable decreases. For example, there is probably a negative relationship between the amount of time you spend on social media in class and your memory for what the professor talked about in class. What that means is that if you spend a lot of time on social media during class, you will remember less of the content of that class, and if you spend very little (or no) time on social media during class, you will remember more of the content of the class.

If you look at the value of r reported in a social science report you can easily tell if the correlation is positive or negative. If the number is between –1.0 and 0, then it's a negative correlation, and if it's between 0 and +1.0, it's a positive correlation. For example:

$$r = -.70 \text{ is a negative correlation}$$
$$r = .70 \text{ is a positive correlation}$$

Note that the "+" usually gets left off of positive correlations. If it's not negative, assume that it's positive.

Strength

The strength of the correlation refers to how closely the two variables are related. It's important to know the strength of the association because variables can vary a lot in terms of the degree to which they are related to each other, and this affects the predictive power of the correlation. For example, if time spent studying and test grades are strongly correlated, then if you wanted to predict how you might do on a test given the amount of time you spent studying, you'd probably be pretty accurate in your prediction. The strong correlation would mean that the variables are very closely related, so as one increases, the other increases in a very similar way, with few exceptions. Imagine, however, that there was a very weak correlation between studying and test grades. This would mean that if you studied a lot, you might or might not do well on your test. Your ability to predict your test grade from the amount you studied would be weak.

Regardless of whether the value of r is negative or positive, the closer the number is to 1.0, the stronger the association between the two variables. There is no such thing as a perfect correlation in the social sciences; you'll likely never see $r = 1.00$, as it would be difficult to imagine two variables related to human behaviour that vary perfectly together. That doesn't mean perfect correlations do not exist. The more gas you pump into your car, the more money it will cost you, and with every extra litre you add, your cost will go up by the same amount, so this is a perfect correlation. However, social scientists aren't all that concerned with how much it costs you to put gas in your car. They are concerned, for example, with the relationship between the price of gas and physical activity, though. There is a positive relationship between gas prices and the number of people who walk and ride bikes (Courtemanche, 2011; Rashad, 2009), and a negative relationship between gas prices and obesity rates (Rabin, Boehmer, & Brownson, 2007). Those correlations are not perfect, though. Some people will choose to drive and some will choose to cycle no matter what the price of gas is, and we know that obesity has many risk factors other than walking rather than driving.

Keep in mind that a correlation of $r = -.62$ is just as strong as a correlation of $r = +.62$. Direction and strength are two different aspects of the correlation, and strength is indicated by the absolute value (i.e., ignore the – or + sign) of r.

INFERENTIAL STATISTICS

Descriptive statistics, such as those we discussed above, are derived from the data you actually have. In other words, the mean age of a group of ten people refers only to that group of ten people and is normally not used to make predictions about the age of anyone who is not in the group. Often, however, social scientists are interested in making predictions about larger groups, or even society at large. For example, a psychologist may be conducting an experiment in which they are testing a treatment for depression on a group of ten individuals, but obviously in addition to hoping to improve the mental health of these people, the psychologist also wants to know if the treatment will work for people outside that group. In other words, they want to be able to generalize their findings to people not in their treatment group. This is an issue of practicality: Therapy is time-consuming and labour-intensive, so it would be expensive and impractical to include every depressed individual in their experiment. In addition, it would be impossible to track down every depressed person in the world. Inferential statistics are what allows researchers to study a small group of people (or things) and then make inferences, or predictions, about what would happen if they had done the same thing to a larger group.

Populations and Samples

The entire group of people or things being studied is referred to as the **population**. That doesn't necessarily mean the population of the world. If you are interested in European drivers, then your population would be all the drivers in Europe (but not in any other part of the world). If you are interested in North American university students, then your population would be all the students currently enrolled in universities in North America. As you can imagine, these groups are huge, and you could never study all the individuals in them. Plus, people enroll in and graduate from university all the time, so you could never get an accurate count of them all. Even fairly small groups, such as elite athletes or YouTube celebrities under the age of 20, would be challenging to study because you'd probably have a hard time reaching them all, even if they did agree to let you study them.

An alternative to hunting down every person or thing in the population you are interested in studying is to draw a **sample** from that population. A sample is a subset of the population. Not all samples are created equal, however. Imagine that you are conducting a study of helping behaviour in children. Which would be a better sample: a group of children who have volunteered to be in your study, or a group of children who have been randomly chosen from a list of all children? Can you see the problem with only using people who volunteered for your study on helping behaviour? If only the helpful people volunteer, but not the unhelpful people, then your sample will not be representative of the population, and your findings will only be generalizable to other helpful people and not the general population. In order for a sample to be representative of the population, two conditions must be met: The participants in the sample must be randomly selected from the population, and everyone in the population must have an equal chance of being selected.

If you select your sample properly, you can conduct your study on your sample and then generalize those findings to the population you are interested in. That's what inferential statistics is all about: making inferences about a population based on a sample. Inferential statistics are what the psychologist testing a treatment for depression would use. Their population would be people who are seeking treatment for depression. From that group, a certain number would be randomly selected for treatment and a certain number would be selected to serve as a control group against which to compare the treatment group (often with mental health research, the control group participants are put on a waiting list for treatment, and they receive it as soon as the study is over). The psychologist would then administer the treatment to the treatment group. At the end of the study, levels of depression would be assessed in both groups. Inferential statistics would then be used to determine if these groups are significantly different—in other words, whether they are different enough to conclude that the treatment works.

Statistical Significance and Beer

What does statistical significance have to do with beer, you ask? Everything! Without beer, the modern statistical significance test would not exist. William Sealy Gosset was a master brewer and scientist working at the Guinness brewery in Dublin, Ireland. He was looking for a way to improve the formula for the beer, especially when brewed in small batches. He developed a statistical test to allow him to be able to generalize the results he found on his small batches to larger batches of beer. This was revolutionary in the field of statistics (and beer), but unfortunately Guinness didn't allow their employees to publish under their own names because they didn't want their competitors to know about the fancy science they were using to brew beer. So, rather than call his test "The Gosset test of significance" (because if you are going to develop a statistical test, why wouldn't you name it after yourself?), he published it under the name "Student," and it became known as Student's *t* distribution.

In order to understand the notion of **statistical significance**, let's back up a little. Remember how researchers draw samples from populations, conduct research with those samples, and then generalize the results back to the population? And how if you randomly select your sample, it should look like a mini version of your population? Well, here's the thing. Sometimes, even if random selection is used, and every person in the population has an equal chance of being selected for the sample, the sample won't quite look like the population. Imagine that you have a deck of cards, which has 17 hearts, 17 diamonds, 17 clubs, and 17 spades. In other words, there are four different types of cards, each representing one-quarter, or 25 percent, of the deck.

If you randomly select a sample of eight cards, theoretically that sample should have the same breakdown as the full deck, with 25 percent of your sample comprising each group (i.e., two hearts, two diamonds, two clubs, and two spades). Go ahead and try this if you have a deck of cards handy. What do you think you would find?

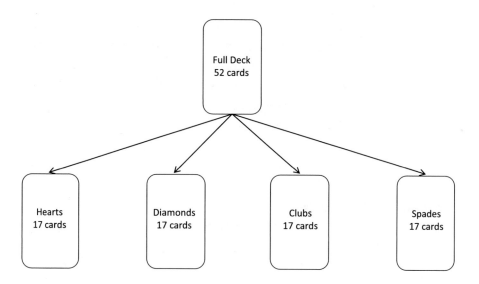

Figure 9.1: Deck of Cards as a Population

What you'll find is that your sample may or may not look exactly like your population. You may have two clubs and two spades but only one heart and three diamonds, or four clubs and four spades, or even eight hearts. Why? It's not because you cheated or made a mistake or deliberately tried to select certain cards. It's just the nature of random chance. Statisticians call it **random sampling error**. Even though theoretically your sample should look like your population, it may not.

This means that researchers cannot just assume that their samples are perfect representations of the populations they are studying. They may be, but they may not be, so there is always a level of uncertainty about how accurate their results might be. And given that researchers study samples because they can't study the entire population, this means they don't really know if their sample is representative of the population, because they don't actually have that information about the population. Sounds like a problem, right?

Fortunately, it's not. Although it does mean that researchers can never be 100 percent sure the findings they get with their sample would be the same as what they would find if they studied the entire population, there are statistical tools that allow them to calculate exactly how confident they can be in their findings. In other words, they can calculate the probability that their findings were due to chance and not to real differences in the groups they are studying.

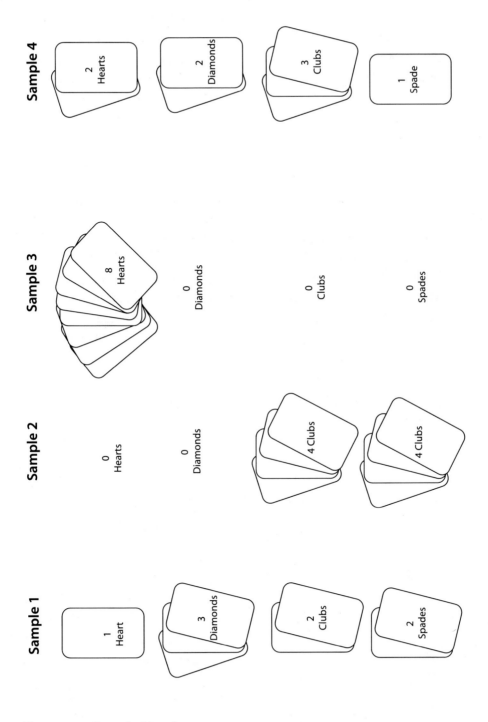

Figure 9.2: Sample Hands

Rather than just using descriptive statistics (the mean of each group), inferential statistics will tell you whether those two groups are significantly different and the degree of confidence you can have in your findings. If you are comparing two groups, the inferential statistical test you would use is a called a *t*-test (remember the Guinness guy? That's his test). It compares your two groups, taking into account the variability within each group. It results in a statistic that indicates the probability that any difference between your two groups is due to chance. That statistic is "*p*", which stands for probability. *p* ranges from 0 to 1.0, where $p = 0$ would be a 0 percent probability that the results are due to chance, and $p = 1.0$ is a 100 percent probability that the results are due to chance. Researchers, as you can imagine, are much happier when their *p*s are closer to 0 than to 1, because it means that their study results are more reliable.

Obviously, no one would care about a study that resulted in a *p* of 1.0, because that would indicate that the results are absolutely, 100 percent due to chance. Imagine that you are trying to figure out whether to take a treatment for which researchers are 100 percent certain that any positive effects that have been found are entirely due to chance. It would be pointless. But what about a 50 percent chance? Would you take it?

In social science, the accepted convention is that if there is a 5 percent probability or more that the results are due to random chance rather than real differences, we discard that finding as not being statistically significant. In other words, we are only willing to accept a 5 percent or lower chance that the findings do not reflect reality (i.e., that they are incorrect). So, the magic number that social scientists, and you, as a consumer of social science research, should look for is this:

$$p < .05$$

It's actually $p \leq .05$, but you'll more likely see the "less than" sign used than the "less than or equal to" sign.

Now that you're familiar with it, you'll see it everywhere in the results sections of articles. What it means is that there is a less than (or equal to) 5 percent chance that the results are due to random sampling error. In other words, there is a more than 95 percent chance that the results accurately reflect reality.

Interpreting Statistical Significance

$p \leq .05$ = statistically significant = the results are most likely not due to chance and you should assume that this finding is important

$p > .05$ = not statistically significant = there is too high a risk that the results are due to chance, so you should assume the finding is not important

READING AND UNDERSTANDING THE "RESULTS" SECTION

You've probably read a lot of journal articles by now. And we're willing to bet that some of them had statistics in them. Be honest: Did you read the parts with the numbers in them, or did you skip over them? Many people skip over them because they think they won't understand them, but if you've read this far in the chapter, you already have the basic tools to interpret these numbers.

Here is an example of a sentence you might come across in a typical results section (although there is much variation in social science research studies, so they won't all look like this). This is from an unpublished study on whether apologies are effective in getting people to forgive. The researchers randomly assigned participants to either receive an apology or not, after experiencing a transgression by another person.

Results

A t-test for independent samples revealed that those in the apology group were significantly more likely to forgive the transgressor (M = 6.52, SD = 1.11) than those in the no apology group (M = 1.49, SD = 1.09), $t(141)$ = 27.39, $p < .05$.

Believe it or not, you know what all of those numbers mean. The first numbers you come to (M = 6.52, SD = 1.11) represent the mean and standard deviation of the forgiveness scores in the treatment group (the people who received an apology). The second group of numbers (M = 1.49, SD = 1.09) represents the forgiveness scores of the control group (the people who did not get an apology). So, the average amount that people forgave when they got an apology was 6.52, whereas the average amount they forgave when they didn't get an apology was 1.49.

Table 9.3: Understanding Statistical Tests

You can understand the results section of a social science research study without knowing how to calculate statistics, but you should be familiar with how those tests are reported in scientific journal articles.

Test name	What it tests	What the statistics look like	What it means
t-test	Whether two groups are significantly different from each other	"A t-test between the groups revealed a significant effect of the treatment, $t(23) = 4.59, p < .05$."	When the two groups are compared, the scores on one of them (in this case, the treatment variable) is significantly (i.e., meaningfully) higher or lower than the other one.
ANOVA (analysis of variance)	Whether two or more groups are significantly different from each other	"An ANOVA revealed a significant difference between the groups, $F(2,102) = 9.26, p < .05$."	In all the groups that were compared, at least one of them differs significantly from the others.
Correlation	The extent to which two variables are related to each other	"The two variables were significantly correlated, $r = .75, p < .05$."	These two variables are positively related in a meaningful way; as one increases, so does the other one.
Linear or multiple regression	The extent to which an outcome variable can be predicted by a predictor variable (linear regression) or group of predictor variables (multiple regression)	"A multiple regression analysis revealed that the model significantly predicted the disease, $F(5,893) = 32.97, p < .01$. R^2 for the model was .67. Table 1 shows the unstandardized and standardized regression coefficients for each variable." This is often followed by a table listing all of the variables and whether they were significant predictors or not.	F refers to whether the overall test is meaningful; in other words is it a good model to predict the disease? If $p < .05$, then it's meaningful. R^2 refers to how meaningful, or strong, the model is. It also indicates which variables are most important in the model. The variables that are significant (i.e., $p < .05$) contribute to being able to predict the score on the outcome variable.

Test name	What it tests	What the statistics look like	What it means
Logistic regression	The extent to which a binary outcome (i.e., an outcome with only two possible outcomes) can be predicted by a group of predictor variables	"A test of the model was significant, $\chi^2(6, N=509) = 54.63, p < .05$. The model was able to correctly classify 82% of those in the 'yes' group and 85% of those in the 'no' group. Table 1 shows the logistic regression coefficient, Wald test, and odds ratio for each of the predictors." This is often followed by a table listing all of the variables and whether they were significant predictors or not.	The χ^2 statistic tells you whether the model, as a whole, is able to correctly predict who falls into which group (in other words, if we know the scores of someone on all of the predictor variables, how accurate would we be in guessing which category they fall into?). The odds ratio tells you how likely a person is to fall in which group, given their score on each individual predictor variable.
Chi-square	Whether the frequency of a particular outcome is different than what would be expected	"A chi-square goodness of fit test showed that the number of people in the 'yes' group was significantly higher than the number of people in the 'no' group, $\chi^2(1, N=104) = 15.28, p < .05$."	Significantly more people said "yes" than "no"; N in the statistic refers to the total number of people in the groups.

The standard deviations for the groups are similar (1.11 compared to 1.09), which suggests that they are similar in their variability (in other words, one group's scores are not more spread out than the other).

So, just comparing the averages of the two groups, it looks like apologies are effective, right? Remember, though, about random sampling error: Maybe the people in the group that was given an apology just happened to be more forgiving. That's why the statistical test was conducted. In this case it's a *t*-test. You don't need to know what all those components of the *t* statistic mean; the important part is the number that follows the "*p*," because it tells you whether the scores of the two groups are significantly different. In this case it's less than .05, so that tells us that we can assume that the two groups are significantly different, with a less than 5 percent chance that we're wrong in this assumption.

WAYS TO LIE WITH STATISTICS

Statistics get a bad rap. Mark Twain is known for claiming that "there are three kinds of lies: lies, damned lies, and statistics" (he didn't make it up—he was quoting someone else, although no one seems to know who; see Velleman, 2008, p. 1). One of the most well-known statistics books of all time is called *How to Lie with Statistics*, written by Darrell Huff in 1954. We like to think that most social scientists want to present their findings honestly and with integrity (with a few exceptions, which you'll remember from Chapter 6), so we're going to recommend approaching the statistics in scholarly research as most likely not a pack of lies. And since most social science research you read in journal articles has been peer-reviewed, which means it has been read by other experts in the field and they haven't found any big errors in it, deliberate attempts to lie with statistics probably would have been caught before they even got published. So, scholarly articles are mostly trustworthy.

Unfortunately, the same is not necessarily true of social science research presented in the media or other non-scholarly venues. Sometimes people want to present data in a way that tells the story they want to tell. Sometimes they have a vested and/or financial interest in making you buy into their claims. And sometimes they just don't know any better. You don't have to be a statistician to notice some of the common ways statistics are used to misrepresent reality. Ironically, these are taken from Huff's (1954) book (with current examples)—it seems that not much has changed since then.

Using the Wrong Measure of Central Tendency

We've already talked about the fact that there are certain conditions under which it is best to use something other than the mean to describe the central tendency of a sample, one being the presence of an outlier, or an extremely high or low score. How can this be used to deliberately misrepresent reality? Imagine that you are researching companies to work for. One factor that may be important to you is the average salary of the employees of a company. Here's something to keep in mind. In Canada in 2015, the top CEOs were paid 159 times the average salary of their workers (Evans, 2016). That translates into about $7.89 million a year. When you are considering the average salary, does that average include the CEO? Think about how the average salary might differ depending on whether the CEO's salary is included. How likely is it that the average salary will reflect your actual salary?

You won't always be able to tell if an outlier is affecting the mean, but there are some places where the mean is commonly used when the median should be. One is with salaries. Another is with real estate. The way some neighbourhoods are divided, they may contain a diversity of houses, with some very reasonably priced houses and some very expensive ones. If a real estate agent brags about how much the "average" house sells for in a particular neighbourhood, check to see if there is a very expensive home in that list that is artificially inflating the mean.

Misrepresenting Small Differences as Significant

When groups are being compared on some variable, it's unlikely that the mean scores of the two groups will be exactly the same. Most of the time, one group will have a higher mean than the other. The mistake people often make is in assuming that this difference is meaningful, or significant. Without doing a statistical test, which will take into account both the differences in the means and the variability of the groups, you won't be able to tell. Small differences may be due to random sampling error, the presence of an outlier, or even just one participant in the study having a bad day. So, even though the means of the two groups might lead you to assume that they are different, they may not be significantly different.

Using Graphs to Exaggerate Differences

Darrell Huff, the author of the book about how to lie with statistics, wrote, "There is terror in numbers. When numbers in tabular form are taboo and words will not do the work well, as is often the case, there is one answer left: Draw a picture" (1954, p. 60). Data can be complicated. People often don't want to do

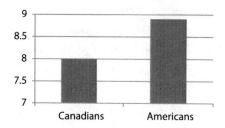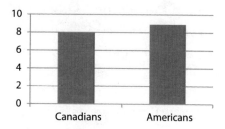

Figure 9.3: Alcohol Consumption: Canadians vs. Americans

the work of interpreting what a list of numbers might mean, and they tend to skip over paragraphs with lots of numbers in them (admit it—you probably have done that a few times while reading this chapter). Instead of terrorizing people with numbers, social scientists and people writing about social science research in popular media often use graphs and charts to visually depict research findings. It makes sense: The data are easier to understand, it's more appealing, and it means you don't have to read tedious paragraphs full of numbers. As we'll see, however, visual depictions of data can be used for good or for evil, and you need to be able to see through attempts to fool you into thinking the findings are more interesting or important than they actually are.

Take a look at the two charts in Figure 9.3. They graphically depict the descriptive statistics we presented earlier regarding yearly alcohol consumption of Canadians and Americans. Which one is more likely to get your attention?

Can you spot the difference? Although neither chart is technically incorrect, the one on the left makes a much more compelling case for a difference between the two groups, doesn't it? This is because of the numbering on the Y axis. Both charts indicate that the mean of the Canadians is 8.0 and the mean of the Americans is 8.9, and that the difference between them is 0.9. But the chart on the left, by truncating the scale to 7 and 9, makes this difference look a lot larger than it actually is. Now, if you had information about statistical significance, you would be able to tell if this difference is meaningful or not, but if all you had to go on was a graph, the graph on the left is misleading.

The same can happen with line graphs. The two line graphs in Figure 9.4 both show the change in the percentage of people who participated in outdoor activities close to home from 2011 to 2015 (Statistics Canada, 2018b). By truncating the scale on the Y axis, it seems like there has been a large change in outdoor activity levels, with more people apparently deciding to just stay in and watch *Game of Thrones* instead of going out to play. When you view the graph with a more realistic scale, you can see that the difference between 75 (in 2011) and 72 (in 2015) is not very large.

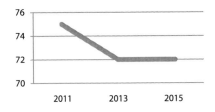
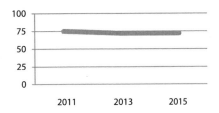

Figure 9.4: Participation in Activities Close to Home

Fortunately, once you are aware of them, these attempts to exaggerate findings are fairly easy to spot. Look at the Y axis: Does it start with zero? If it does not, is there a good reason for the chart being truncated? Be skeptical, and if the findings look too good to be true, they probably are.

A FINAL WORD ON STATISTICS

No one expects you to be a statistics expert after reading this chapter, but hopefully you have a better understanding of how statistics are used (and misused) in quantitative social science research. There's no need to be afraid of them (they can't hurt you), and if you give them a chance, you might even surprise yourself by understanding more than you think you do.

We should also mention that just because we included an entire chapter on statistics in this textbook, it does not mean that we think that statistics and quantitative methods are the only way to learn about social science phenomena. In the same way, just because we included a section on how to lie with statistics does not mean we think statistics and quantitative methods should not be used to learn about social science phenomena. Some research questions are best answered with numbers and some are not, and part of being a wise consumer of social science research is to understand whether the techniques used to answer the research question are appropriate.

REVIEW IT

1. What is a descriptive statistic? What descriptive statistics can you think of, that you might already know?
2. Describe the difference between mean, median, and mode.
3. What does the standard deviation of a group of scores tell you?

4. Describe what a negative correlation means. Can you think of an example?
5. What's the difference between a population and a sample?
6. Explain, in your own words, what it means if the difference between the means of two groups is statistically significant.

APPLY IT

1. Calculate the mean, median, and mode of the following group of numbers:

    13
    15
    18
    1
    15
    11
    9
    15
    19
    15
    12

    Which measure of central tendency is the most appropriate to use with this group of scores? Why?

2. In a study on the effect of music on consumer behaviour, Milliman (1986) experimentally manipulated the type of music that was playing in a restaurant: Some patrons heard music with a fast tempo, and some heard music with a slow tempo. He measured how quickly they were served, how long they lingered over the meal, and how much alcohol they drank (among other things) to see if there were different effects of the two types of music. He reported the following statistics (p. 288):

Variable	Slow music	Fast music	Significance level
Service time	29 minutes	27 minutes	$p > .05$
Customer time at table	56 minutes	45 minutes	$p = .01$
Amount of bar purchases	$30.47	$21.62	$p = .01$

What would you conclude from these results? Be sure to incorporate the significance level into your answer.

Answers: 1. Mean = 13; Median = 15; Mode = 15. The median or the mode would be more appropriate than the mean, since the score of "1" is an outlier and is making the mean smaller. 2. If the significance level (p) is less than .05, then the two means are significantly different. The tempo of the music had no effect on how quickly they were served (because p is greater than .05), but it did have a significant effect on how long they spent at their table (slow music made them stay longer) and how much they spent on alcohol (slow music made them spend more) (because the p values are both less than .05).

10 "Junk" Science: Distinguishing Science from Pseudoscience

If you've been keeping up with us, you should be pretty good at finding, critically assessing, and communicating about scholarly research in the social sciences by now. These skills will serve you well when you are writing papers for your courses. But what about when you are sitting on your couch reading or watching the news and a report comes on claiming that fruit and vegetables are bad for you? Do you immediately cancel your trip to the farmer's market, or do you think reasonably about the issue and dig a little deeper? If you do this, you will sometimes discover that the claims being made are either ridiculous or impossible, or both. You'll encounter a lot of bad, or "junk," science in your life outside of school, and you'll save yourself a lot of grief (and will still get to enjoy a balanced diet) by refining your junk science detection skills.

LEARNING OBJECTIVES

1. Learn to critically assess scientific claims made in popular literature
2. Identify some commonly held beliefs about the social world that are not supported by research
3. Learn how to avoid making inaccurate claims about the social world

---

WHAT IS JUNK SCIENCE AND WHERE DOES IT COME FROM?

From Climate Change Denial to Detox Diets: Examples of Junk Science

When we talk about junk science, we don't mean the science of junk (although that would be an interesting field to study). By **junk science**, we mean the misconduct or misrepresentation of scientific research, resulting in the dissemination of misinformation about scientific findings. You'll also hear it referred to as pseudoscience, bad science, and utter nonsense. It can happen either when bad research inadvertently sneaks through the peer-review process and gets published, or when good research is misrepresented to the public.

Why do we care so much about junk science? There are some pretty frightening examples of what can happen when people come to believe things that aren't true. Take climate change, for example. Despite irrefutable empirical evidence that human behaviour has increased greenhouse-gas emissions and that these emissions are implicated in the warming of the planet, some people refuse to believe that climate change is a real danger to the survival of the planet and its inhabitants. Those who fail to see the evidence also fail to act in ways that will help stop or slow down climate change.

Another example of how the spreading of junk science can have significant negative consequences concerns the soundly debunked claim that vaccines can cause autism. The original research article that made this claim has been retracted, and countless research studies have failed to find any connection between vaccines and autism, and yet some parents still choose not to vaccinate their children because of the original claim. As a result, incidence rates of diseases that had all but been eradicated have shot up in recent years (Larson, Cooper, Eskola, Katz, & Ratzan, 2011; Poland & Spier, 2010).

Not all junk science is as potentially dangerous as the misinformation about climate change or vaccinations and autism, but some of it might affect you and the choices you make. The box below lists some common pseudoscientific claims. Do any of them surprise you?

Junk Science

1. **Detox diets**. The idea of a detox diet is to flush toxins out of your system by limiting what kinds of food you eat. At best, they get you eating healthier foods like vegetables and fruits and limiting less healthy stuff like sugar and processed food. At their worst, they may deprive your body of necessary nutrients, especially those diets that limit you to only one type of food (like a juice fast). The science is pretty clear on the idea of using a special diet as detoxification: It's junk. Your body has a built-in detoxification system (your liver and kidneys) so it's not necessary to cleanse it.

2. **Astrology and horoscopes**. What's your sign? Some people believe that the astrological sign under which you were born gives you characteristics in common with others born under the same sign. For example, if you are a Pisces (i.e., born between February 19 and March 20), you are believed to be creative and gentle, but also overly trusting. There are 12 astrological signs, each with its own profile. Those who believe in astrology also believe that your sign can also predict what will happen to you in the future (search for "horoscope" to see what your day is presumably going to be like). While they may be fun to read and are mostly harmless, horoscopes have been soundly debunked. In a smart but simple experiment, Forer (1949) had participants do a personality test and then gave them a written profile that they were told had been generated based on their answers on the test. Most of the participants reported that the profile accurately described them. However, Forer had actually given everyone exactly the same profile. It was just written in a vague enough way that participants could easily see themselves in it. For example, it included statements such as "While you have some personality weaknesses, you are generally able to compensate for them." Horoscopes tend to use the same strategy: Even if you are not a Pisces, there is probably some part of you that is creative and gentle, and perhaps you trust more than you should sometimes.

3. **Polygraphs (i.e., lie detectors)**. You've probably seen polygraphs being used in movies to determine if suspected criminals are guilty. The (junk) science behind them is that when a person is not telling the truth, their face may be able to hide this fact but their body cannot. Polygraphs measure a person's heart rate/blood pressure,

respiration, and skin conductivity while they are being asked questions. The claim is that changes in these physiological measures are indicative of lying. Unfortunately, the evidence does not support their effectiveness, and scientists generally agree that polygraph tests are not a reliable and valid way to detect deception (APA, 2004). Although it would be great to have a foolproof method of determining whether someone is lying or not, polygraphs are not the answer.

How Bad Things Happen to Good Science

The science junkyard is littered with outrageous claims, impossible conclusions, and outright lies, some more damaging than others. Sometimes it's hard to know what to believe, especially in an era in which there is a tendency to discount information that one doesn't agree with as "fake news." Do scientists and those reporting on science set out to deliberately fool people into believing nonsense? Maybe we have an unrealistically rosy view of human nature, but we don't think so, at least most of the time. So how does junk science happen? Why can't only high-quality, confirmed facts be studied, published, and reported on? There are a number of reasons for this; we discuss five of them below.

Bad Research

Even though the peer review process ensures that most research that gets published meets a minimum standard, sometimes a study that is heavily flawed or poorly conducted sneaks through. By now you are skilled at critically assessing this research (for a refresher, go back and read Chapters 2 and 5). Don't assume that just because a study has flaws that it is bad research, however. As we've said before, there is no such thing as a perfect study. All studies have some limitations, and most of the time these limitations do not detract from the main points the study is making. For a study to qualify as junk science it would have to be really bad. A study describing an experiment in which many participants dropped out of the experimental group before the study was finished would be considered to be flawed; a study that doesn't even include a control group but makes causal claims anyway would be bad research. A study in which the interviewer fails to follow up on an interesting comment made by one of the participants is flawed; a study in which the interviewer is clearly biased and deliberately leads the participants into agreeing with their views would be bad research.

Publication Bias

Not all research gets published. Sometimes this is because it doesn't make it through the peer review process because it is too flawed, but there are other reasons why some research studies never see the light of day. Sometimes researchers do not even try to publish their findings because the study did not reveal any significant findings. There is a preference in social science (and other fields) to publish studies that find differences between groups or big effects of one variable on another or that have counterintuitive and/or unexpected findings. This means that research that investigates whether, say, students study better in the morning or at night and finds no difference in their grades regardless of when they study is less likely to get published than a study that finds that the time of day does make a difference when it comes to studying. This may not seem like that big a deal, but imagine a study on the effectiveness of a drug. If drug trials that find no effect of the drug are less likely to be published, then the published literature will be biased. A drug may have been found to be ineffective in ten studies, but if one study finds it to be effective, that study is much more likely to be published. If a medical professional wanted to know whether to prescribe this particular drug or not, all they have to base their decision on is the one study that found the drug to be effective, and not the ten studies that found that it doesn't work. At best they are wasting time by prescribing a drug that is likely to be ineffective, but when a life-saving drug is needed, the consequences of this could be much worse. The problem with publication bias is that it is invisible—we have no idea how much research doesn't get published.

Lack of Replication

In the same way that academic journals tend not to want to publish non-significant findings, they also tend not to publish studies that replicate the findings of other studies. This means that a study with really interesting, unexpected findings might not be the best study on that topic; it just may have been the first. If another researcher tried to confirm these findings by conducting a similar study, that study would be less likely to be published. You can see the problem here: If the replication study finds something completely different because the first study was flawed, the scientific community will never know because it has not been published. This contributes to publication bias. Even if the replication study confirms the findings, this is helpful to know too, as it provides more evidence of the interesting and unexpected finding. Either way, all we have to go on is the original study because the other studies likely won't be published. There is a push in the field of social science to put more emphasis on replication studies because it's clear that we can have more confidence in a research finding, especially if it is counterintuitive, if other researchers have been able to get the same results.

Poor Reporting by the Media

For the average person (and by that we mean a non-student), most of their social science news comes from the media rather than from scholarly sources. This puts a lot of responsibility on journalists and other writers to report accurately and fairly on the research that is done by social scientists. The problem is that most often they are not scientists—they may not have had the benefit of a course like the one you are taking—and so they don't have the skills to fully understand the research they are reporting on. This is one reason why you see so many headlines claiming that something you love (e.g., wine, coffee, or chocolate) either causes or prevents something you probably don't want (e.g., poor health, weight gain, or premature aging). Even though we all know that correlation does not equal causation, the media repeatedly confuses the two. In fact, this is probably the most common problem in social science reporting. This is partly due to lack of training on the part of the people reporting on the science, but partly it's because people are much more likely to click on or read a story with a strong, definitive headline ("Eating chocolate makes you smarter!") rather than a less interesting but more realistic one ("Researchers find a small but significant positive correlation between intelligence and amount of chocolate ingested, but caution that this could be due to lots of things so we shouldn't make too big a deal about it").

Public Desire for Quick, Interesting News

Be honest: When was the last time you read an entire news article from start to finish? We mean a news article from an actual newspaper, like the *New York Times*, *Washington Post*, or the *Globe & Mail*, and not something from a less reputable site that contains stories with more pictures than words. With more information being thrown at us, we have less time to read any one thing in detail. This desire by the public for easy, bite-sized news means that long, nuanced reporting is becoming less and less common. The problem is that scientific findings can be very nuanced, and no research study can be fully explained in a few sentences. If the public is not willing to spend the time reading about social science research, the news media will not write detailed articles about it. In addition, if people are more likely to click on a headline such as "Eating chocolate makes you smarter" rather than "Researchers fail to replicate poorly conducted study that claims that eating chocolate makes you smarter," guess which study the media will report.

BEING FOOLED BY JUNK SCIENCE—IT HAPPENS TO THE BEST OF US

You got to this point in the book without giving up, and you are probably well on your way to writing an entire literature review. Maybe you are doing all this in addition to taking a bunch of other courses or working full-time. So, you're pretty smart. However, despite your awesomeness, we're about to tell you how easy it is to fool you with bad science. Don't worry—it's not just you. We're all susceptible to falling for stuff that isn't true. It's because our brains are trying to be efficient, but it doesn't always serve us well. And if that's not bad enough, once we think we know something, it's incredibly difficult to change our minds.

Why We Believe Junk Science: Heuristics and Cognitive Bias

You take in and process a lot of information over the course of a day, and while your brain is really great, it can only do so much. That's why we rely on **heuristics**, or mental shortcuts, to interpret the world. If every time you saw a table and chair you had to figure out what they were and what to do with them, it would take you forever to get down to doing your homework or eating your dinner. When you see a piece of furniture with four legs and a flat top, your brain knows it's a table because it has created a mental shortcut to say this configuration of pieces equals a table. The same goes for other things that we see and experience. When a stranger approaches you with a smile, you don't have time to get to know them to determine whether they are a nice person or not, so you take their smile as an indication of their friendliness, and you smile back.

Heuristics are shortcuts like this. They are general rules-of-thumb that we follow in order to save time and mental processing. However, the downside to heuristics is that they can sometimes make us more likely to believe things that aren't true. Some heuristics are particularly good at making us susceptible to junk science.

Availability Heuristic and Bias toward Extremes

The **availability heuristic** is based on the fact that we tend to place more emphasis or value on things that more readily come to mind. This strategy helps us make decisions quickly, without having to do a lot of extra research. For example, if you were asked what the most common types of house pets are, you would probably correctly guess dogs or cats. Chances are dogs and cats come to mind easily because you either have one, know someone who has one, or you've seen them on television. The fact that they come to mind quickly helps you guess the correct answer.

Sometimes, however, the availability heuristic can lead us to be biased because what most readily comes to mind may not be the right answer; it might just be the most memorable or extreme one. Say, for example, you read on the news that there has been a shooting in your neighbourhood. Immediately after, someone asks you how safe you think your neighbourhood is. Rather than think about all the years you have lived at this address with no incidences of violent crime at all, the shooting will probably come to mind first, and your response might be that your neighbourhood is not safe and has lots of crime. This **bias toward extremes** can make us susceptible to misinformation. If a government agency or news report is trying to convince citizens that a community should be "tougher on crime," they may refer to an extreme but isolated incident like this in order to make people support increased funding for prisons and police, even if it is not warranted.

Bias toward extremes does not only make us susceptible to misinformation, it can also lead us to make irrational choices. It has, for example, made some people afraid of swimming in the ocean because they are afraid of sharks. Shark attacks, even though they are very uncommon, come to mind pretty easily thanks to the graphic and memorable way they have been depicted in the media and in movies. Logically, you are highly unlikely to be attacked by a shark, but the availability heuristic is what causes the music from the movie *Jaws* to start playing in your head when you go near the ocean.

The availability heuristic, and the resulting bias toward extremes, can be prevented by doing what we've been encouraging you to do throughout this book: look for evidence. Statistics and incidence rates are usually pretty easy to find, whether they involve shark attacks, crime rates, or some other event that scares you, so do your own research before putting too much stock in extreme examples, especially when these extreme examples are being used to sway opinion.

Representativeness Heuristic and the Misperception of Randomness
The **representativeness heuristic** involves how we make judgments about the probability of an event happening. When faced with a novel event, we compare

it to a prototype or exemplar that we already have. In other words, rather than collect new information about an event, we try to categorize it with something we already know about. As with other heuristics, this can save us time. For example, say you have a test in Professor Hardtest's course, but you haven't had a test in this particular course yet so you aren't sure how much to study. However, you did have Professor Hardtest in a course last year, and you found that she certainly lived up to her name. By categorizing this test as most likely being typical of her other exams, you rightly conclude that you should study a lot for this test.

The problem with the representative heuristic is that we can mistakenly add someone or something to a category. This is how stereotyping happens: when we hold views about groups of people and assume that anyone who belongs to that group will be similar. The representativeness heuristic can also negatively affect our ability to predict whether an event is a random occurrence or not. Let's say you flipped a coin ten times. Which of the following set of outcomes do you think is more likely (where H = heads and T = tails)?

Outcome #1:   H   H   H   H   H   T   T   T   T   T

Outcome #2:   H   T   T   H   T   H   H   T   T   H

Many people would pick the second outcome because it looks more random. But in reality each of these outcomes is equally likely. Every time you flip a coin, the chance of getting heads is 50 percent. Whether the next coin toss comes up heads or tails is independent of the results of the preceding toss, so although statistically you should get roughly half heads and half tails if you toss the coin a number of times, it's equally possible that you could get all the heads first and all the tails last or a mixture of heads and tails. This mistake happens because of the **misperception of randomness**: we think we know what randomness looks like (i.e., a chaotic distribution with no discernable pattern), but in fact, not all random events fit this description.

The misperception of randomness can have negative consequences because it can make you miscalculate the probability of a given event happening. On a personal level this can, for example, cause you to lose money at gambling or playing the lottery because you mistakenly believe that the longer you keep playing, the more likely you are to win. In fact, this is not true (this actually has a name; it's called the gambler's fallacy). On a societal level, this can make some people believe that one random cold day means climate change is not real, or that a cluster of cancer diagnoses in one area means the area is contaminated. The better you understand the representative heuristic and how the concept of randomness works, the better you will be able to make your own judgments and predictions and critically evaluate the judgments and predictions of others.

Representativeness Heuristic and Regression toward the Mean

The representative heuristic can also make us bad at understanding cause and effect. And we don't just mean mistaking correlation for causation. Imagine you go to the doctor for a routine check-up, and it turns out that your blood pressure is a bit high. The doctor puts you on blood pressure medication and asks you to go back in a month. When you go back you learn that your blood pressure has returned to normal. Yay for medicine—a pill cured your high blood pressure! Or did it? As it turns out, blood pressure fluctuates, sometimes randomly and sometimes because a visit to the doctor's office can make some people a bit uneasy and their blood pressure goes up a bit. The point is, your blood pressure may have been a bit high that day, but it might not have signalled a problem. What you'd probably find is that after a day when your blood pressure was high, it would most likely be lower the next time you measure it. Conversely, after a day when your blood pressure was low, it would most likely be higher the next time you measure it. What's happening is that your blood pressure is returning to its average level after a high or low reading. This phenomenon, whereby variables tend to return to their average rating after extreme high or low measurements, is called **regression toward the mean**. This can cause us to attribute the change in a score or measurement to something we did (like take a pill for high blood pressure), when in fact the score or measurement would have gone down on its own. Regression toward the mean is a consequence of the representativeness heuristic because people sometimes assume that the changes they are seeing are representative of what they expect to see rather than what is more likely to be the cause.

Often people don't take action until something is either happening too much or not enough (for example, a medical intervention for high blood pressure or an academic intervention for poor test scores). Regression toward the mean may be the reason why the issue of concern gets better (i.e., returns to normal), but people may mistakenly believe it was their intervention that caused the improvement. When you see claims like this being made, don't be too quick to discount the effectiveness of the intervention because they often do work, but consider whether the changes may have been due to regression toward the mean instead.

The "Stickiness" of Junk Science: Why It's So Hard to Debunk Misinformation

It's bad enough that our overly efficient brains cause us to sometimes believe things that aren't true, but once we come to believe these things, it can be very difficult to convince us that we're wrong. Even hard evidence is sometimes not enough to change our minds. That's why some people still believe that climate change is a hoax or that vaccines cause autism or that the US government has been covering up evidence of an alien spacecraft that crashed onto Earth. Even though these myths have been soundly disproven by science and hard facts, they remain "sticky" for some people. Why is it so hard to debunk this misinformation?

Lewandowsky and his colleagues have spent years trying to understand this. In their review of the literature on misinformation (Lewandowsky et al., 2012), they describe four possible reasons for what they call the "continued influence effect"—we'll call it the "stubbornly holding on to incorrect information even though it's been debunked" effect.

Mental Models

When you receive information about an event, your brain creates a mental model of it—kind of like a story or short film. If some of the information about the event were found to be untrue, to remove it from your mental model would leave a gap in the narrative, or a plot hole. Missing information, even if it was incorrect, would cause discomfort for us because our mental model of the event would no longer makes sense. Our motivation to store *complete* stories outweighs our motivation to store *accurate* stories, and so even misinformation is better than no information.

Retrieval Failure

Remember Chapter 1, when we talked about the three components of memory: encoding, storage, and retrieval? When one of these components fails, memory will be compromised. This theory of why we hold on to incorrect information suggests that the failure occurs in retrieving all of the relevant information from memory. Even if the new, correct information is encoded and stored, when the information is being recalled, somehow the fact that it is incorrect does not get retrieved. This results in only the original incorrect information being recalled.

Fluency and Familiarity

The more times we hear something, the better it is encoded in our memory (which is why you should always go to class). Unfortunately, when incorrect information is encoded in our memory, the correction of this information may serve to reinforce the original misinformation. You may only listen to the part of the message that repeats the original untrue fact and ignore the correction. Imagine that you heard on the news that aliens landed just outside your hometown ten years ago, but that it was covered up by the government. Later, when you hear a report of how this information was not true, the part about the aliens landing will be more familiar to you so that's what you'll pay attention to, ignoring the part about it not being true. Retractions and corrections of misinformation may backfire because, ironically, we only listen to the part that restates the misinformation.

Reactance

Sometimes people just react negatively to being told that what they have been led to believe is not actually true. Some people may be particularly scornful of retractions that come from official sources, like the government or a person with authority. This theory holds that people may not be discounting the information itself; instead, they are reacting to the source of the information.

This has big implications for those trying to undo misinformation. When the original article claiming that vaccinations cause autism was found to be unethical and scientifically unsound, it was retracted. The failure of this retraction to convince some people that vaccinations do not cause autism could be due to any or all of the reasons above. For example, a parent may have learned about the supposed connection between vaccinations and autism on the news, and decided that this story made sense in the context of their child, who started to develop signs of autism after receiving a vaccine. Now that they have a mental model of why their child is acting the way he or she is, removing the cause (i.e., the vaccine) would leave a large gap in their model. Or a retrieval failure may happen, in that the retraction of the article may not be retrieved from their memory at the same time as the reason for their child's autism. It could also be that every time they hear that vaccinations do not cause autism, what they selectively hear is the connection between the vaccine and autism, thus reinforcing their incorrect belief. Finally, they may just be resistant to what they perceive as a cover-up by government or pharmaceutical companies (who develop and profit from vaccinations), and hence misinterpret the intention of the retraction.

It makes sense, then, that in order to debunk misinformation, you need to address these issues. For example, if by retracting the study claiming that vaccinations lead to autism you will leave a gap in someone's understanding of why their child is behaving in a certain way, then you need to fill that gap with a plausible explanation. Unfortunately, researchers don't have an equally simple explanation for how autism develops, which is one reason why this mistaken belief about vaccines and autism is so difficult to dispel.

CUTTING THROUGH THE CRAP: HOW DO YOU KNOW WHAT TO BELIEVE?

What we've learned so far is that not only are we prone to believing things that aren't true, but we are shockingly resistant to the correction of this misinformation. You may feel that it's a good time to just give up on the truth at all, but we want to encourage you not to lose hope. In this world of "fake news" and "alternative facts," there is one powerful tool you can use to make sure you don't fall prey to misinformation: skepticism.

Sounds easy, right? Just be skeptical of everything, and you'll never be fooled! Unfortunately, that may not be the best tactic. It takes time to debunk false claims, and if you assume everything is a false claim then you'll use up an awful lot of mental energy. Instead, we recommend a more rational approach that won't cause you to question everything and alienate your friends. It's really no more than simply asking for evidence, something we've been suggesting throughout this book. If a claim cannot be backed up with evidence, then you should be skeptical.

The checklist below is a combination of suggestions from two people who are famous for their advice on "baloney detection," or how to evaluate scientific claims. Astronomer Carl Sagan, who was well-known for his ability to write about science in a clear and accessible way, wrote a chapter called "The Fine Art of Baloney Detection" (Sagan, 1996). In it, he lists many tools that we should use when evaluating claims. Michael Shermer (2001), who earned his PhD in the history of science and is the founder of the Skeptics Society, has developed his own "Baloney Detection Kit," a list of questions to ask when evaluating the validity of scientific claims. We've combined their advice to give you some general guidelines for distinguishing fact from fiction. In general, these guidelines involve asking questions about three aspects of the claim: the source, the claim itself, and the evidence. Following the checklist below will help you assess whether something is junk science or not. If any of these questions raise a flag, it doesn't necessarily mean you should discount the claim; it might mean that you have to do some more digging to find more information.

The Skeptic's Checklist

CHECK THE SOURCE

- Is it reliable?
- Is it biased?
- Do other sources agree?
- Is the source claiming to be an authority?

CHECK THE CLAIM

- Does it make sense?
- Do the conclusions follow logically?
- Is it the only explanation that works?
- Is it an actual claim, or is it simply attacking other explanations?
- Can it be falsified?
- Is it the simplest explanation, all things being equal?
- Does it adequately explain the phenomenon?

CHECK THE EVIDENCE

- Is there data or another type of evidence to back up the claim?
- Was the scientific method used to evaluate it?
- If causal claims are being made, have controlled experiments been conducted?

You don't have to go out of your way to hear false claims about the way the world works; an hour or so on social media, or even watching the evening news, should be sufficient. Some of these claims will be ridiculous and obviously false, but some will be very convincing. And some of them you may not pay attention to because they don't directly affect you, but others will affect you or those you care about. If you use the information from this chapter, as well as the other chapters in this book, you will become a better, more critical consumer of this information. Sometimes you'll need to seek out additional information. When you do, be sure to use your critical research skills (and the CRAAP test) to evaluate the information you find.

When you think about it, this entire book has been leading up to you becoming an educated skeptic about social science research. What will you do when you come across a seemingly outrageous claim about something in the news? Let's say it's something you care about deeply, like the psychological benefits of nature (our apologies if you don't care about trees as much as we do; in that case, think of something meaningful to you). Imagine that the article has just informed you that nature is bad for you, and you should stop going outside immediately. What should you do?

Use this book as a resource! Here's how:

Chapter 2 explains how social science research should be conducted, so use it to determine if the research seems to be sound. Are they relying on actual evidence, or some other way of knowing? Did they use the scientific method to test their claims? If the news article is claiming that nature causes illness, did they conduct experiments to support these causal claims?

Chapter 3 shows you how to find scholarly research, so look for original research articles on nature and illness (or wellness). If the news report is referring to a specific research study, track it down to see if it was reported accurately. See if you can find a meta-analysis, which summarizes and assesses all of the published research on the topic.

Chapter 5 describes how to critically evaluate the articles and websites you find. Use these skills to assess both the original article (if there is one) and any websites that have reported on it.

Chapter 6 will help you evaluate whether the research has been conducted in an ethical manner. Did they get informed consent from the participants? Is there any evidence of research fraud?

Chapters 7 and 8 will help you explain your findings to others, if you feel like sharing.

Chapter 9 will help you evaluate the statistics, if there are any. It will also help you determine if they are using the statistics in a manipulative or deceitful way.

Chapter 10 will help you think about and evaluate why you might believe or disbelieve the information being presented. If you already dislike going outside, your cognitive biases will probably lead you to not even question this news report, whereas if you love nature, you'll likely search harder for confirmation that the article is junk science.

By using this book as a guide, you'll be able to confidently and accurately assess claims like this. When you take the time to critically evaluate these claims, you can then make educated decisions about whether, for example, you should go out and enjoy nature (quick answer: science says you should!), start that fad diet (science says probably not), or use a product because a celebrity endorses it (science suggests you do your research).

Do Your Research! How to Check for False Claims

Here are some sources we have found useful in evaluating the accuracy of scientific (and non-scientific) claims. This list is far from exhaustive—there are many excellent resources out there—but it's a place to start. We've made every attempt to ensure that the links are up-to-date, but if they do not work, we've given you the name of the organization too.

Bad Science (a collection of columns by Ben Goldacre, a very smart, very funny epidemiologist and science writer)—http://www.badscience. net

Calling Bullshit (an entire course on evaluating scientific claims)— http://www.callingbullshit.org

Centres for Disease Control and Prevention—http://www.cdc.gov

Factcheck.org (a wide-ranging fact-checking source, but they have a special page on science fact checking)—http://www.factcheck.org

Health Canada—http://www.canada.ca/en/health-canada.html

Potholer54 (the YouTube channel of Peter Hadfield, a journalist/geologist who likes to debunk scientific claims)—https://www.youtube.com/ user/potholer54

Snopes (a reputable fact-checking site)—http://www.snopes.com

Tim Minchin (this may not help you evaluate scientific claims, but his song, "If You Open Your Mind Too Much Your Brains Will Fall Out (Take My Wife)," will make you smile)—https://www.youtube.com/ watch?v=RFO6ZhUW38w

AUTHOR BIOGRAPHIES

Judy Eaton is a member of the department of psychology at the Brantford campus of Wilfrid Laurier University. She teaches a variety of courses, including statistics, introductory psychology, positive psychology, and social science literacy. Her two main areas of research are the resolution of interpersonal conflict through apology and forgiveness, and strategies for student success. Her work has been published in psychology, criminology, education, and interdisciplinary journals, and in 2008 she was the recipient of the Canadian Psychological Association President's New Researcher Award. In her spare time she enjoys hiking, reading, and eating, usually not at the same time, and has been trying to learn how to play the banjo for about 10 years. She lives in Hamilton, Ontario, with her family.

David N. Morris is a geographer at the Brantford campus of Wilfrid Laurier University. His undergraduate degree is from Laurier Brantford, and his graduate degrees are from the University of Waterloo. Although his primary research interest is in ecological restoration in the Carolinian zone of southern Ontario, he is also interested in local food systems. David self-identifies as a treehugger: he has a passion for propagating, growing, and collecting trees of all kinds. Fortunately, David and his wife, Monica, have a farm in rural Brant County, Ontario, that provides David with space to grow his tree collection.

GLOSSARY

academic literacy—the ability to find, understand, and communicate information

applied research—research intended to be put into practice, to purposefully address some particular problem or issue

availability heuristic—a heuristic or mental shortcut that describes our tendency to place more emphasis or value on things that more readily come to mind

basic research—research intended solely to help us better understand human nature on a more abstract level; it is conducted for the purpose of understanding

bias toward extremes—a heuristic or mental shortcut that describes our tendency to notice and remember unusual or extreme events, rather than typical or usual events

biophilia hypothesis—the theory that humans have an inborn need to connect with nature and other living things

canon—a fundamental principle or rule as to how the world works

canons of science—four principles or rules that scientists hold to be true: determinism, empiricism, parsimony, and testability

common knowledge—information that people can reasonably be expected to know; this may vary depending on the intended audience; for an academic paper it would mean information a reasonably well-educated person might be expected to know

confirmation bias—a phenomenon whereby we tend to notice evidence that fits with, or confirms, our theories and ignore evidence that does not fit with our theories

confound—in an experiment, a variable that could have an effect on the dependent variable, making it difficult to determine whether the change in the dependent variable is due to the independent variable or to the confound

content analysis—a research method used by both qualitative and quantitative researchers, whereby traditionally qualitative artifacts (e.g., books, songs, photos) are examined to identify common themes control condition—in an experiment, the condition that serves as a comparison group to the experimental condition; participants are treated the same as those in the experimental condition, except that they are not exposed to the independent variable

correlation—a quantitative (i.e., numerical) assessment of whether two variables are related

critical thinking—carefully and objectively assessing claims or statements to determine whether there is sufficient evidence to support them

deductive approach—a top-down approach to theory building, in which a theory is proposed and then evidence is sought to support that theory

dependent variable—in an experiment, the variable that is measured, in order to determine what effect, if any, the independent variable has on it

descriptive research—research that is conducted to learn more about specific variables, such as how often and under what conditions they occur

descriptive statistics—the use of numbers to summarize or describe a variable

determinism—one of the four canons of science; the assumption that all events or phenomena have causes, and that things happen for a reason

elaborative interrogation—a study strategy in which questions are posed and an attempt is made to figure out the answers before reading about the topic in more detail

empiricism—one of the four canons of science; the assumption that we learn about things by carefully and systematically observing them

encoding—the part of the memory process that involves getting, or encoding, information into the brain

experiment—a quantitative research method that involves manipulating a variable under carefully controlled conditions and observing whether any changes occur in a second variable as a result

experimental condition—in an experiment, the condition in which participants are exposed to the independent variable; also sometimes called the treatment condition explanatory research—research conducted to learn more about why things happen; in other words, to explain the relationships between variables

exploratory research—research conducted to learn more about a phenomenon when not much is known about it; often used to uncover key variables and to develop methods for measuring those variables

field research—a type of qualitative research method in which a researcher collects data in a natural setting (i.e., a setting that is not created for the purpose of the research study)

focus group—a qualitative research method in which a researcher interviews a group of research participants together rather than just one at a time

generalizability—the extent to which the findings of a research study (using a sample) are applicable to the larger group under study (i.e., the population)

heuristics—mental shortcuts that we use to save time and mental processing when we are interpreting events or situations; sometimes called rules of thumb

idea map—a method of narrowing a general idea into a specific, researchable question by drawing an image in which the general idea is surrounded by increasingly specific concepts or questions

independent variable—in an experiment, the variable that is manipulated, in order to see if it has any effect on the dependent variable

inductive approach—a bottom-up approach to theory building, in which observations are made and then a theory that best explains those observations is proposed

inferential statistics—the use of numbers to make predictions or inferences about variables; used in making predictions about whether the results found in a study using a small number of people can be generalized to a larger group of people

interleaved practice—a study strategy in which different topics are studied in the same session, rather than studying only one topic at a time

interview—a qualitative research method in which a researcher asks a research participant questions and then documents the answers; the answers serve as data in-text citations—a method used to give credit to sources in the body of a paper or article without listing the full citation; in APA style, this includes the author(s) last name and the year of the publication

junk science—the misconduct or misrepresentation of scientific research, resulting in the dissemination of misinformation about scientific findings

literature review—an overview of what is known about a particular topic, in which all of the published research on the topic is synthesized, which includes identifying themes, common findings, areas where the research findings do not agree, and any gaps in the research (i.e., unanswered questions)

mean—the average of all the numbers in a group or sample; a measure of central tendency

measure of central tendency—a type of descriptive statistic, whereby a single number is used that best represents the group or sample (e.g., mean, median, mode)

measure of variability—a type of descriptive statistic that indicates how spread out, or variable, the scores in a distribution are (e.g., range, standard deviation)

median—the exact midpoint of the scores in a group or sample; a measure of central tendency

mindset theory—the theory that we make assumptions about the malleability of personal attributes or characteristics (i.e., that they are either fixed, or unchangeable, or that they are malleable, or changeable), and that these assumptions can affect our motivation and behaviour

misperception of randomness—a common cognitive bias, whereby individuals mistakenly think that randomness necessarily involves a chaotic distribution with no discernable pattern (when in fact, randomness can look very ordered)

mode—the number in a group or sample that occurs most frequently; a measure of central tendency

natural sciences—the disciplines that study phenomena and processes in nature, such as biology, chemistry, and physics open-ended interview—a type of qualitative research method in which a researcher begins with a general question to pose to a research participant, but develops follow-up questions based on the participants' responses; few, if any, predetermined questions are used

operationalization—the process of specifying how a variable is measured

outliers—in groups of scores, scores that are significantly higher or lower than the rest; also called extreme scores

paradigms—frames of reference, or worldviews, that we use to organize and make sense of the world; for social scientists, paradigms provide a standard set of assumptions, rules, and methods for conducting research

paraphrasing—completely rewriting a point made by a source, keeping the meaning and intent of the original but using your own words; does not mean to simply replace a few words with synonyms

parsimony—one of the four canons of science; the assumption that, when faced with different theories to explain some phenomenon, the best theory is the simplest one

peer review—the process by which research, before it is published, is read and reviewed by experts in the field to ensure that it is free from bias and errors, that it is well conducted, and that it makes a meaningful contribution to the scientific community

population—the entire group of people or things being studied; does not necessarily refer to everyone in the world

practice tests—a study strategy in which ungraded tests are used as a rehearsal for retrieving information stored in the brain

primary source—a description of original research, conducted by the author

programmatic research—the process by which research progresses from exploratory to descriptive to explanatory; it aims first to explore the phenomenon, then describe it, and then provide an explanation as to why it happens

qualitative data—data or observations that are expressed as words, images, sounds, or objects qualitative research—a type of research design in which researchers aim to learn more about phenomena by collecting data or observations that are expressed as words, images, sounds, objects, or in other non-quantifiable ways

quantitative data—data or observations that are expressed as numbers

quantitative research—a type of research design in which researchers aim to learn more about phenomena by measuring them with as much accuracy as possible using numbers

random assignment—in an experiment, a way of assigning participants to groups so that everyone has an equal chance of being selected for any given group

random sampling error—the fact that even if a sample is randomly chosen from a population, the sample may not be a representative sample; the error is the difference between the sample and the population

range—in a group of scores, the distance between the lowest score and the highest score; a measure of variability

regression toward the mean—the fact that variables tend to return to their average rating after extreme high or low measurements

representativeness heuristic—a mental shortcut that describes our tendency, when faced with a novel event, to compare it to a prototype or exemplar that we already have or to categorize it with something we already know about

research fraud—the act of committing research misconduct, which may include making up data, misrepresenting the results of a research study, fabricating one's credentials, conflicts of interest, and plagiarism

retrieval—the part of the memory process that involves getting, or retrieving, information from the brain (i.e., remembering)

sample—a subset of the population being studied

scholarly source—an article or book that is written by an expert in the field, often describing original scientific research

search terms—significant words or phrases related to a topic; also called keywords

secondary analysis—a type of quantitative research method in which data that has already been collected is re-examined in order to address new research questions

secondary source—a source that describes, analyzes, or contextualizes primary sources; examples include literature reviews, academic opinion articles, academic books, and textbooks

self-explanation—a study strategy in which the learner tries to explain the answer to a question to themselves, as a test of their understanding of the topic

semi-structured interview—a type of qualitative research method in which a researcher poses predetermined questions to a research participant, but with the flexibility to include additional questions that may arise during the interview

social science—"the scientific study of social, cultural, psychological, economic, and political forces that guide individuals in their actions" (Hunt & Colander, 2011, p. 1)

spaced practice—a study strategy in which studying is spaced out over a period of time, rather than being done all at once; the opposite of cramming

standard deviation—a measure of how much, on average, all the scores in a distribution differ from the mean of the distribution; a measure of variability

statistical significance—a low probability that the results of a research study are due to chance (i.e., random sampling error); in the social sciences, the accepted convention is that if there is less than a 5 percent probability the results are due to random chance rather than real differences, we conclude that the finding is statistically significant

storage—the part of the memory process that involves keeping, or storing, information in the brain

structured interview—a type of qualitative research method in which a researcher poses predetermined questions to a research participant; all the questions are determined beforehand, and the researcher does not deviate from the script synthesizing—when writing a literature review, weaving the findings of the various scholarly sources together into core themes, to tell an interesting and original story about the research topic

testability—one of the four canons of science; the assumption that in order to be valid, a theory must be testable, in that it must be possible to prove or disprove it

theory—a proposed explanation as to why things happen; used to explain the relationship between variables

REFERENCES

Agnew, R. (1992). Foundation for a general strain theory of crime and delinquency. *Criminology, 30*, 47–88. doi:10.1111/j.1745-9125.1992.tb01093.x

Alexitch, L. R. (2002). The role of help-seeking attitudes and tendencies in students' preferences for academic advising. *Journal of College Student Development, 43*, 5–19.

American Psychological Association. (2004). *The truth about lie detectors (aka polygraph tests)*. Retrieved from http://www.apa.org/research/action/polygraph.aspx

American Psychological Association. (2010). *Publication manual of the American Psychological Association* (6th ed.). Washington, DC: Author.

American Psychological Association. (2017). *About APA*. Retrieved from http://www.apa.org/about/index.aspx

Atkinson, R. C., & Shiffrin, R. M. (1971). *The control processes of short-term memory.* Stanford, CA: Stanford University.

Bahrick, H. P., & Hall, L. K. (2005). The importance of retrieval failures to long-term retention: A metacognitive explanation of the spacing effect. *Journal of Memory and Language, 52*, 566–577. doi:10.1016/j.jml.2005.01.012

Bamber, M. D., & Schneider, J. K. (2016). Mindfulness-based meditation to decrease stress and anxiety in college students: A narrative synthesis of the research. *Educational Research Review, 18*, 1–32. doi:10.1016/j.edurev.2015.12.004

Banks, M. R., & Banks, W. A. (2002). The effects of animal-assisted therapy on loneliness in an elderly population in long-term care facilities. *The Journals of Gerontology Series A: Biological Sciences and Medical Sciences, 57*, M428–M432. doi:10.1016/j.jamda.2007.11.007

Bastardi, A., Uhlmann, E. L., & Ross, L. (2011). Wishful thinking: Belief, desire, and the motivated evaluation of scientific evidence. *Psychological Science, 22*, 731–732. doi:10.1177/0956797611406447

Baumeister, R. F., & Leary, M. R. (1997). Writing narrative literature reviews. *Review of General Psychology, 1*, 311–320. doi:10.1037//1089-2680.1.3.311

Bentley, M., Peerenboom, C. A., Hodge, F. W., Passano, E. B., Warren, H. C., & Washburn, M. F. (1929). Instructions in regard to preparation of manuscript. *Psychological Bulletin, 26*, 57–63. doi:10.1037/h0071487

Berry, C. (1981). The Nobel scientists and the origins of scientific achievement. *The British Journal of Sociology, 32*, 381–391. doi:10.2307/589284

Blakeslee, S. (2004). The CRAAP test. *LOEX Quarterly, 31*(3), 6–7. Retrieved from http://commons.emich.edu/cgi/viewcontentcgi?article=1009&context=loexquarterly

Bohnert, N., Chagnon, J., & Dion, P. (2015). *Population projections for Canada (2013 to 2063), provinces and territories (2013 to 2038)*. Ottawa, ON: Statistics Canada. Retrieved from http://www.statcan.gc.ca/pub/91-520-x/91-520-x2014001-eng.pdf

Bratman, G. N., Hamilton, J. P., Hahn, K. S., Daily, G. C., & Gross, J. J. (2015). Nature experience reduces rumination and subgenual prefrontal cortex activation. *Proceedings of the National Academy of Sciences, 112*, 8567–8572. doi:10.1073/pnas.1510459112

Brown, P. C., Roediger, H. L., & McDaniel, M. A. (2014). *Make it stick*. Cambridge, MA: Harvard University Press.

Burke, M., Marlow, C., & Lento, T. (2010, April). Social network activity and social well-being. In E. Mynatt, G. Fitzpatrick, S. Hudson, K. Edwards, & T. Rodden (Eds.), *Proceedings of the SIGCHI Conference on Human Factors in Computing Systems* (pp. 1909–1912). New York, NY: ACM.

Canadian Institute for Health Information. (2017). *Alcohol harm in Canada: Examining hospitalizations entirely caused by alcohol and strategies to reduce alcohol harm*. Ottawa, ON: Author.

Canadian Institutes of Health Research, Natural Sciences and Engineering Research Council of Canada, & Social Sciences and Humanities Research Council of Canada. (2014). *Tri-council policy statement: Ethical conduct for research involving humans*. Retrieved from http://www.pre.ethics.gc.ca/pdf/eng/tcps2-2014/TCPS_2_FINAL_Web.pdf

Carpenter, S. K. (2009). Cue strength as a moderator of the testing effect: The benefits of elaborative retrieval. *Journal of Experimental Psychology: Learning, Memory, and Cognition, 35*, 1563–1569. doi:10.1037/a0017021

Cepeda, N. J., Pashler, H., Vul, E., Wixted, J. T., & Rohrer, D. (2006). Distributed practice in verbal recall tasks: A review and quantitative synthesis. *Psychological Bulletin, 132*, 354–380. doi:10.1037/0033-2909.132.3.354

Churchill, M., Safaoui, J., McCabe, B. W., & Baun, M. M. (1999). Using a therapy dog to alleviate the agitation and desocialization of people with Alzheimer's disease. *Journal of Psychosocial Nursing, 37*, 16–22.

Cohen-Mansfield, J. (1986). Agitated behaviors in the elderly: II. Preliminary results in the cognitively deteriorated. *Journal of the American Geriatrics Society, 34*, 722–727. doi:10.1111/j.1532-5415.1986.tb04303.x

Courtemanche, C. (2011). A silver lining? The connection between gasoline prices and obesity. *Economic Inquiry, 49*, 935–957. doi:10.1111/j.1465-7295.2009.00266.x

Cox, M., Garrett, E., & Graham, J. A. (2005). Death in Disney films: Implications for children's understanding of death. *Omega: Journal of Death and Dying, 50*, 267–280. doi:10.2190/Q5VL-KLF7-060F-W69V

Creagan, E. T., Bauer, B. A., Thomley, B. S., & Borg, J. M. (2015). Animal-assisted therapy at Mayo Clinic: The time is now. *Complementary Therapies in Clinical Practice, 21*, 101–104. doi:10.1016/j.ctcp.2015.03.002

Crozier, J. (2002). A unique experiment. *China in Focus, 12.* Retrieved from http://www.sacu.org/examinations.html

Curcio, G., Ferrara, M., & De Gennaro, L. (2006). Sleep loss, learning capacity and academic performance. *Sleep Medicine Reviews, 10*, 323–337. doi:10.1016/j.smrv.2005.11.001

Daltry, R. M., & Mehr, K. E. (2015). Therapy dogs on campus: Recommendations for counseling center outreach. *Journal of College Student Psychotherapy, 29*, 72–78. doi:10.1080/87568225.2015.976100

De Grez, L. (2009). *Optimizing the instructional environment to learn presentation skills* (Unpublished doctoral dissertation). University of Ghent, Belgium.

Dempster, F. N. (1988). The spacing effect: A case study in the failure to apply the results of psychological research. *American Psychologist, 43*, 627–634. doi:10.1037/0003-066X.43.8.627

Department of Health, Education, and Welfare. (1979). *The Belmont report: Ethical principles and guidelines for the protection of human subjects of research.* Washington, DC: OPRR Report.

Deters, F. G., & Mehl, M. R. (2013). Does posting Facebook status updates increase or decrease loneliness? An online social networking experiment. *Social Psychological and Personality Science, 4*, 579–586. doi:10.1177/1948550612469233

Diekelmann, S., & Born, J. (2010). The memory function of sleep. *Nature Reviews Neuroscience, 11*, 114–126. doi:10.1038/nrn2762

Dunlosky, J., Rawson, K. A., Marsh, E. J., Nathan, M. J., & Willingham, D. T. (2013). Improving students' learning with effective learning techniques: Promising directions from cognitive and educational psychology. *Psychological Science in the Public Interest, 14*, 4–58. doi:10.1177/1529100612453266

Dweck, C. S. (1986). Motivational processes affecting learning. *American Psychologist, 41*, 1040–1048. doi:10.1037/0003-066X.41.10.1040

Dweck, C. S. (2000). *Self-theories: Their role in motivation, personality, and development.* London, UK: Psychology Press.

Dweck, C. S. (2006). *Mindset: The new psychology of success.* New York, NY: Random House.

Dweck, C. S., Chiu, C. Y., & Hong, Y. Y. (1995). Implicit theories and their role in judgments and reactions: A word from two perspectives. *Psychological Inquiry, 6*, 267–285. doi:10.1207/s15327965pli0604_1

Dyson, J. (2003). *Against the odds: An autobiography.* New York, NY: Texere.

Eachus, P. (2001). Pets, people and robots: The role of companion animals and robopets in the promotion of health and well-being. *International Journal of Health Promotion and Education, 39*, 7–13. doi:10.1080/14635240.2001.10806140

Ebbinghaus, H. (1885/1913). *Memory. A contribution to experimental psychology (Über das Gedchtnis. Untersuchungen zur experimentellen Psychologie)*. New York, NY: Teachers College, Columbia University.

Education Advisory Board. (2014). Strategies for combatting academic misconduct. Retrieved from https://www.eab.com/research-and-insights/student-affairs-forum/custom/2014/05/strategies-for-combatting-academic-misconduct

Ellis, Y., Daniels, B., & Jauregui, A. (2010). The effect of multitasking on the grade performance of business students. *Research in Higher Education Journal, 8*, 1–10.

Emmons, R. A., & McCullough, M. E. (2003). Counting blessings versus burdens: An experimental investigation of gratitude and subjective well-being in daily life. *Journal of Personality and Social Psychology, 84*, 377–389. doi:10.1037/0022-3514.84.2.377

Evans, P. (2016, September 16). Top Canadian CEOs paid almost 159 times the average worker's salary last year. *CBC News*. Retrieved from http://www.cbc.ca/news/business/ceo-pay-compensation-1.3766091

Fallows, S., & Steven, C. (2000). Building employability skills into the higher education curriculum: A university-wide initiative. *Education + Training, 42*, 75–83. doi:10.1108/00400910010331620

Fenesi, B., Lucibello, K., Kim, J. A., & Heisz, J. J. (2016). Sweat so you don't forget: How exercise breaks during instruction can promote learning. *Journal of Exercise, Movement, and Sport, 48*, 165.

Ferguson, S. A., Hardy, A. P., & Williams, A. F. (2003). Content analysis of television advertising for cars and minivans: 1983–1998. *Accident Analysis & Prevention, 35*, 825–831. doi:10.1016/S0001-4575(02)00087-8

Fey, T. (2013). *Bossypants*. New York, NY: Reagan Arthur Books.

Fick, K. M. (1993). The influence of an animal on social interactions of nursing home residents in a group setting. *American Journal of Occupational Therapy, 47*, 529–534. doi:10.5014/ajot.47.6.529

Filan, S. L., & Llewellyn-Jones, R. H. (2006). Animal-assisted therapy for dementia: A review of the literature. *International Psychogeriatrics, 18*, 597–611. doi:10.1017/S1041610206003322

Forer, B. R. (1949). The fallacy of personal validation: A classroom demonstration of testing. *Journal of Abnormal and Social Psychology, 44*, 118–123.

Gage, S. (2014, April 22). A bottle of wine a day is harmless? The evidence suggests otherwise. *The Guardian*. Retrieved from https://www.theguardian.com/science/sifting-the-evidence/2014/apr/22/drinking-wine-health-evidence-alcohol-units

Garfield, S., (2000). *Mauve: How one man invented a color that changed the world.* New York, NY: Norton.

Gauvin, L., Rejeski, W. J., & Norris, J. L. (1996). A naturalistic study of the impact of acute physical activity on feeling states and affect in women. *Health Psychology, 15,* 391–397. doi:10.1037/0278-6133.15.5.391

Gelso, C. (2006). Applying theories to research: The interplay of theory and research in science. In F. T. Leong & J. T. Austin (Eds.), *The psychology research handbook* (pp. 455–465). Thousand Oaks, CA: Sage.

Gillen-O'Neel, C., Huynh, V. W., & Fuligni, A. J. (2013). To study or to sleep? The academic costs of extra studying at the expense of sleep. *Child Development, 84,* 133–142. doi:10.1111/j.1467-8624.2012.01834.x

Gould, L. F., Dariotis, J. K., Greenberg, M. T., & Mendelson, T. (2016). Assessing fidelity of implementation (FOI) for school-based mindfulness and yoga interventions: A systematic review. *Mindfulness, 7,* 5–33. doi:10.1007/s12671-015-0395-6

Greer, K. L., Pustay, K. A., Zaun, T. C., & Coppens, P. (2001). A comparison of the effects of toys versus live animals on the communication of patients with dementia of the Alzheimer's type. *Clinical Gerontologist, 24,* 157–182. doi:10.1300/J018v24n03_13

Haines, L. (2005, November 23). Canon braces for arse-induced copier carnage. *The Register.* Retrieved from https://www.theregister.co.uk/2005/11/23/xmas_copier_emergency/

Hall, K. G., Domingues, D. A., & Cavazos, R. (1994). Contextual interference effects with skilled baseball players. *Perceptual and Motor Skills, 78,* 835–841. doi:10.2466/pms.1994.78.3.835

Hawking, S. W., Perry, M. J., & Strominger, A. (2016). Superrotation charge and supertranslation hair on black holes. *Journal of High Energy Physics, 5,* 1–33. doi:10.1007/JHEP05(2017)161

Hilton, L., Hempel, S., Ewing, B. A., Apaydin, E., Xenakis, L., Newberry, S., ... & Maglione, M. A. (2017). Mindfulness meditation for chronic pain: Systematic review and meta-analysis. *Annals of Behavioral Medicine, 51,* 199–213. doi:10.1007/s12160-016-9844-2

Hoerrner, K. L. (1996). Gender roles in Disney films: Analyzing behaviors from Snow White to Simba. *Women's Studies in Communication, 19,* 213–228. doi:10.1080/07491409.1996.11089813

Horkheimer, M. (1972). *Critical theory: Selected essays.* New York, NY: Continuum Publishing.

Huff, D. (1954). *How to lie with statistics.* New York, NY: Norton.

Hunt, E. F., & Colander, D. C. (2011). *Social science: An introduction to the study of society.* Boston, MA: Pearson.

Jivanda, T. (2014, April 19). A bottle of wine a day is not bad for you and abstaining is worse than drinking, scientist claims. *The Independent*. Retrieved from http://www.independent.co.uk/life-style/food-and-drink/news/a-bottle-of-wine-a-day-is-not-bad-for-you-and-abstaining-is-worse-than-drinking-scientist-claims-9271010.html

Kaminski, M., Pellino, T., & Wish, J. (2002). Play and pets: The physical and emotional impact of child-life and pet therapy on hospitalized children. *Children's Health Care, 31*, 321–335. doi:10.1207/S15326888CHC3104_5

Kang, S. H. K., & Pashler, H. (2012). Learning painting styles: Spacing is advantageous when it promotes discriminative contrast. *Applied Cognitive Psychology, 26*, 97–103. doi:10.1002/acp.1801

Kessler, R. C., Stein, M. B., & Berglund, P. (1998). Social phobia subtypes in the National Comorbidity Survey. *American Journal of Psychiatry, 155*, 613–619. doi:10.1176/ajp.155.5.613

Kongable, L. G., Buckwalter, K. C., & Stolley, J. M. (1989). The effects of pet therapy on the social behavior of institutionalized Alzheimer's clients. *Archives of Psychiatric Nursing, 3*, 191–198.

Kruger, K. A., & Serpell, J. A. (2006). Animal-assisted interventions in mental health: Definitions and theoretical foundations. *Handbook on Animal-Assisted Therapy: Theoretical Foundations and Guidelines for Practice, 2*, 21–38.

Kuhn T. S. (1996). *The structure of scientific revolutions* (3rd ed.). Chicago, IL: University of Chicago Press.

Lang, J. M. (2013). *Cheating lessons*. Cambridge, MA: Harvard University Press.

Larson, H. J., Cooper, L. Z., Eskola, J., Katz, S. L., & Ratzan, S. C. (2011). Addressing the vaccine confidence gap. *The Lancet, 378*, 526–535. doi:10.1016/S0140-6736(11)60678-8

Lauter, D. (2016, November 8). The USC/L.A. Times poll saw what other surveys missed: A wave of Trump support. *Los Angeles Times*. Retrieved from http://www.latimes.com/politics/la-na-pol-usc-latimes-poll-20161108-story.html

Lawson, A., & Fouts, G. (2004). Mental illness in Disney animated films. *The Canadian Journal of Psychiatry, 49*, 310–314. doi:10.1177/070674370404900506

Lax, E. (2004). *The mold in Dr. Florey's coat: The story of the penicillin miracle*. New York, NY: Henry Holt.

Lewandowsky, S., Ecker, U. K., Seifert, C. M., Schwarz, N., & Cook, J. (2012). Misinformation and its correction: Continued influence *and successful debiasing*. *Psychological Science in the Public Interest, 13*, 106–131. doi:10.1177/1529100612451018

Loui, M. C. (2002). Seven ways to plagiarize: Handling real allegations of research misconduct. *Science and Engineering Ethics, 8*, 529–539. doi:10.1007/s11948-002-0005-6

Machi, L. A., & McEvoy, B. T. (2009). *The literature review*. Thousand Oaks, CA: Corwin Press.

MacKerron, G., & Mourato, S. (2013). Happiness is greater in natural environments. *Global Environmental Change, 23*, 992–1000. doi:10.1016/j.gloenvcha.2013.03.010

Marshall, T. C., Lefringhausen, K., & Ferenczi, N. (2015). The Big Five, self-esteem, and narcissism as predictors of the topics people write about in Facebook status updates. *Personality and Individual Differences, 85*, 35–40. doi:10.1016/j. paid.2015.04.039

Maxwell, J. C. (2007). *Failing forward*. Nashville, TN: Thomas Nelson Inc.

Mayer, R. E. (2009). *Multimedia learning*. New York, NY: Cambridge University Press.

McCabe, D. L., Butterfield, K. D., & Treviño, L. K. (2012). *Cheating in college: Why students do it and what can be done about it*. Baltimore, MD: Johns Hopkins University Press.

Michael, E. B., Keller, T. A., Carpenter, P. A., & Just, M. A. (2001). fMRI investigation of sentence compression by eye and by ear: Modality fingerprints on cognitive processes. *Human Brain Mapping, 13*, 239–252. doi:10.1002/hbm.1036

Milgram, S. (1963). Behavioral study of obedience. *Journal of Abnormal and Social Psychology, 67*, 371–378. doi:10.1037/h0040525

Milgram, S. (1974). *Obedience to authority*. New York, NY: Harper Perennial.

Milliman, R. E. (1986). The influence of background music on the behavior of restaurant patrons. *Journal of Consumer Research, 13*, 286-289.

Morahan-Martin, J., & Schumacher, P. (2003). Loneliness and social uses of the Internet. *Computers in Human Behavior, 19*, 659–671. doi:10.1016/S0747-5632(03)00040-2

Mueller, P. A., & Oppenheimer, D. M. (2014). The pen is mightier than the keyboard: Advantages of longhand over laptop note taking. *Psychological Science, 25*, 1159–1168. doi:10.1177/0956797614524581

Nolen-Hoeksema, S., Wisco, B. E., & Lyubomirsky, S. (2008). Rethinking rumination. *Perspectives on Psychological Science, 3*, 400–424. doi:10.1111/j.1745-6924.2008.00088.x

O'Flaherty, W. (2015, December 5). (CCSLQ-13) Right thing. Retrieved from http://www.essentialcslewis.com/2015/11/22/ccslq-13-right-thing/

Organisation for Economic Co-operation and Development. (2016). *Society at a glance 2016: OECD social indicators* (Summary). Paris, France: OECD Publishing. Retrieved from doi:10.1787/c665889e-en

Padilla-Walker, L. M., Coyne, S. M., Fraser, A. M., & Stockdale, L. A. (2013). Is Disney the nicest place on earth? A content analysis of prosocial behavior in animated Disney films. *Journal of Communication, 63*, 393–412. doi:10.1111/jcom.12022

Paffenbarger, R. S., Jr., & Hyde, R. T. (1988). Exercise adherence, coronary heart disease and longevity. In R. K. Dishman (Ed.), *Exercise adherence: Its impact on public health* (pp. 41–73.). Champaign, IL: Human Kinetics Books.

Peterson, C., Park, N., & Seligman, M. E. (2005). Orientations to happiness and life satisfaction: The full life versus the empty life. *Journal of Happiness Studies, 6*, 25–41. doi:10.1007/s10902-004-1278-z

Plante, T. G., Gustafson, C., Brecht, C., Imberi, J., & Sanchez, J. (2011). Exercising with an iPod, friend, or neither: Which is better for psychological benefits? *American Journal of Health Behavior, 35*, 199–208. doi:10.5993/AJHB.35.2.7

Poland, G. A., & Spier, R. (2010). Fear, misinformation, and innumerates: How the Wakefield paper, the press, and advocacy groups damaged the public health. *Vaccine, 28*, 2361–2362. doi:10.1016/j.vaccine.2010.02.052

Pressley, M., McDaniel, M. A., Turnure, J. E., Wood, E., & Ahmad, M. (1987). Generation and precision of elaboration: Effects on intentional and incidental learning. *Journal of Experimental Psychology: Learning, Memory, and Cognition, 13*, 291–300. doi:10.1037/0278-7393.13.2.291

Rabin, B. A., Boehmer, T. K., & Brownson, R. C. (2007). Cross-national comparison of environmental and policy correlates of obesity in Europe. *The European Journal of Public Health, 17*, 53–61. doi:10.1093/eurpub/ckl073

Rashad, I. (2009). Associations of cycling with urban sprawl and the gasoline price. *American Journal of Health Promotion, 24*, 27–36. doi:10.4278/ajhp.071121124

Rawson, K. A., & Dunlosky, J. (2011). Optimizing schedules of retrieval practice for durable and efficient learning: How much is enough? *Journal of Experimental Psychology: General, 140*, 283–302. doi:10.1037/a0023956

Roediger, H. L., III, & Karpicke, J. D. (2006). Test-enhanced learning: Taking memory tests improves long-term retention. *Psychological Science, 17*, 249–255. doi:10.1111/j.1467-9280.2006.01693.x

Roediger, H. L., III, Putnam, A. L., & Smith, M. A. (2011). Ten benefits of testing and their applications to educational practice. *Psychology of Learning and Motivation, 44*, 1–36. doi:10.1016/B978-0-12-387691-1.00001-6

Roth, J. (2000). Pet therapy uses with geriatric adults. *International Journal of Psychosocial Rehabilitation, 4*, 27–39.

Ruscio, A. M., Brown, T. A., Chiu, W. T., Sareen, J., Stein, M. B., & Kessler, R. C. (2008). Social fears and social phobia in the USA: Results from the National Comorbidity Survey Replication. *Psychological Medicine, 38*, 15–28. doi:10.1017/S0033291707001699

Sagan, C. (1996). *The demon haunted world: Science as a candle in the dark.* Toronto, ON: Random House.

Salmon, P. (2001). Effects of physical exercise on anxiety, depression, and sensitivity to stress: A unifying theory. *Clinical Psychology Review, 21*, 33–61. doi:10.1016/S0272-7358(99)00032-X

Saxe, J. G. (2017). *The blind men and the elephant.* Retrieved from http://www.allaboutphilosophy.org/blind-men-and-the-elephant.htm

Schunk, D. H. (1991). Self-efficacy and academic motivation. *Educational Psychologist, 26*, 207–231. doi:10.1080/00461520.1991.9653133

Seidman, G. (2013). Self-presentation and belonging on Facebook: How personality influences social media use and motivations. *Personality and Individual Differences, 54*, 402–407. doi:10.1016/j.paid.2012.10.009

Shermer, M. (2001). Baloney detection. *Scientific American, 285*, 36.

Sitkin, S. (1992). Learning through failure: The strategy of small losses. *Research in Organizational Behavior, 14*, 231–266.

Spitzer, H. F. (1939). Studies in retention. *Journal of Educational Psychology, 30*, 641.

Stasi, M. F., Amati, D., Costa, C., Resta, D., Senepa, G., Scarafioiti, C., ... & Molaschi, M. (2004). Pet-therapy: A trial for institutionalized frail elderly patients. *Archives of Gerontology and Geriatrics, 38*, 407–412. doi:10.1016/j.archger.2004.04.052

Statistics Canada (2015). *Canadian megatrends. Canada's crime rate: Two decades of decline.* Catalogue no. 11-630-X. Retrieved from https://www150.statcan.gc.ca/n1/en/pub/11-630-x/11-630-x2015001-eng.pdf?st=nlZalG6u

Statistics Canada. (2018a). *About us.* Retrieved from http://statcan.gc.ca/eng/about/about?MM=as

Statistics Canada. (2018b). *Table 153-0153: Households and the environment survey, participation in outdoor activities, Canada, provinces and census metropolitan areas (CMA), every 2 years (percent).* CANSIM (database). Retrieved from http://www5.statcan.gc.ca/cansim/a26?lang=eng&id=1530153

Steptoe, A., Wardle, J., Fuller, R., Holte, A., Justo, J., Sanderman, R., & Wichstrom, L. (1997). Leisure-time physical exercise: Prevalence, attitudinal correlates, and behavioral correlates among young Europeans from 21 countries. *Preventive Medicine, 26*, 845–854. doi:10.1006/pmed.1997.0224

Stossel, S. (2014). Performance anxiety in great performers. *The Atlantic*, January/February. Retrieved from https://www.theatlantic.com/magazine/archive/2014/01/what-hugh-grant-gandhi-and-thomas-jefferson-have-common/355853/

Sumner, W. G. (1940). *Folkways: A study of the sociological importance of usages, manners, customs, mores, and morals.* New York, NY: Ginn and Co.

Taylor, K., & Rohrer, D. (2010). The effects of interleaved practice. *Applied Cognitive Psychology, 24*, 837–848. doi:10.1002/acp.1598

Velleman, P. F. (2008). Truth, damn truth, and statistics. *Journal of Statistics Education, 16*, 1–14. doi:10.1080/10691898.2008.11889565

Walsh, P. G., & Mertin, P. G. (1994). The training of pets as therapy dogs in a women's prison: A pilot study. *Anthrozoös, 7*(2), 124–128. doi:10.2752/089279394787002014

Walsh, P. G., Mertin, P. G., Verlander, D. F., & Pollard, C. F. (1995). The effects of a "pets as therapy" dog on persons with dementia in a psychiatric ward. *Australian Occupational Therapy Journal, 42*, 161–166. doi:10.1111/j.1440-1630.1995.tb01331.x

Wayman, T. (1993). *Did I miss anything? Selected poems 1973–1993*. Madeira Park, BC: Harbour Publishing.

Wikipedia. (2017). *Wikipedia editing policy*. Retrieved from https://en.wikipedia.org/wiki/Wikipedia:Editing_policy

Wilson, E. O. (1984). *Biophilia*. Cambridge, MA: Harvard University Press.

Woloshyn, V. E., & Stockley, D. B. (1995). Helping students acquire belief-inconsistent and belief-consistent science facts: Comparisons between individual and dyad study using elaborative interrogation, self-selected study and repetitious-reading. *Applied Cognitive Psychology, 9*, 75–89. doi:10.1002/acp.2350090106

Yardley, J., Rodríguez, M. D., Bates, S. C., & Nelson, J. (2009). True confessions? Alumni's retrospective reports on undergraduate cheating behaviors. *Ethics & Behavior, 19*, 1–14. doi:10.1080/1050842080248709

INDEX